ROBERT MORKOT

THE PENGUIN
**HISTORICAL ATLAS
OF ANCIENT GREECE**

PENGUIN BOOKS

Published by the Penguin Group
Penguin Books Ltd, 80 Strand, London WC2R 0RL, England
Penguin Group (USA) Inc., 375 Hudson Street, New York, New York 10014, USA
Penguin Group (Canada), 90 Eglinton Avenue East, Suite 700, Toronto, Ontario, Canada M4P 2Y3
(a division of Pearson Penguin Canada Inc.)
Penguin Ireland, 25 St Stephen's Green, Dublin 2, Ireland
(a division of Penguin Books Ltd)
Penguin Group (Australia), 250 Camberwell Road,
Camberwell, Victoria 3124, Australia (a division of Pearson Australia Group Pty Ltd)
Penguin Books India Pvt Ltd, 11 Community Centre,
Panchsheel Park, New Delhi – 110 017, India
Penguin Group (NZ), cnr Airborne and Rosedale Roads, Albany,
Auckland 1310, New Zealand (a division of Pearson New Zealand Ltd)
Penguin Books (South Africa) (Pty) Ltd, 24 Sturdee Avenue,
Rosebank, Johannesburg 2196, South Africa

Penguin Books Ltd, Registered Offices: 80 Strand, London WC2R 0RL, England

www.penguin.com

First published in Penguin Books 1996
Published simultaneously by Viking
13

Text copyright © Robert Morkot, 1993
Design and maps copyright © Swanston Publishing Ltd, 1996
All rights reserved

Printed and bound in Italy by L.E.G.O. Spa

ISBN: 978–0–1405–1335–6

Foreword

Traditionally, the Greeks have been held up as our ancestors, particularly in matters of culture and politics: freedom and democracy as we understand them are supposed to have begun with Greece. The ancient Greeks were like us, but earlier. As such, they were unlike other ancient peoples such as the Phoenicians and the Egyptians. It is increasingly obvious that, not only is this view of the Greeks a myth, but that the Greeks were probably more unlike us than we have ever allowed. Democracy, even of the limited Athenian kind, was not the universal (or even dominant) political system of the Greek world. The Greeks themselves attributed much of their culture to stimuli from Egypt and Phoenicia, and increasingly this reality is being acknowledged. As archaeology reveals to us more of the Minoan and Mycenaean civilizations and anthropology challenges our assumptions about the Classical world, our perceptions of Greece must change radically. While we would not begin to devalue the glory of Periklean Athens or its enormous influence in ancient and recent times, we increasingly recognize that it is one, relatively short, period in the development of Greek civilization. Perhaps due to the nature of the international age in which we live, we have also begun, at last, to appreciate the contribution and the importance of the three hundred years of the Hellenistic world.

The history and culture of Greece were deeply influenced in all phases by the other civilizations of the eastern Mediterranean and western Asia. Greece eventually came to dominate them politically and culturally. The perspective on the Greek world presented here tries to place Greek history within that broader context. This volume is an introduction and by its nature emphasises historical events (which turn out, all too frequently, to be military) and political changes. It describes rather than explains. I have relied on the studies of numerous specialists some of whose works, which do offer more authoritative explanations, are recommended in the Further Reading.

There is an increasing tendency to use Greek spellings rather than the Latinized forms which were once prevalent. This has resulted in some inconsistencies, but in that we are at least consistent with most other books. The use of the occasional anachronistic name has also proved unavoidable.

My thanks to the cartographers and production team for their creative response to the material and particularly to Stephen Haddelsey for his keen eye and skilful use of the editorial pen. Most of all, my thanks go to those who have taught and guided me in all phases of Greek history over the years.

Robert Morkot
Exeter, February 1996

Contents

Timeline: 7000 BC to 1500 BC

GREECE	NEAR EAST AND NORTH AFRICA	EUROPE AND THE MEDITERRANEAN	CULTURE AND TECHNOLOGY
			c. 7000 Early experiments with copper ores in Anatolia. First pottery in the Near East
c. 6500 First farming in Greece and the Aegean	6250–5400 Catal Hûyûk, the largest city of its day flourishes in Anatolia	6500 Adoption of farming in the Balkans signals beginning of European Neolithic period	
	6000 Sheep, barley and wheat introduced to Egypt from western Asia	6200 Farming villages established in western and central Mediterranean	
	5500 Halaf culture in Mesopotamia		
	c. 5000 Colonization of Mesopotamian alluvial plain by peoples practising irrigation. First agricultural settlements in Egypt	5200 Farmers of central Europe spread northwest as far as the Netherlands	5000 Gold and copper used in manufacturing in the Balkans
			4500 Copper smelting in eastern Europe. Beginning of rich burial patterns in eastern and central Europe. Cattle used as plough animals in lower Danube region. First megalithic tombs in western Europe
			4400 Domestication of horse on Eurasian steppes
			4200 World's earliest known copper mines in eastern Europe at Aibumar and Rudna Glava
		3800 Formation of defended villages in western Europe	*c.* 4000 Bronze casting begins in Near East. Use of plough commences
	3400 First walled towns in Egypt	3500 Increasing use of animals in farming	3500 Invention of wheel and plough (Mesopotamia) and sail (Egypt)
3200–2000 Early Cycladic civilization in Aegean	3100 Emergence of Egyptian state, new capital at Memphis	3200 First wheeled vehicles in Europe. Construction of megalithic stone circles, predominantly in north-west France and British Isles	3100 Pictographic writing invented in Sumur
3000 Construction of walled citadels in Mediterranean	2700 Beginning of Egyptian Old Kingdom		3000 First evidence of Egyptian heiroglyphics
			2650 First Egyptian stepped pyramid at Saqqara
		2300 Full European Bronze Age begins	2600 Pyramid of Maidum, Egypt – the first true pyramid
	2180 Collapse of Egyptian Old Kingdom		
	2040 Establishment of Egyptian Middle Kingdom		
c. 2000 Indo-Europeans invade and settle Peloponnese. Rise of Minoan civilization on Crete	1990 New Egyptian capital at El-Lisht		2000 Sail used on seagoing vessels in the Aegean. Stonehenge constructed
	1800 Shamshi-Adad founds Assyrian state. Horse introduced to Egypt		
	1783 Fall of Egyptian Middle Kingdom		
	c. 1750 Foundation of Babylonian empire. Foundation of Hittite empire in Anatolia.		1700 Bronze body armour first used in Near East
			1650 "Linear A" script
c. 1600 Rise of Mycenaean civilization on mainland Greece	*c.* 1560 Rise of the Egyptian New Kingdom		*c.* 1500 "Linear B" script

Timeline: 1501 BC to 480 BC

GREECE	NEAR EAST AND NORTH AFRICA	EUROPE AND THE MEDITERRANEAN	CULTURE AND TECHNOLOGY
c. 1450 First destruction of Minoan Crete			
c. 1200 Collapse of Mycenaean civilization. Second destruction of Minoan Crete.	c. 1200 Collapse of Hittite empire. Jewish exodus from Egypt	c. 1200 "Sea People" active in Mediterranean	
	1151 Death of Pharaoh Ramesses III		
	1100 Spread of Phoenicians in Mediterranean		c. 1100 Development of alphabetic script by the Phoenicians
		1000 Hillforts in western Europe	1000 Establishment of iron industry in the Aegean
900 End of Greek Dark Age and beginning of Geometric period	c. 900 Assyrian expansion begins	850 First settlement at Rome	c. 9th C Homer active
		800 Establishment of Celtic Iron Age culture (Hallstatt). Rise of Etruscan city-states	8th C Hesiod active
	814 Foundation of Carthage by Phoenicians	753 (trad) Romulus founds Rome	776 First Olympic Games held in Greece
c. 750 Spread of Greek colonization throughout Mediterranean and Black Sea	721–650 Apogee of Assyrian empire	750 Iron-working spreads to Britain	c. 750 Homer's *Iliad* and Hesiod's poetry first written down
700 Beginning of Archaic period in Greece			
	671 Assyrian conquest of Egypt		690 Etruscan script developed from Greek
c. 650 Rise of the tyrants. Reforms of Lykourgos in Sparta.	664 Pharoah Psamtik I ascends Egyptian throne		c. 650 First Greek coins. Rise of Greek lyric poetry
	630 Foundation of Kyrene		
c. 624 Drakon codifies Athenian law	620 Foundation of Naukratis		
	612 Collapse of Assyrian power		
c. 594 Reforms of Solon in Athens	593 Psamtik II campaigns against Kush, using Greek mercenaries	600 Foundation of Greek colony at Massalia (Marsailles). Trade between Celts northwest of the Alps and Greek colonies in western Mediterranean. Rome established as urban centre	600 Development of Latin script
			585 Beginnings of Greek rationalist philosophy
	c. 550 Cyrus II founds Persian empire		c. 530 Pythagoras, active
	525 Persian conquest of Egypt		525 Aischylos, tragic dramatist, born at Eleusis. Dies c. 456.
			c. 522 Pindar, chief lyric poet of Greece, born near Thebes. Dies at Argos c. 440
514 Assassination of Hipparchos by Harmodios and Aristogeiton the "tyrannicides"	521 Darius I rules Persian empire		510 Temple of Jupiter Optimus Maximus completed at Rome
c. 505 Kleisthenes founds democracy in Athens	c. 510 Darius I completes canal connecting Nile with Red Sea	509 Last of kings expelled from Rome. Treaty with Carthage	
	500 Construction of Persian Royal Road from Sardis to Susa. Tribute reliefs carved at Persepolis	c. 500/490 Darius sends embassy to Carthage	5th C Pheidias and Polykleitos (sculptors) and Polygnotos (painter) active
	494 Persians suppress Ionian Revolt	496 Battle of Lake Regillus: Rome against Latin League	496 Sophokles, tragic dramatist, born at Kolonos. Writes 123 plays. Dies at Athens, 406
490 Persian invasion of Greece defeated at Marathon			c. 485 Herodotos, historian, born at Halikarnassos. Dies 425
480 Battles of Salamis and Plataiai, Persians defeated		480 Second stage of European Iron Age	c. 480 Euripides, dramatist born. writes 80 plays. Dies in 406

Timeline: 479 BC to 326 BC

GREECE	NEAR EAST AND NORTH AFRICA	EUROPE AND THE MEDITERRANEAN	CULTURE AND TECHNOLOGY
		c. 480–460 Carthage under Hanno expands African territory	479 Death of Confucius
478 Foundation of Confederacy of Delos, becomes Athenian Empire			479–338 Period of Greek Classical culture
			469 Sokrates, philosopher, born in Athens. Father of the Sokratic method of philosophy. Condemned to death, 399
460–446 First Peloponnesian War	460 Papyrus replaces clay tablets in Persian administration		c. 460 Hippokrates, physician, born at Kos. Author of over 70 medical treatises. Dies at Larisa, Thessaly, c. 377. Birth of Thucydides, historian of the Peloponnesian War. Dies c. 400
450 Apogee of Athens	459–454 Revolt of Inaros in Egypt, aid sent by Athens		
449 Peace of Kallias brings temporary end to Athenian–Persian hostility		449 Secession of Roman plebeians leads to constitutional reform	
443–429 Perikles dominates Athenian politics			c. 448 Birth of Aristophanes, greatest of the Greek comic dramatists. Author of 54 plays. Dies c. 388
			433 Parthenon completed in Athens
431–404 Peloponnesian War between Sparta and Athens			
		410 Carthage invades Sicily	c. 429 Plato born, possibly in Athens. Practises philosophy in Athens and founds his own academy. Dies in Athens, 347
		409 Carthage sends embassy to Athens	
	404 Egypt independent		
	401 Revolt of Cyrus against Artaxerxes II. Battle of Kunaxa, Cyrus killed	400 Celtic settlement of northern Italy	4th C Praxiteles (sculptor) active
		390 Celts sack Rome	
	387–386 King's Peace of Artaxerxes II	380s Roman expansion in Italy begins	384 Aristotle, philosopher, scientist and physician, born in Thrace. Becomes student of Plato and tutor to Alexander the Great. Dies at Chalkis, Euboea, 323
371 Battle of Leuctra, defeat of Sparta			
357–355 "Social War" and "Sacred War"			
356 Philip II rules Macedon			c. 350 Mausoleum constructed at Halikarnassos
349 Philip of Macedon invades Chalkidike	342 Egypt reconquered by Persians	348 Rome renews treaty with Carthage	
		340-38 Latin War: Rome gains control of Latium	341 Epikourous philosopher, born at Samos. Author of over 300 volumes on many subjects. Establishes school of philosophy at Athens. Dies at Athens, 270
338 Battle of Chaironeia, Macedonian victory over Greece			
336 Assassination of Philip at Pella, Alexander the Great succeeds to Macedonian throne	334 Alexander the Great invades Persian empire. Persians defeated at Granikos		
	333 Macedonian victory at Issos		
	332 Alexander conquers Egypt		
	331 Persians defeated at Gaugemela		
	330 Persepolis captured		
	329–328 Alexander campaigns in Bactria and Sogdia		
	326 Macedonian victory at Hydaspes, subjugation of the Punjab	c. 326–304 War between Rome and Samnites	

Timeline: 325 BC to 30 BC

GREECE	NEAR EAST AND NORTH AFRICA	EUROPE AND THE MEDITERRANEAN	CULTURE AND TECHNOLOGY
	323 Death of Alexander at Babylon. Empire divided among Alexander's marshals		
317 Philip III of Macedon assassinated			
	312–311 Commencement of Seleukid era	310 Roman expansion into Etruria	c. 310 Theokritos, pastoral poet, born at Syracuse. Dies 250
	312 Battle of Gaza, defeat of Antigonos		
308 Deaths of Alexander IV and Roxana			
307 Athens captured by Antigonos	305/306 Seleukos I at war with Chandragupta Maurya		
	304 Ptolemy I founds independent dynasty in Egypt		
	301 Battle of the Kings at Ipsos results in defeat of Antigonos and Demetrios	300 Appearance of Celtic coinage as Celts move toward formation of states. Development of trade between Carthage and Egypt.	c. 300 Euclid founds mathematical school in Alexandria
			290 Foundation of library at Alexandria
	283 Death of Ptolemy I		
281 Battle of Korupedion, Lysimachos defeated by Seleukos I. Seleukos assassinated		280–275 Rome at war with Pyrrhos of Epirus	280 Colossus of Rhodes built
277 Celtic armies defeated at Lysimacheia			c. 279 Lighthouse of Alexandria built
258 Naval battle of Kos results in Seleukid victory over Ptolemaic forces	276–272 First Syrian War ends with Egyptian expansion into Palestine	264–241 First Punic War between Rome and Carthage	
		250 All of peninsular Italy under Roman jurisdiction	
	246 Deaths of Ptolemy II and Antiochos II		
	246–241 Third Syrian War ends with defeat of Ptolemaic navy	229/228 Romans in Illyria	
	223–187 Reign of Antiochos III	218–201 Second Punic War	
		218 Hannibal defeats Roman army at Lake Trasimene	212 Mathematician Archimedes killed by Romans during capture of Syracuse
		206 Roman conquest of Spain	
197 Rome defeats Philip V of Macedon at Kynoskephalai		200 Rome declares war on Philip V of Macedon	200 Romans invent concrete
			190 Victory of Samothrace
	188 Peace of Apameia deprives Seleukids of all territory west of Taurus Mountains	171-167 Roman War against Perseus of Macedon	170 Altar of Zeus at Pergamon
150 Macedonia becomes Roman province	149 Third Punic War		c. 150 Laocoon of Agesander of Rhodes
146 Mummius sacks Corinth			
	133 Pergamon bequeathed to Rome	133 Reforms of T. Gracchus	
	88–85 Pontos and Rome at war	91-89 Social War: Rome defeats rebellious Italian allies but grants major concessions	
	64 Pompey the Great conquers Syria; end of Seleukid empire		
	54 Battle of Carrhae, Roman forces defeated by Parthian army		
48 Pompey the Great defeated by Caesar at Pharsalos	48 Pompey executed on the orders of Ptolemy	44 Assassination of Julius Caesar	
31 Forces of Mark Antony and Kleopatra VII defeated at Actium	30 Suicide of Mark Antony and Kleopatra		

I: Crete, Mycenae and the Heroic Age

To formulate a coherent history of Greece prior to the Archaic period historians have been required to knit together a confusing collection of features gleaned primarily from archaeology and legend.

History, Archaeology and Myth

"If we trace the ancestry of Danae, the daughter of Akrisios, we find that the Dorian chieftains are genuine Egyptians ... But there is no need to pursue the subject further. How it happened that Egyptians came to the Peloponnese, and what they did to make themselves kings in that part of Greece, has been chronicled by other writers."

Herodotos, *The Histories, Book VI*

The history of Greece in the Classical and Hellenistic periods is extremely well documented, through the historical writings of Herodotos, Thucydides, Xenophon and others and in the many surviving fragments of other, now lost, works epitomized by the encyclopaedists of the Hellenistic and Roman periods, such as Diodoros, Strabo and Pliny. The expansion of Roman rule into the Hellenistic world is also recounted by Roman writers such as Livy and Polybius (actually a Greek). Inevitably there are many conflicting interpretations of these sources, particularly the earlier writers such as Herodotos, but it is reasonable to say that from the time of the Persian Wars we are in an historical world. Earlier than that our prime source, inevitably, must be archaeology.

Archaeology was a rather late development among the tools for learning about and understanding the past. The literary tradition was, of course, paramount, and from the Renaissance onwards played an enormous role in the development of western European culture. Also important were the remains of the Roman world. The influence of Greece on Rome was well-known, and the first rudimentary excavations were often the result of Papal rebuilding in the Eternal City. In 1506 Michelangelo was witness to the discovery of a statue group depicting Laocoon and his sons strangled by serpents (today in the Vatican Museum). The subject was an episode from the Trojan wars, but more importantly, the sculpture itself was familiar as one described by the Roman writer Pliny as standing in the palace of the emperor Titus, and was known to be the work of Agesander of Rhodes. So the sculptures described in the ancient literature could be seen (even if in later copies).

The collections formed in Rome over the next two centuries by the cardinals and princes and those gathered by travellers from other European countries led to the next stage: their chronological ordering and from that the writing of art history. This was first achieved by J.J. Wincklemann whose history of ancient art commenced with Egypt. Wincklemann argued that Greek was superior to Roman (although a lot that he thought was Greek was, in fact, Roman copy, or late Hellenistic).

As part of the Ottoman empire Greece was less visited than Italy. Interest in Greek art increased with the "discovery" of Paestum and of Greek pottery in Italy (mistakenly called "Etruscan"). The Napoleonic wars opened up the eastern Mediterranean to the western European powers and tourists and collectors soon followed. Even though the early 19th century saw the removal from Greece of some important collections of sculptures, from the Parthenon and from the temple of Aphaia at Aegina, the historical importance of Greece was still somewhat subordinated to Rome.

The history of Greece from the Archaic period (8th century BC) onwards could be reconstructed from the surviving ancient literary sources; for the pre-Classical world historians used myth. They believed that the myths contained an historical remembrance of actual events, and tried to unravel the myths to reconstruct the earliest history. Their interpretations were, however, coloured by other factors, notably the "discovery" of the Indo-European language group, to which Greek belongs, and the supposition that it and other languages in the group were all spoken by "Aryans". Archaeology began much later and focussed first on the monuments of the great centres of Classical Greece, such as Athens, Delphi and Olympia.

In Egypt and other parts of the Near East, it was the biblical tradition which provided the stimulus for achaeology (as opposed to treasure-hunting). As archaeologists there excavated with the Bible in one hand, so Heinrich Schliemann visited the city-mounds of western Turkey, with a copy of the *Iliad*. Schliemann was fired by the dream of discovering Priam's city of Troy. Schliemann correctly identified the mound of Hissarlik as Troy and began excavations there in 1870 (they continued until 1890). He followed his first seasons at Troy with excavations at Mycenae (1874), where he believed he had discovered the burial of Agamemnon) and at Tiryns (1884). Schliemann's archaeological technique was little worse than that practised by many "professional" archaeologists at the time. It certainly improved when he collaborated with Wilhelm Dörpfeld, who continued his work. Schliemann also examined sites on Crete. Although he did no digging there, Schliemann recognized at Knossos the "Palace of Minos" which was later excavated by Sir Arthur Evans (1900 onwards).

A Cycladic figurine which has become popularly known as the "star-gazer" because the eyes are lifted to the skies. Dating to around 2800—2700 BC the piece belongs to the Louros type of the Grotta-Pelos culture.

Schliemann was able to identify the many city levels at Troy, and it was clear which of them pre-dated the Archaic and Classical levels. It was, however, far more difficult to date them precisely. The solution came from the founder of archaeology in Egypt, Sir Flinders Petrie. In his excavations at the sites of Naukratis and Defenneh (Daphnae) in the Nile Delta, Petrie found Greek pottery of the 6th century BC. He later found pottery of the type excavated by Schliemann at Mycenae, firstly at the site of Gurob and then at many other sites, notably Amarna. The chronology of Egypt was thought to be firmly established, so the archaeological contexts of Mycenaean and Greek material in Egypt should give their corresponding dates BC. For the later material (such as that from Naukratis) this seemed to work reasonably well. However, for the earlier, Mycenaean, pottery, it seemed not to work. The end of the Mycenaean civilization had been set at around 800 BC, Petrie's ties between Egypt and Greece placed the Mycenaean Age some four hundred years earlier, between 1600 and 1200. Not surprisingly, Petrie's contribution was not received with enthusiasm by the archaeologists of Greece. However, over the past hundred years it has gradually been accepted, and the four centuries between the end of the Mycenaean and the emergence of the Archaic worlds are now known as the Dark Age.

In reconstructing Greek history the tendency has been, for obvious reasons, to value archaeology for the earlier periods and literary sources for the later. But recent trends in historical research have been informed by anthropology, and they increasingly show how unlike us the ancient Greeks actually were.

Who were the Greeks?

In all attempts to define the identity and origins of an ancient people there must be many alternative and often conflicting perspectives and interpretations. The ethnography of the ancient Greeks is no exception. Through repetition ideas achieve a general acceptance and gradually assume the dignity of "established fact". Many of the ideas about racial origins were developed in the 19th century and, although they may have had some foundation in historical tradition, archaeology or linguistics, they were usually combined with other more dubious presumptions. Only in recent years have historians begun to challenge the theories which were first formulated a century ago.

One of the most significant formative influences on the 19th century interpretation of ancient Greek history was the "discovery" of the Indo-European language group, which includes both Greek and Latin. All speakers of these languages were thought of as branches of the "Aryan race". Originating somewhere in central Asia, one group invaded India, whilst the others moved gradually westwards in a series of migrations. The Victorians proposed that these peoples invaded Greece on three separate occasions. The earliest, taking place around 1900 BC, was that of the Achaeans (later thought of as the founders of the Mycenaean civilization). The Ionians also arrived sometime in the early 2nd millenium. The last invasion was that of the Dorians, which was placed variously at 1200 and 1000 BC.

As the Dorians pushed southwards from the Balkans the earlier settlers of Greece were once again forced to become mobile. The populations of north-central Greece were the first to be affected: some went across the sea to Lesbos and the adjacent coast, where they became the Aeolians. In southern Greece the resident population fled before the invaders, either into the mountain fastnesses of Arcadia, or across the sea to the coast of Asia Minor around the bay of Smyrna—the future Ionian coast. Some managed to hold out in southern Attica. The result of these migrations was the division of Greece into the different dialects known from the Classical period: Ionian in Attica and parts of Asia; Doric over much of the Peloponnese and the conquered islands (Crete, Rhodes and Kos); Aeolic in Thessaly, Boiotia and the northern coast of Asia.

Historians attributed certain characteristics to these groups, but it is clear that their impositions are little more than backward projections of stereotypical generalizations from the Classical period combined with rather dubious and unsubstantiated racial theories. For intance, the Ionians were supposed to be indolent, but intellectually refined, while the Dorians were austere, morally rigorous and admirers of physical prowess.

This reconstruction of early Greek history was based upon ancient sources such as Herodotos and predated the discovery of the Minoan and Mycenaean civilizations. These same early sources refer to an indigenous population called the Pelasgians, who were conquered by the descendants of Hellen, the son of Deukalion. Dorus, son of Hellen, was the eponymous ancestor of the Dorians; Aeolos was the ancestor of the Aeolians; Ion of the Ionians. In contrast to the Spartans, the Athenians claimed to be an indigenous people, and this mythical ancestry was used during the Classical period to claim for Athens a legitimate primacy as defender of Greece.

The Dorian invasion of the Peloponnese became confused, even in ancient times, with another myth, narrating the return of the Heraklids (the descendants of Herakles). In the ancient sources the Dorians were settled in central Greece, and after various moves around Thessaly, graduated southwards into the Peloponnese. Historians in the 19th century decided (though without any real evidence to support their theory) that the Dorians had come from much farther afield. According to this idea, the Dorian movement into central Greece from the Balkans was merely the last stage in a much lengthier migration. Ultimately, the Dorians became closely associated with other population movements, most notably those of the so-called "Sea Peoples".

Archaeology tends to confirm the view that mainland Greece has been populated ever since man's first appearance on the planet. Undoubtedly there have been immigrations, whether these were the great waves envisioned by

19th century historians is altogether more debateable. Historical processes tend to be rather more complex: the conquest of a country by a relatively small group can have enormous impact on a population, just as a large-scale immigration of "barbarians" can become rapidly acculturated.

The most recent examination of the problem of the Dorian invasion follows the view of Herodotos more literally than the historians of the last century. Herodotos' version of events tells us that the Dorians were settled in the Pindos mountains to the north and west of Boiotia, from where they moved to the region around Mount Olympus and then back to the coast of Thessaly. It has now been suggested that, rather than a military invasion, the Dorian infiltration of the Peloponnese probably happened in the Dark Ages, when they occupied many sites abandoned after the crisis which brought about the collapse of the Mycenaean civilization around 1200.

Archaeologists and historians today are much more aware of the problems and complexities (and political manipulation) of racial history than their predecessors of the 19th and early 20th centuries. Ethnicity, language and culture are phenomena which are linked in many complex ways. No-longer do archaeologists say that a new culture (usually associated in archaeology with discoveries of pottery) necessitates the advent of a new people in a given region. The decipherment of the Linear B tablets revealed that Greek was

The architectural recreations of Sir Arthur Evans at Knossos have been severely criticized over the years as being founded upon insufficient archaeological knowledge and for being irreversible. Despite this scholarly uncertainty, however, many visitors to the site have found the reconstructions to be great aids to the imagination. This view is of the main corridor looking south towards the Main Court. The remains of the North Entrance dominate the scene.

being spoken by the Mycenaeans, and this discovery forced a revision of the old theory that the Mycenaeans were pre-Greeks—instead they were viewed as earlier invaders. Overall, the Greeks are perhaps best defined by culture, as they were in the Hellenistic period, when individual ethnic origins were of less importance.

The Civilizations of Crete and Mycenae

The earliest evidence of agriculture in Greece comes from Thessaly and at Knossos on Crete, at the beginning of the 7th millenium BC. But the limits of archaeology must be remembered. There may be equally early sites in Greece which have yet to be identified, or which lie below the remains of later settlements. There are indications of cross-Aegean traffic even at this early date, and the exploitation of the obsidian resources of Melos seems to have begun before the island was permanently settled.

The settlement of the Cyclades took place in the late 6th and 5th millenium. There was a wide range of trading contacts by this time, and influences from Anatolia are discernable in pottery styles. The early Bronze Age culture which developed on the Cyclades is most noted for its marble figures. The type was perhaps first developed on Paros and Naxos, where the finest marble in the islands is found. Highly stylized, some are simple standing (or perhaps lying) figures, others depict musicians, seated figures and groups. Imitations were made on Crete and in Attica. The function of the figures is still uncertain, although they are assumed to be religious as most come from graves. Although the historical processes are unclear, the islands ultimately came under the cultural dominance of Crete.

It was on Crete that civilization first flowered in the Greek world. The great palace complex of Knossos was begun around 1900, but it stands above many layers of earlier settlement. It has been claimed that these "Minoans" came from Egypt or western Asia. Certainly there were stimuli from the east, and these are reflected in the myths relating to Minos, but the culture has a highly individual character.

In the first phase of Minoan civilization there were trading contacts with Ugarit in Syria and with Egypt and these increased considerably in the "Second Palace Period" (c. 1700—1400). This was the period of the Late Bronze Age in the Near East and it has been termed the "first international age". It was also the time of the great empires. Egypt expanded to control much of Syria-Palestine, and eventually the Hittites came to dominate much of Anatolia and north Syria. The search for raw materials, particularly metal, led to wide-ranging trade and diplomatic contacts. This was also the time of the rise of Mycenaean power on the mainland. The main palaces of Minoan Crete, at Khania, Phaistos, Knossos and Mallia, have revealed a culture of great sophistication and cultural influence now spread from Crete over the Aegean and the mainland.

On Crete the extensive trade links are revealed by the materials used. Lapis lazuli came via Mesopotamia (ultimately from Afghanistan); gold, ivory and alabaster came from Egypt and ostrich eggs from both Egypt and Libya. Northerly links are demonstrated by the existence of amber beads. One of the most important commodities of the period was copper, some of it exported from Cyprus.

The volcanic explosion which destroyed Thera has been blamed for the end of the Minoan civilization. Thera lies just 60 miles north of Crete, and its

explosion must have been devastating. The excavations on Thera suggested to its archaeologists that the explosion of the island was remembered in the legend of the destruction of Atlantis, and the idea was quite widely accepted. However, a new analysis of all the ancient sources on Atlantis, particularly the work of Plato, has convincingly shown that the famous city was probably near Mount Sipylos in Ionia, a little to the east of the later city of Magnesia. The destruction of Thera probably took place around 1650. On Crete at the same time there was a destruction of some of the palaces, but Knossos was rebuilt, and came under Mycenaean sway around 1400 BC.

Mycenae's power rose rapidly around 1600, and specialists are still divided as to the causes. The archaeological evidence does little to clarify matters. Some archaeologists attribute the Mycenaean ascendancy to local rulers who had strong contacts with Crete. However, the evidence for the introduction of chariot warfare suggests the possibility that the rulers were themselves foreign. Recently, a radically revised version of one of the older theories has proposed that it was a relatively small migration of Indo-European Greek speakers which created this Mycenaean golden age. Whatever the origins of Mycenae, an enormous cultural influence came from Minoan Crete. The treasures of the shaft graves are certainly Minoan-influenced and in many cases they may in fact be imports from Crete.

International trade during this phase increased even further. The shipwrecks at Ulu Burun and Cape Gelidonya off the Turkish coast show the variety and volume of international trade at this time, and further details can be gleaned from the contemporary letters in the Amarna archive from Egypt. Written in Akkadian (the language of Mesopotamia) which was the diplomatic language of the day, the Amarna letters detail gifts sent from or to the Egyptian pharaoh. Egyptian paintings and reliefs (principally from tombs) also show the foreign "tribute" presented to the pharaoh. Whilst there are many aspects of the economy which remain uncertain, it seems fairly safe to assume that international trade was in the hands of the pharaoh in Egypt, and similarly controlled by the rulers elsewhere in western Asia. The ancient sources show that it was conducted as gift-exchange. Gifts were sent whenever a messenger or embassy went from one ruler to another, other gifts were sent for specific royal occasions (accession, royal festivals, marriages etc), and for the building of palaces and temples. The gifts sent as dowry were on a vast scale. It is clear from the texts that everything was weighed and its exact value calculated—so that the gift sent in return was of equal value (bearing in mind the rank of the sender and receiver). The role of private trade within this period is much more difficult to assess. There has been a tendency to assume that while in Egypt foreign trade was controlled by the pharaoh or the priests, throughout western Asia it was in the hands of private merchants. It seems more likely that all international trade in the Late Bronze Age was controlled by the palaces. The objects and raw materials which appear in the Mycenaean context reveal that they were part of this system. Egyptian paintings depict people who are quite probably Mycenaean or Cretan; even more striking are the names written in hieroglyphic which are shown as "subject" to the pharaoh Amenhotep III (1386—1349). These have been identified with Amnisos, Phaistos, Lyktos, Knossos and Kydonia on Crete, Mycenae, Messenia, Nauplia and Kythera in Greece, and, perhaps, Troy. Objects bearing the name of the same pharaoh have been found on Crete and at Mycenae. At the same time, there is also good evidence for connections with the Hittites. Hittite texts beginning with the reign of Suppiluliuma (1380—1346) refer to the land of *Ahhiyawa*, which is widely accepted as meaning the Achaeans. More specifically, there are references to *Millawanda*, which is thought to be Miletos, where there was a major Mycenaean settlement.

As elsewhere, writing developed as a response to the demands of a centralized economy and probably through growing international contacts. The earliest Cretan script seems to have been a local invention. Linear A is found at sites all over Crete from around 1700 to 1450. It is also found at other places in the Aegean and was the ancestor of Linear B. The language which Linear A communicates is still a matter of dispute, Linear B, however, is certainly a form of Greek. Found from around 1400 it was used for economic texts and is associated with palace and similar sites on Crete and the mainland. The swift disappearance of written texts suggests that literacy was very limited and that with the collapse of the palace economies, it was no longer required.

The restriction of writing to economic texts has ensured that the Minoan and Mycenaean worlds are almost without documented history. Archaeology can tell us much about developments, but little about events. However, in the search for Mycenaean history, scholars have been repeatedly drawn to the Greek myths and particularly to the Homeric epics.

The Age of Heroes

Beginning with Schliemann and Evans, "discovering" the world of the Greek myths has been a motivation, even an obsession, of some archaeologists. However, in many cases what is discovered does not always match what we assume should be there.

Any portrait of Homer must, perforce, be speculative since no accounts of his appearance are extant. Indeed, throughout the centuries there has been heated debate over whether the Iliad *and the* Odyssey *were written by a man at all, perhaps the author was a woman, or a group of people. The legend of his blindness may also be apocryphal since the earliest likenesses make no reference to this disability.*

Of all the heroic cycles, the *Iliad* and the *Odyssey* are without doubt the greatest. The date of the conflict and the fall of Troy has been a subject of fascination both in ancient and modern times. The ancient writers give dates which fall (in modern terms) between 1346 and 1127 BC, one of the most favoured being around 1184. Following the excavations at Troy, levels VI and VIIa are those most usually suggested as candidates for the Homeric city. On the evidence of the Mycenaean pottery, the date for their destruction can be calculated at *c.* 1300 and 1200. The earlier level, which has massive walls, seems to fit Homer's description more closely than the later city, but it appears to have been destroyed by an earthquake rather than by human force. The later city, which was destroyed by fire, appears to have been rather poor in comparison. Archaeologists were thus reluctant to identify it with the city of Priam.

It has been assumed that the Homeric epics record a late Mycenaean world, certainly some of the details suggest this. The boar's tusk helmet, which is described in detail, is typically Mycenaean. Yet the description of battle follows practices of the Archaic period more closely. In the epics, chariots are used primarily to convey warriors to the scene of the conflict, the fighting is on foot. It has been assumed, therefore, that the myths were substantially transformed during the "Dark Age," either through oral transmission, or when they were turned into the epics by Homer in the 8th century. There is evidence that in the Archaic period Bronze Age burials became the focus of cults. The Greeks regarded the Mycenaean tombs as those of the heroes. The opening of these graves may have brought to light weapons and armour which were then described in the epics.

Other myths of the heroes are asssociated with the Minoan and Mycenaean world and perhaps reflect the international contacts of the time. The Phoenician princess Europa, carried off from Tyre by Zeus in the guise of a bull, was taken to Crete where she gave birth to Minos, ruler of Knossos, and to Rhadamanthys, a law-giver who became one of the judges in the underworld. Europa's brother, Kadmos, was sent in search of her and during his travels founded the city of Thebes, which was certainly a major centre of the Mycenaean period. The descendents of Kadmos (such as Oedipus) continued to rule in Thebes, although their history was tragic and became a favoured subject for the great Athenian dramatists of the Classical period.

Theseus, a key figure in the political history of Athens, was also linked in tradition with the time of the Trojan War. Son of Aegeus, king of Athens, Theseus was renowned for his valiant exploits, the most famous being his journey to Crete to kill the Minotaur (a monster created by the union of Minos' wife and a bull sent by Poseidon) in the Labyrinth below the palace of Knossos. This legend has been viewed as an allegorical description of Attica's rejection of Minoan influence and details such as the lair of the Minotaur can be equated with the multi-layered complexity of Bronze Age Knossos as it was revealed to archaeologists at the beginning of this century. Later developments of the myth made Theseus stop at Delos on his return journey, thereby giving to Athens an ancient precedent for authority over the island. Theseus was also counted responsible for the *synoecism*, the bringing together of the villages of Attica into a political union, with Athens at its heart. This was long regarded as myth by historians, who preferred to date the process to the Archaic period, but archaeological evidence now suggests the possibility that Attica was indeed coalescing into a unified state during the late Mycenaean period.

Historians will certainly continue to debate the relationship between myth, history and archaeology but the remarkable levels of coincidence between "myth" and archaeological "fact" mean that it is no longer possible to entirely dismiss the ancient Greek legends as mere unsubstantiated "fairy tales".

The End of the Bronze Age

The Mycenaean world came to an end sometime after 1200 BC. But it was not alone: throughout the great empires and kingdoms of western Asia there was crisis and in many places the palaces were looted and burnt.

Numerous theories have been put forward to explain this wholesale destruction. One popular idea was a widespread cultural decline analagous with the decline and fall of the Roman empire. It was argued that the empires became "worn out" and then fell before the onslaught of more vigorous "barbarians". This explanation was particularly favoured in the later 19th century, when a theory of cultural "decadence" was developed.

One of the most widely accepted theories attributed the collapse of the great empires to the incursions of the "Sea Peoples". The evidence for the existence of the Sea Peoples comes mainly from Egypt, where a number of attempted invasions are recorded by inscriptions of the reigns of the pharaohs Merneptah (c. 1212—1202) and Ramesses III (c. 1182—1151). The most important source is a series of reliefs of the reign of Ramesses III depicting a battle at sea.

This explanation, which gained much widespread acceptance, argued that the movement of a new Indo-European population, the Illyrians, into the Balkans forced out the resident populations, one group into Anatolia, the other into Greece. The invaders of Anatolia, the Phrygians, were supposed to have destroyed the Hittite empire and, like a tidal wave, caused the migration of the Sea Peoples. The Sea Peoples were thus displaced populations from Anatolia who then moved southwards, destroying cities in Cyprus, Syria and Palestine before being repulsed at the borders of Egypt. Some of these groups then settled (the *Peleset*—Philistines—in the region which became known as Philistia), while others sailed westwards, such as the *Shardana* who eventually settled in Italy and the islands.

Despite having been favoured until quite recently, this idea of the Sea Peoples migration can no longer be accepted; there is no real evidence to support it. Essentially the Sea Peoples theory was a convenient and plausible invention of the 19th century, designed (largely by the historian Gaston Maspero) to fit the very limited available facts.

Egyptian texts name a number of different peoples who took part in the incursions repelled by Merneptah and Ramesses III. The facts that their names are usually linked with Libyan invasions and that they appear to have been present in only small numbers would seem to imply that they may, in fact, have been employed as mercenary troops by the Libyan rulers. Among these mercenaries we discover the *Shardana* from Sardinia, the *Lukka* (who may have originated in Lycia), the *Ekwesh* (who have been identified with the Achaeans), and the *Peleset* (who were certainly the Philistines).

A recent re-assessment of the Sea Peoples theory has argued that the destructions of 1200 should be attributed to these groups of free-booters who finding how successful they were in military confrontation with the eastern empires, began to form raiding parties. It is quite clear that in some places, such as Crete, the settlements which replaced the sacked centres were located in deliberately remote and easily defended positions.

Other theories have been suggested for the collapse of the Late Bronze Age empires. It has been proposed that climatic changes caused problems throughout western Asia and that the centralized economies were unable to control their agricultural subsistence. Alternatively, there may have been close links between the great palace centres of Egypt, Mesopotamia and the Hittites and their mutual reliance meant that the collapse of one would have a devastating "domino effect".

Although natural catastrophe, such as earthquake, has been accepted as a factor at individual sites, it has been less enthusiastically received as a more general explanation. However, recent archaeological work has suggested the possibility that such a disaster may have been the cause of severe problems in Mycenaean Greece. The great earthquake which levelled Sparta in 465 caused an uprising of the subject population, and although Sparta was able to reassert her position, the incident gives a clear indication of the devastating effects of just one severe tremor. The repercussions of a series of such earthquakes may have been sufficient to destabilize a civilization. The most recent evidence comes from Mycenaean Tiryns, first excavated by Schliemann. A geological survey carried out by the German Archaeological Institute has revealed clear indications that the destruction was the result of severe seismic activity. The force of the earthquake which devastated Tiryns would have caused massive destruction in the other cities of the plain, Mycenae and Argos. The natural catastrophe which enveloped these cities did not bring the civilization to an end, but the following phase has a different character. Whatever the factors which began the crisis in the eastern Mediterranean, the result was the same: fragmentation, economic recession and the beginning of a Dark Age which saw the emergence of new kingdoms, new warfare and new forms of trade.

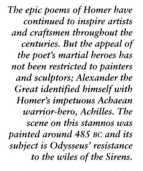

The epic poems of Homer have continued to inspire artists and craftsmen throughout the centuries. But the appeal of the poet's martial heroes has not been restricted to painters and sculptors; Alexander the Great identified himself with Homer's impetuous Achaean warrior-hero, Achilles. The scene on this stamnos was painted around 485 BC and its subject is Odysseus' resistance to the wiles of the Sirens.

Origins

The origins of the Greek civilization remain intractably obscure, but it is certain that the 5th millennium witnessed a startling expansion of trade and cultural interchanges.

The origin of the Greeks is a still much-debated subject. Greek is part of the Indo-European language group, and earlier scholars associated it with a branch of the "Aryan" people, emerging from somewhere in central Asia. Waves of these settlers who spoke different dialects supposedly invaded Greece and subjected the indigenous populations. According to this theory, the last of these invasions, that of the Dorians, brought about the destruction of the Bronze Age civilization of Mycenae (around 1200 BC). Given the undoubtedly dubious racial theories underlying much of this reconstruction, recent scholars have treated it more sceptically. But it has to be admitted that our knowledge of prehistoric Greece, and of the transitions between the Neolithic, Bronze Age and Archaic-Classical worlds is still quite limited.

Crete (particularly Knossos) and Thessaly have provided the most information on the Neolithic phases, the 7th to 4th millennia BC, during which agriculture and animal domestication became widespread. Archaeology has suggested that there were new populations, but equally the changes could be the result of local populations having stronger contacts with other regions. Some Cretan pottery, for example, has similarities with that of western Anatolia. The stimulus in Thessaly was probably from the other cultures of the northern Balkan regions. As yet, there is only evidence of much smaller, scattered settlement in southern Greece.

From 5000 there was an expansion of the trade routes, and, perhaps as a result, greater settlement throughout the Cyclades and Crete. Obsidian from Melos has been found at Knossos and in Thessaly, showing that wide-ranging trade began early. Other island sites, such as Saliagos and Grotta (on Naxos), reveal that there were connections with, and influences from, the eastern Aegean. Some Cycladic pottery also shows Anatolian influence. In the eastern Mediterranean, Cyprus became important in the trade networks of the Bronze Age. By the end of the Bronze Age there are signs of settlement by Greek-speakers in Cyprus.

The archaeological phases of the Bronze Age (*c.* 3300—1000 BC) have been named according to their pottery development: Minoan on Crete, Helladic for the mainland and Cycladic for the islands. These are grouped into longer phases termed Prepalatial (3300—2100), First (2100—1700), Second (1700—1450) and Third (1450—1200) Palace Periods and Postpalatial, the more precise dating of the pottery phases is achieved through the connections with Cyprus, western Asia and Egypt (although there are still academic disputes about detail). These phases saw the growth and flourishing of the Minoan and Mycenaean civilizations, and their eventual collapse.

On the mainland there is evidence for monumental buildings and fortifications developing during the Prepalatial period, notably at Lerna and Tiryns. The function of these structures is still uncertain, but many archaeologists have assumed that they were temples or palaces. Whatever their purpose, they indicate a process of state-formation.

Crete provides us with the earliest evidence for the development of larger settlements. The principal ones, such as Knossos, Phaistos, Gournia and Khania, can be termed towns, having public spaces, a fairly regular layout of streets, and multi-roomed houses. These towns came to be dominated by the

For thousands of years the Neolithic farmers of the Cycladic islands created simple figures, such as this white marble idol dating to around 2500—2000 BC, by grinding the stone to the desired shape.

massive palace complexes. Knossos was already a large settlement at the beginning of the Bronze Age and eventually became pre-eminent amongst the Cretan towns. Some of the larger Cretan centres were probably "capitals" of territories with smaller towns and villages subject to them. Most of the population of these towns was engaged in agricultural work, although there must have been increasing numbers of artisans and administrators, as well as "traders". Writing developed on Crete, probably as a result of contacts with western Asia, the earlier form "Linear A" in the Second Palace Period, and the more sophisticated "Linear B" in the early Third Palace Period.

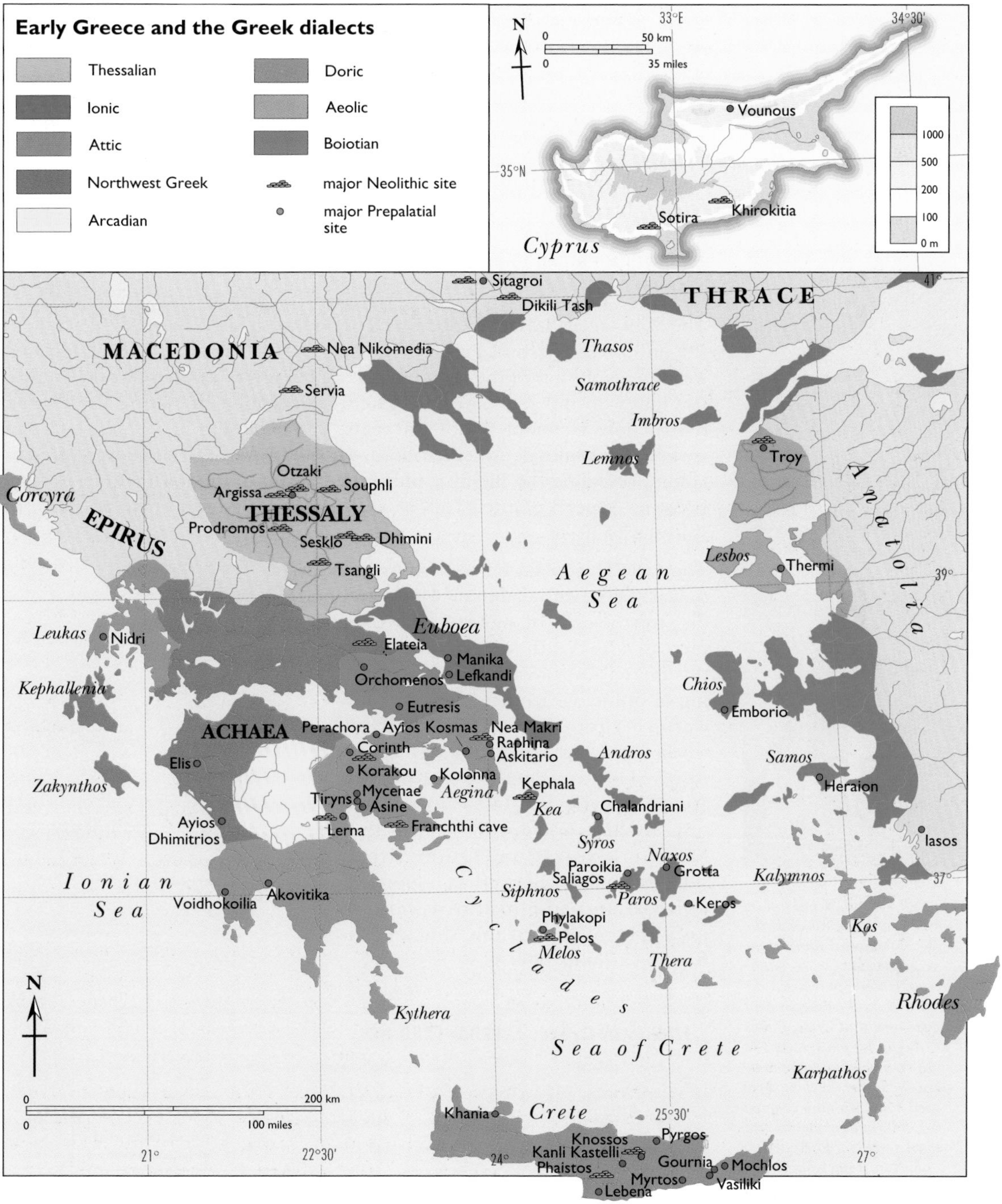
Early Greece and the Greek dialects
Thessalian
Ionic
Attic
Northwest Greek
Arcadian
Doric
Aeolic
Boiotian
major Neolithic site
major Prepalatial site
N
0
50 km
0
35 miles
33°E
34°30'
35°N
Vounous
Sotira
Khirokitia
Cyprus
1000
500
200
100
0 m
Sitagroi
Dikili Tash
THRACE
MACEDONIA
Nea Nikomedia
Servia
Thasos
Samothrace
Imbros
Lemnos
Troy
Anatolia
Otzaki
Argissa
Souphli
THESSALY
Prodromos
Sesklo
Dhimini
Tsangli
Corcyra
EPIRUS
Lesbos
Thermi
Aegean Sea
39°
41°
Leukas
Nidri
Kephallenia
Euboea
Elateia
Manika
Orchomenos
Lefkandi
Eutresis
Chios
Emborio
ACHAEA
Perachora
Ayios Kosmas
Nea Makri
Raphina
Askitario
Corinth
Elis
Korakou
Kolonna
Andros
Samos
Heraion
Zakynthos
Tirryns
Mycenae
Asine
Aegina
Kephala
Kea
Chalandriani
Ayios Dhimitrios
Lerna
Franchthi cave
Syros
Iasos
Naxos
Paroikia
Saliagos
Grotta
Kalymnos
37°
Ionian Sea
Voidhokoilia
Akovitika
Siphnos
Paros
Keros
Phylakopi
Pelos
Melos
Kos
Cyclades
Thera
Rhodes
Kythera
Sea of Crete
Karpathos
0
200 km
0
100 miles
Khania
Crete
25°30'
Knossos
Pyrgos
Kanli Kastelli
Gournia
Mochlos
Phaistos
Myrtos
Vasiliki
Lebena
21°
22°30'
24°
27°

King Minos and Knossos

Bronze Age Crete was dominated by the palace civilization of Knossos. Victorian and later excavations would reveal a sophisticated society boasting considerable artistic and agricultural development.

The civilization of Crete was named by the excavator of Knossos, Sir Arthur Evans, after the mythical King Minos: the complexity of the palaces at Knossos allowed a suitable comparison with the Labyrinth to be made. Although no archaeological evidence can be invoked to confirm the legend, or even Minos' existence, Knossos was undoubtedly the most powerful of the Cretan cities.

The towns contained palaces, administrative and religious centres. There were also many cult sites in the countryside (the peak sanctuaries and the sacred caves).

The Minoans maximised the agricultural potential of Crete, and their success in this endeavour is demonstrated by the terraces and dams at Pseira. The so-called "villas", found particularly in the east, have settlements associated with them, and were probably important in the production of wine and olive oil.

The Minoan civilization experienced periods of crisis. A major destruction at the end of the Second Palace Period (*c.* 1450), has often been associated with the explosion of the island of Thera. However, on present calculations, the dates do not coincide, the Thera catastrophe predating the Cretan destructions by about 100 or 150 years. The explosion of Thera, which was certainly enormous, preserved the town site of Akrotiri, perhaps a Minoan colony, revealing the highly sophisticated layout of the town and its houses, boasting superb painted frescos and drainage systems equal to those of Knossos itself.

The early Third Palace Period at Knossos was particularly rich, with elaborate tombs and burials, new cycles of ornate frescos and increased links with western Asia. During this phase, Knossos rose to its peak ruling or influencing much of central and western Crete. This was the period when the Linear B script was developed. The destruction of Knossos (probably in the late 14th century) was not, as once thought, the end of the Minoan civilization. Other sites, notably Khania, survived as important political and administrative centres until the collapse of the Minoan civilization, around 1200 BC.

The Bull Verandah and pillars of the Hypostyle Room at the Palace of Knossos, as reconstructed by Sir Arthur Evans. Having purchased the site from the independent government of Crete, Evans began his excavations in 1899. The palace which he unearthed over the next three and a half decades covered 13,000 square metres and boasted a multi-floored design of astonishing complexity.

Gramvousa
Grambousa

Arkoudiotissa
Akrotiri
(cave of Lera)
Kydonia ★● Khania
Apter

White Mountains

Khrysoskalitissa
Thrimbokambos

24°

I/Minoan Crete, c. 1500–1250 BC

△	palace	⌒	tholos tomb	▬	finds of Linear A texts
△	lesser palace & villa	⌂	sacred cave	▬	finds of Linear B texts
●	town	●	peak sanctuary		places mentioned in Linear B texts
○	village	⛵	port	★	

2000
1500
1000
500
200
0 m

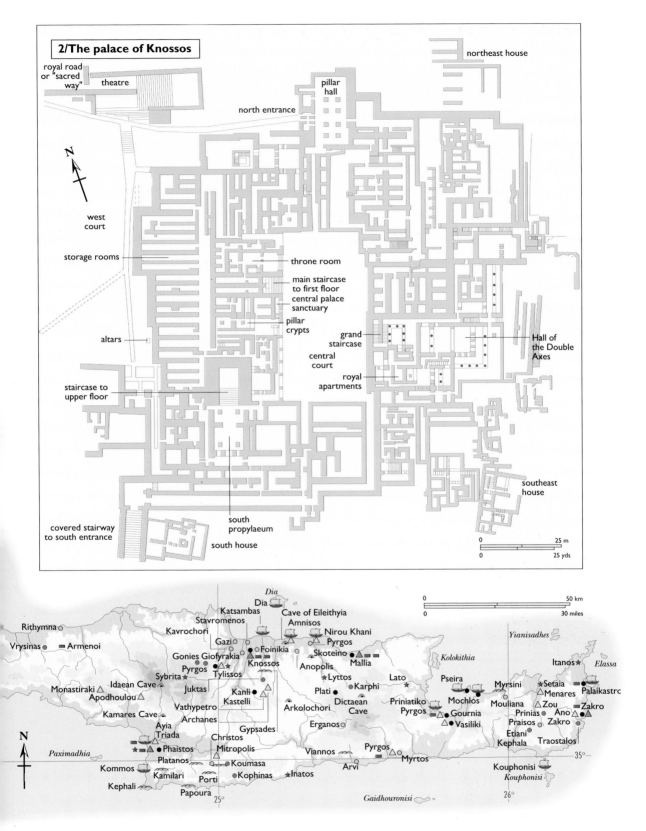

2/The palace of Knossos

royal road or "sacred way"

theatre

northeast house

pillar hall

north entrance

N

west court

storage rooms

throne room

main staircase to first floor

central palace sanctuary

pillar crypts

grand staircase

Hall of the Double Axes

altars

central court

staircase to upper floor

royal apartments

southeast house

covered stairway to south entrance

south propylaeum

south house

0   25 m
0   25 yds

Rithymna

Vrysinas

Armenoi

Dia

Dia

Katsambas

Stavromenos

Kavrochori

Cave of Eileithyia

Amnisos

Nirou Khani

Pyrgos

Gazi

Foinikia

Skoteino

Yianisadhes

Gonies Giofyrakia

Knossos

Anopolis

Mallia

Kolokithia

Itanos

Elassa

Pyrgos

Sybrita

Tylissos

Lyttos

Lato

Pseira

Myrsini

Setaia

Idaean Cave

Juktas

Plati

Karphi

Menares

Palaikastro

Monastiraki

Apodhoulou

Kanli Kastelli

Priniatiko Pyrgos

Mochlos

Mouliana

Zou

Zakro

Kamares Cave

Vathypetro

Archanes

Arkolochori

Dictaean Cave

Gournia

Vasiliki

Prinias

Praisos

Ano Zakro

Ayia Triada

Christos

Gypsades

Erganos

Etiani Kephala

Traostalos

N

Paximadhia

Phaistos

Mitropolis

Viannos

Pyrgos

Myrtos

35°

Platanos

Koumasa

Arvi

Kouphonisi

Kommos

Kamilari

Porti

Kophinas

Inatos

Kouphonisi

Kephali

Papoura

25°

Gaidhouronisi

26°

0   50 km
0   30 miles

The Mycenaean World

The Mycenaean civilization boasted considerable wealth and power and its supremacy was reflected in both its colossal architecture and the skill of its craftsmen.

The Third Palace Period (1450—1200) saw the greatest expansion and sophistication of the mainland states. The economic structure seems to have followed that of western Asia and Crete, being centralized upon the palaces. Mycenae was the most powerful of the mainland states, with Tiryns as a subject city for at least part of this period. There were other palace-based states at Pylos, Thebes, Athens and perhaps Orchomenos and Gla. Linear B tablets and jar-inscriptions have been found at these sites.

The rulers of Mycenae, and perhaps the other states had diplomatic relations with Egypt, and are probably to be identified with the kings of Ahhiyawa referred to in the Hittite royal archives. At Mycenae the richly-equipped burials discovered by Heinrich Schliemann in the Shaft Graves

"There are parts of the ring-wall left, including the gate with lions standing on it. They say this is the work of Kyklopes, who built the wall of Tiryns for Proitos ... In the ruins of Mycenae are the underground chambers of Atreus and his sons where they kept the treasure-houses of their wealth. There is the grave of Atreus and the graves of those who came home from Troy, to be cut down by Aigisthos at his supper-party ... another tomb is Agamemnon's."
Pausanias, *The Guide to Greece*

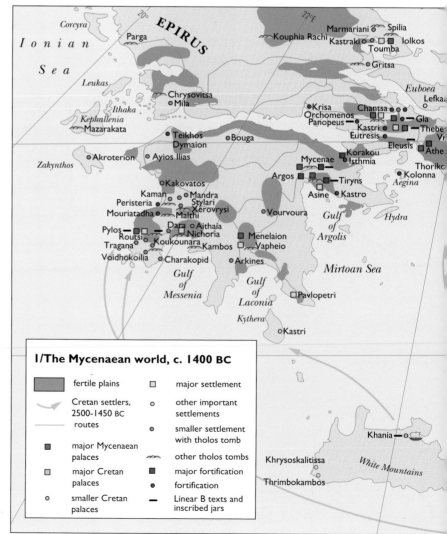

I/The Mycenaean world, c. 1400 BC

▨	fertile plains	□	major settlement
⤳	Cretan settlers, 2500-1450 BC	○	other important settlements
—	routes	◎	smaller settlement with tholos tomb
■	major Mycenaean palaces	⌢	other tholos tombs
□	major Cretan palaces	■	major fortification
○	smaller Cretan palaces	●	fortification
		—	Linear B texts and inscribed jars

Although known traditionally as the Lion Gate, the carvings above the main entrance to Mycenae may be griffins.

belong to the 16th century, early in the city's rise to preeminence. Gold masks, crowns and costume decorations, jewellery of gold, silver, amethyst and amber, vases of gold, silver, faience and alabaster, drinking vessels made from ostrich eggs, and objects of ivory, all attest the rulers' considerable wealth derived from local resources and foreign trade.

During the high point of Mycenae's power, massive "cyclopean" city walls were constructed. Other sites, notably Tiryns, also had fortifications, although the wide spread of small settlements suggests that this was not due to constant warfare (as was once proposed). The fortifications may have been to emphasize the importance of the centres, and perhaps to protect the wealth which was stored within them. A network of roads and bridges radiated from Mycenae, connecting it with the other major centres and were perhaps to make movement by chariot easier. The palaces and houses were decorated with frescos and, like the Cretan palaces, had bathrooms and drainage systems. There were many craftsmen, including specialists in ivory working and faience, techniques developed in western Asia and Egypt. This sophisticated culture was to come to a sudden and catastrophic end.

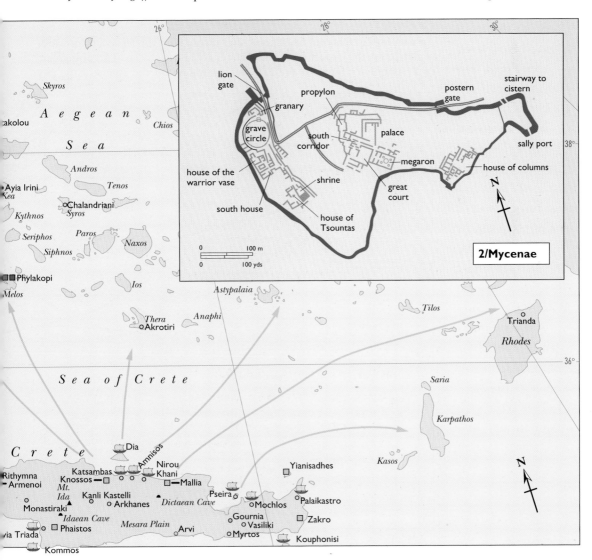

Bronze Age Trade

The movement of goods, whether through trade or the exchange of gifts, indicates a rapidly expanding communications network throughout the eastern Mediterranean in the Bronze Age period.

"A message from the King of Alashiya (Cyprus) to the King of Egypt. My brother, I send a messenger to you with 100 talents of copper. Now may your messenger bring to me one ebony bed trimmed with gold, one chariot and two horses, fourteen beams of ebony, and bales of the finest linen. You have not been put on the same level as the King of Hatti or the King of Shankhar (Babylon). Whatever greeting-gift my brother sends to me, I for my part send you back double."

Letter from the Amarna archive

We have far less evidence from the Prepalatial and First Palace Periods than from the later phases of the Bronze Age. In both, it is only Crete that has produced material of Egyptian and western Asiatic origin, and only Minoan material has been found in those countries. With the Second Palace Period there was a growth of Minoan influence throughout the eastern Mediterranean and in the mainland centres of southern Greece. Contacts with other parts of Europe also developed. At the same time there was an expansion of western Asiatic, particularly Cypriot, activities. This increased still further in the Third Palace Period, resulting in complex international networks. Metals, particularly copper (from Cyprus and Anatolia) and gold (from Egypt and Kush) were an important item of exchange. Other materials came from more remote regions: ebony and ivory (mostly from Kush via Egypt), lapis lazuli (from Afghanistan) and amber.

Archaeological material from many sites throughout the Near East provides evidence for the export of Mycenaean and Minoan objects. The diplomatic correspondence between the Egyptian pharaoh and the rulers of the city

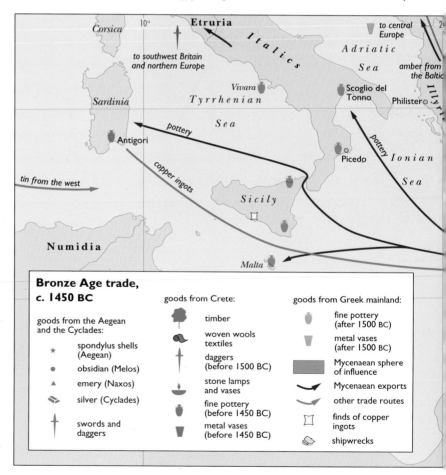

Bronze Age trade, c. 1450 BC

goods from the Aegean and the Cyclades:

- ★ spondylus shells (Aegean)
- ● obsidian (Melos)
- ▲ emery (Naxos)
- 🦪 silver (Cyclades)
- ✝ swords and daggers

goods from Crete:

- 🌳 timber
- 🐚 woven wools textiles
- ✝ daggers (before 1500 BC)
- 🛢 stone lamps and vases
- 🏺 fine pottery (before 1450 BC)
- ▼ metal vases (before 1450 BC)

goods from Greek mainland:

- 🏺 fine pottery (after 1500 BC)
- ▼ metal vases (after 1500 BC)
- ▢ Mycenaean sphere of influence
- ↶ Mycenaean exports
- ↷ other trade routes
- ▢ finds of copper ingots
- 🦪 shipwrecks

states of Syria, Palestine and the kingdoms of Anatolia and Mesopotamia, highlight the method and type of the commodities exchanged. Perhaps most strikingly, the ship-wrecks at Cape Gelidonya and Ulu Burun off the coast of Anatolia, provide an invaluable record of cargoes. A site near Mersa Matruh has yielded Cypriot and Mycenaean material and is evidence of trading contacts with the Libyans.

Controversy still surrounds the issue of "trade" in the Bronze Age. Some specialists argue that much international exchange during the Late Bronze Age was gift-exchange between rulers, made at the sending of embassies, as dowries, or on royal occasions such as accession or jubilee. But whether "trade" or "gift" the result was essentially the same: raw materials and manufactures from one region were exchanged for those of another. This could be indirect: for example, ivory might pass from Kush (modern Sudan) to Egypt and thence to one of the cities of the Phoenician coast (such as Ugarit) or Cyprus and from there to Mycenae. There is also good evidence for direct contacts between the Mycenaean/Minoan world and Egypt.

As well as producing exquisite works of art in gold and bronze, the Mycenaean artisans and craftsmen used more homely materials to create items of immense character and charm. One such artefact is this delightful pottery goblet decorated with a stylized cuttlefish, dating from around 1350 BC.

Both Minoan and Mycenaean pottery (containing perfumed oils) seem to have become regular items of exchange and have been found in sites in Cyprus, Egypt, Sudan, western Asia (Carchemish and Masat) and in Sicily, Etruria, Malta and Sardinia. Although archaeology emphasises the precious materials such as metals and ivory, other commodities, such as olive oil and perhaps wine, were important exports from Greece and the Aegean.

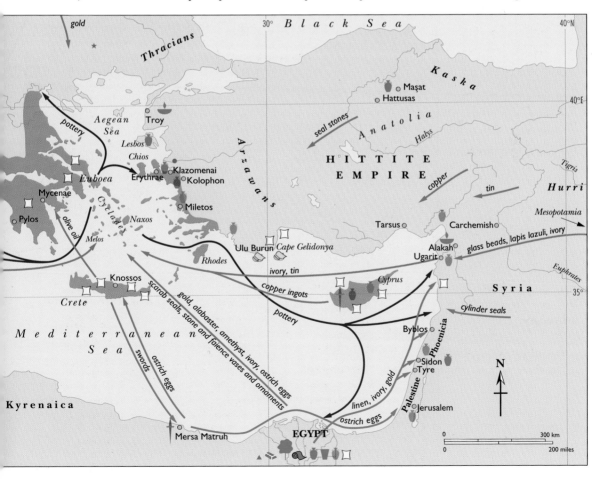

The Sea Peoples Controversy

During the 12th century BC a tide of destruction swept across the eastern Mediterranean but controversy still rages as to what caused such wide-spread devastation.

"The isles were restless, disturbed among themselves. They poured out their people all together. No land stood before them … they destroyed them and assembled in one camp in the midst of the Amorite country."
Inscription of Ramesses III on the temple walls of Medinet Habu, *c.* 1190 BC

Around 1200 BC there was crisis in the eastern Mediterranean which resulted in the collapse of the Late Bronze Age empires. In mainland Greece, Thebes, Lefkandi, Tiryns, Mycenae and Pylos and on Crete, Khania, all suffered destruction, partial or complete. Mostly these cities and their palaces seem to have gone up in flames. In Anatolia, all of the major Bronze Age sites have a destruction level which can be dated to around this time. The Hittite capital of Hattusas was plundered and burned, as were the chief cities of Cyprus. On the coast of north Syria, the trading city of Ugarit was destroyed and never reoccupied. Further south in the Levant many other sites show similar destruction. This wave of destruction did not spread east to Mesopotamia, and although it moved southwards, Egypt possessed the strength to withstand it.

Of the various theories put forward to explain the crisis, that which has been most highly favoured attributes it to ethnic movements, principally from the

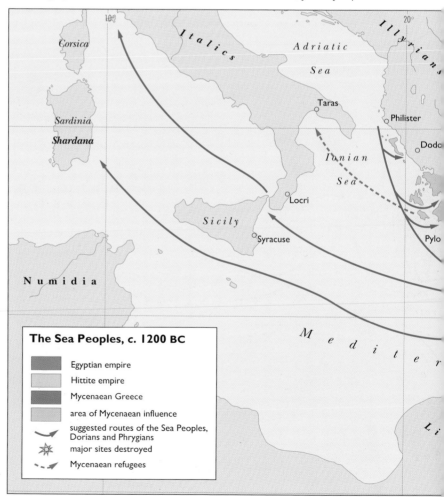

The Sea Peoples, c. 1200 BC

- Egyptian empire
- Hittite empire
- Mycenaean Greece
- area of Mycenaean influence
- suggested routes of the Sea Peoples, Dorians and Phrygians
- major sites destroyed
- Mycenaean refugees

A frieze carved at Abydos during the reign of Ramesses II constitutes one of the only visual representations of the Sea Peoples available to modern scholars. The figure wears a horned helmet and carries both a shield and a sword.

north. In Greece, it was attributed to the invasion of the Dorians, and in western Asia, to the Phrygians and the "Sea Peoples". The identity of the Sea Peoples is based on Egyptian inscriptions and reliefs of the reigns of the pharaohs Merneptah and Ramesses III. The names of some of the groups preserved in the Egyptian sources clearly relate to known place-names. For example, the *Shardana* have long been associated with Sardinia. It was suggested that, following the repulse of the invasion by the pharaoh Ramesses III, this group sailed off and eventually colonised Sardinia.

A recent re-examination of the whole "Sea Peoples" problem has questioned the accuracy of this 19th-century interpretation of events. A new theory has been proposed which challenges the idea that the crisis was caused by a mass movement of populations. This new interpretation does not deny the destructions but attributes them to changed warfare at the time. It is possible, for instance, that such groups as the *Shardana* were mercenary troops coming *from* Sardinia. The dating and nature of the "Dorian invasion" of Greece is now also generally discounted. Nevertheless, there certainly was upheaval throughout the eastern Mediterranean, but population movements may have been a result, rather than a cause of the crisis. Exactly what brought about the end of the Mycenaean kingdoms and the Bronze Age empires of western Asia is still unexplained.

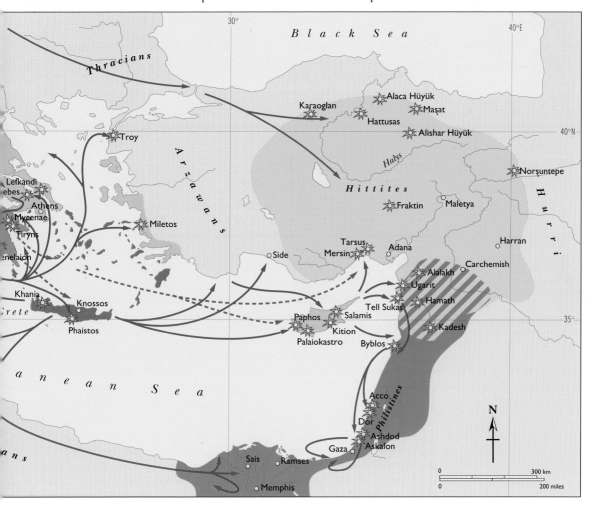

The Collapse of Mycenae

Around 1200 BC the Mycenaean world was plunged into chaos and economic collapse, some settlements were re-established whilst others remained deserted.

"The Lacedaemonians were the most eminent of the Dorian peoples and the Athenians of the Ionian. These two ... were the most powerful of the Greek people ... The Dorians have been constantly on the move ... they settled in Pindos, and were known as Macedonians; thence they migrated ... to the Peloponnese, where they got their present name of Dorians."

Herodotos, *The Histories, Book I*

Mycenaean power came to an end around 1200 BC. The close of the Third Palace Period is marked by destruction, often by fire, at many sites. Some towns were abandoned and never reoccupied, others were rebuilt and some even grew in size. Tiryns, notably, expanded, probably becoming the most important centre in the Argolid. There was a dramatic decline in overseas trade and although the Mycenaean pottery traditions continued, there was certainly an economic recession.

The northernmost sites to show these signs of destruction are in Thessaly, where Iolkos was probably burned, but occupation continued. At Thebes there are signs of devastation followed by rebuilding and another destruction. Lefkandi was burned but immediately rebuilt. The evidence from Athens is less clear, but the Postpalatial settlement was much smaller than the earlier one. Korakou on the isthmus of Corinth was perhaps damaged and reoccupied. Many sites in the Argolid were destroyed or abandoned after 1200. Prosymna, Barbati, both close to Mycenae, were abandoned, but without signs of devastation. This was perhaps the case at Lerna also, but nearby Zygouries and Midea were destroyed by fire. At Tiryns and Mycenae the citadels and towns were consumed by fire. The citadel of Mycenae was rebuilt and reoccupied, and the new city at Tiryns was larger than before. Asine was another site which grew in size. In the southern and western Peloponnese, Iria and Menelaion went up in flames, as did Nichoria, Pylos, Mouriatadha and Malthi.

The regions of Elis and Arcadia are less well-known, but there are indications of population decline. There are many more sites known further north in Achaea and it has been suggested that people now moved to this more protected region. Some sites, such as Teikhos Dymaion had been burnt but were now protected with fortifications.

The evidence from the islands is much scantier, although there is evidence for similar destruction and looting of palaces on Paros, at Koukounaries, which was then rebuilt with fortified walls, Mycenaean sites at Phylakopi on Melos, Ayia Irini on Kea and Grotta on Naxos survived. Further east, Ialysos on Rhodes seems to have increased enormously in population, the settlement at Seraglio on Kos continued.

Crete, presents a different problem. The destruction of Knossos seems to predate this catastrophe, and is probably due to different causes. Khania was destroyed around 1200. In the east of the island, coastal sites were abandoned and larger settlements in remote and well-protected places seem to be preferred. So Amnisos, Mallia and Palaikastro were deserted, to be replaced by Karphi, Vrokastro and Kavousi.

This wave of destruction, much of which can be dated by the pottery evidence to around 1225—1100, has been blamed on the invasions of the Sea Peoples and the Dorians. Theories put forward in the last century, which gained wide acceptance until quite recently, argued that the end of the Mycenaean world was brought about by massive "barbarian" invasions from the central Balkans. Other population movements from the Balkans eastward into Anatolia were seen to account for the destruction of Troy and the Hittite capital of Hattusas. Most Hittite scholars have discarded this migration (for which the evidence was only very circumstantial). Similarly the movement of the Dorians into southern Greece may have been into the less-populated regions created by migrations to Cyprus and the coast of Anatolia (where they became the Ionians). Who or what then was responsible for the widespread destruction and the fall of Mycenae? Over-centralization and economic decline, famine, technological change and proletarian revolution have all been proposed for the collapse of Mycenaean Greece. Most recently the destructions have been attributed to organized groups raiding by sea from bases in Thessaly. Controversy about Mycenaean collapse will doubtless continue to divide the academic world. What we can be certain of, is that Greece was plunged into a "Dark Age".

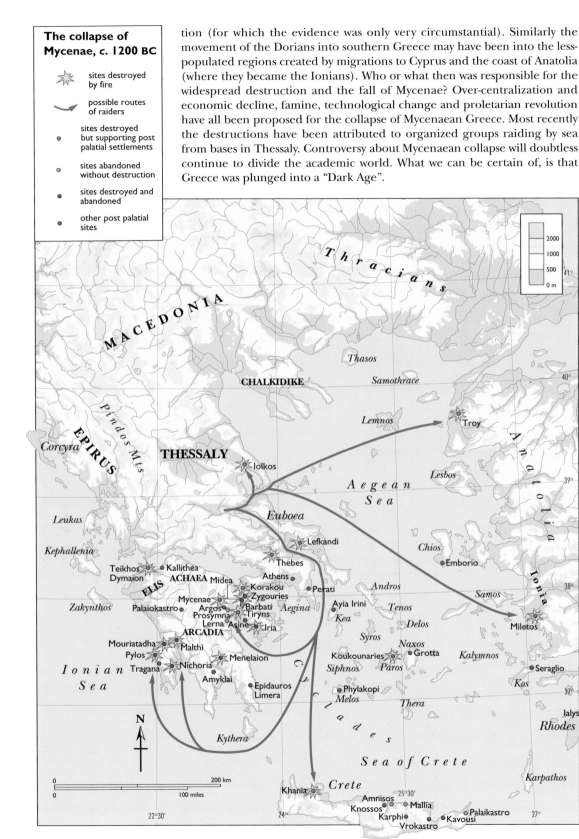

The collapse of Mycenae, c. 1200 BC

- sites destroyed by fire
- possible routes of raiders
- sites destroyed but supporting post palatial settlements
- sites abandoned without destruction
- sites destroyed and abandoned
- other post palatial sites

The Trojan Wars

For thousands of years the works of Homer have been a source of inspiration to writers, artists and craftsmen and the doubts over their authorship and historical accuracy do not diminish their real worth.

"Alas! So the gods did beckon me to my death! ... Athene has fooled me. Death is no longer far away; he is staring me in the face and there is no escaping him ... So now I meet my doom. Let me at least sell my life dearly and have a not inglorious end, after some feat of arms that shall come to the ears of generations still unborn."

Hektor's last vow in the *Iliad*, Book XXII

Since ancient times, the *Iliad* and the *Odyssey* have attracted speculation. More recently the question has been, was Homer a real person, or were the poems a collection of oral epics only woven together at a later date? Even the Greeks and Romans had doubts about Homer's existence. It seems possible that the poems are the work of one person, developing traditional material, and a date in the 8th century is now favoured for the composition, although they were first written down in the 6th.

Beginning with Herodotos many writers attempted to calculate the date of the Trojan war, with widely differing results. In our terms they ranged between 1346 and 1127 BC, the most favoured being 1184. As the Bible provided the stimulus for archaeology in the Near East, so the Homeric poems fired the early excavators such as Heinrich Schliemann. But increased

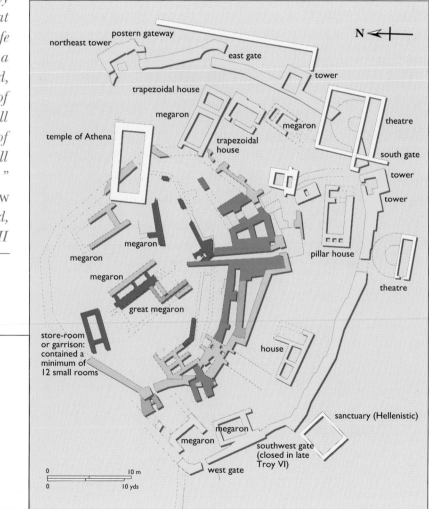

I/The construction phases of Troy

- Troy I
- Troy IIa
- Troy IIb
- Troy IIc–IIg
- Troy VI
- Troy IX

Of the nine major archaeological layers discovered at Troy it is the layer known as Troy VII which has been most closely identified with Homer's Troy. Primarily this identification is based upon the discovery of Mycenaean pottery and on the fact that this city was destroyed by fire.

knowledge from archaeology has only confused the issue further. Many details of the epics (such as the boar's tusk helmets) would seem to place the events in the Late Bronze Age, but other features do not fit. So it is assumed that the world of the Mycenaean period was ornamented, and to some extent garbled, with the contemporary (ie 8th century) details. The evidence from Troy itself has been confusing. Schliemann correctly identified the mound of Hissarlik with the ancient city, and of its many city levels two, Troy VI and Troy VII, offer the most likely equation with the city of Priam. Troy VI with its massive city walls seems to be that most closely resembling Homer's description, but its destruction, around 1300 BC, was both too early for the peak of Mycenaean power, and apparently caused by an earthquake. The succeeding Troy VII, however, was a very much poorer city.

Despite the numerous aspects of the epics which might be seen as illustrative of life and warfare in the Bronze Age, or the Dark Age, it would be folly to use them as such. The Homeric poems (whether by "Homer" or not) should be read as one of the greatest epic cycles in world literature, which has been a constant source of inspiration to playwrights, artists and musicians, and not as a reliable historical text.

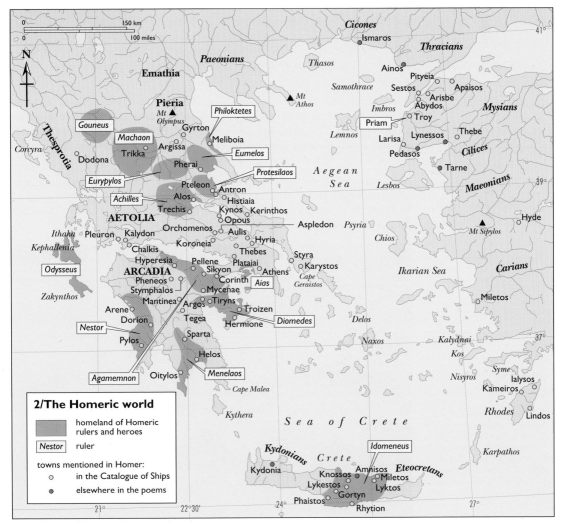

2/The Homeric world

homeland of Homeric rulers and heroes

Nestor ruler

towns mentioned in Homer:
○ in the Catalogue of Ships
● elsewhere in the poems

Minoan and Mycenaean Art

The power and influence of the Minoan and Mycenaean civilizations are evidenced most potently by their varied and often beautiful achievements in architecture and art.

"It gives me great joy to announce ... that I have discovered the tombs that have traditionally been known as the graves of Agamemnon, Cassandra, Eurymedon and their associates. In the tombs, I have found, immense treasures consisting of archaic objects of pure gold."
Heinrich Schliemann to George I of Greece, 1876

The art of mainland Greece owed much in technique and style to that developed on Minoan Crete. The great palaces of Crete, such as Knossos, were on two floors, the ground floors usually built of rubble held in mortar and strengthened with timbers. The upper floors were of brick. Important features were faced with dressed stone and throughout the interiors the walls were decorated with the frescoes which are one of the most renowned products of Minoan art. Throughout the Palatial Periods the range of colours increased, as did the elaboration of the paintings. The earliest, with a limited palette, were flat paintings, later many scenes included figures in plaster relief. Geometric panels flanked the important figurative groups. The subject matter was wide, including all forms of animal life, human and divine figures. The impression is naturalistic (and had a deep influence on the earlier interpretations of Minoan civilization). Not only walls, but ceilings and floors too, were decorated with fresco: the Dolphin fresco from Knossos was probably one such floor painting. Many of the human figurative groups are related to ritual, but the splendid frescoes from Akrotiri depict landscape, ships and town scenes. The famous scenes of bull-leaping are also found on the mainland, and an example has recently been excavated at a site in the Egyptian Delta.

The Mycenaean palaces were less magnificent than those of Crete, but this was probably compensated by the more massive and imposing construction of the citadels. The technique of fresco was widely adopted on the mainland, notably at Tiryns and Mycenae itself, although technically the Mycenaean frescoes are inferior to the Cretan models.

The rulers of Crete and the mainland had access to a wide variety of precious materials, many of them brought from western Asia. The techniques of working these materials were also imported, as well as decorative motifs. But all were adapted to local requirements.

A detail of the restored Dolphin fresco on the wall of the Queen's Room in the Minoan palace at Knossos. The rosette pattern below the dolphins is typically Minoan and the whole fresco probably dates from the last phase of the New Palace, around 1450—1400 BC.

The richest source of jewellery and other precious palace objects are the Shaft Graves of Mycenae. All of the usual types of jewellery are known and much of the work is in gold. Figures and decorations stamped out of a sheet of gold, or foil, were attached to dresses or used to make up necklaces. A wide variety of designs was used: the octopus was a popular Minoan motif, but others, such as griffins and winged sphinxes, show the influence of western Asia. Diadems and head bands were also cut from gold sheets and decorated with embossed relief and pendants. A necklace of large amber beads found at Mycenae shows contacts with more northerly regions. The weapons of the Mycenaean rulers were decorated as lavishly as any jewellery. The hilts of their swords were encased with gold and ivory, the blades decorated with inlays of gold and silver. Some were geometric, others showed marine life or scenes of the chase. One of the most notable is a dagger inlaid with a lion hunt in gold, the figures held in place with *niello* (an adhesive including lead)—a technique employed at (and probably imported from) Byblos.

The so-called "Mask of Agamemnon", was the first of five gold masks discovered by the German entrepreneur and archaeologist Heinrich Schliemann during his excavasions at Mycenae during the 1870s. The beautifully refined masks were manufactured by pressing a thin sheet of gold over a wooden sculpture.

An exquisitely carved ivory box demonstrates both the high quality of Mycenaean craftsmanship and the dependence of the craftsmen on imports from around the Mediterranean. The ivory used to create this delicate work of art would originally have been exported from the African kingdom of Kush to Egypt, and from Egypt to the cultural centres of the Aegean.

Ivory was frequently used as inlay, but was also used to make valuable objects. The *pyxis* (a round or cylindrical box with lid) was particularly favoured as it was the natural shape of a cross-section of the tusk. Figures were also carved of ivory, and one of the most striking is a recently-discovered composite figure (perhaps representing Zeus Kouros) from Palaikastro on Crete. Originally half a metre high, the figure fitted into a base. All of the flesh parts were carved of ivory, the costume and other details made of stone and gold. This divine image was a predecessor of the great gold and ivory statues of the Classical period.

The technique of faience manufacture was introduced to Crete from Egypt or western Asia, but there was soon a flourishing local industry. Faience was used for making mosaic inlays, jewellery and vessels. Knossos remained an important centre and seems to have been continuously affected by the developments in faience elsewhere. The technique was transplanted to the mainland, and faience vessels were manufactured at Mycenae in the 13th century.

Although vessels of stone, faience and metal were used in the palaces, pottery remained the commonest material, and reached great sophistication in technique, forms and decoration, on both Crete and the mainland. Most of the decoration was painted, but a particular type, known as Kamares ware, developed on Crete which was decorated with moulded relief and applied ornaments. Fine decorated wares, notably the stirrup jars (but also Kamares ware) have been found all over the Mediterranean, western Asia and Egypt. They may have been exported as attractive items in their own right, but probably also for their valuable contents (perhaps perfumed oils). The vestiges of the Mycenaean style can be found on proto-Geometric pottery.

It is now clear that the Mycenaeans were speakers of the Greek language—but due to the Dark Age which separates the Mycenaean world from that of Geometric and Archaic Greece, the artistic legacy is obscured. It has been generally (but perhaps incorrectly) assumed that the artists of Archaic Greece started out afresh.

II: Dark Age to Athenian Ascendancy

For around 300 years Greece was lost in the obscurity of a Dark Age—but in the 9th century she emerged to lay the foundations of her cultural, colonial and political ascendancy.

Dark Age to Orientalizing Revolution

The Dark Age is undoubtedly one of the most controversial periods of Greek history. The Mycenaean world is usually thought to have come to an end (for whatever reason) around 1200 BC or in the decades following and Greece did not emerge from the Dark Age until the 9th century. The archaeology of Greece during the Dark Age is not a total blank, but it is confusing. There are many features which are found in the archaeology of Greece both in the Mycenaean age and again in the immediate aftermath of the Dark Age, but there is a lack of material to indicate whether these phenomena were continued through the Dark Age in Greece itself (and simply missing from the archaeological record) or reintroduced from western Asia.

It is certain that the centralized economies based on the palaces were disrupted and that there was extensive destruction at many important settlements. There are indications that people left Greece for Cyprus, Rhodes and the coast of Asia Minor. On the mainland, the evidence has led some archaeologists to assume that a much reduced population was now scattered in small pastoralist communities.

Recently, it has been argued that dates currently assigned to the end of the Mycenaean period (*c.* 1200) should be lowered to the middle of the 10th century. This proposition (based on the re-evaluation of Egyptian and western Asiatic archaeology) has proved highly controversial and is not widely accepted, but it would go a long way towards explaining the continuities from Mycenaean palace centres to the city-states.

Greece's emergence from the Dark Age was contemporaneous with the entry of the rest of the Near East into a new phase. From the 9th century, the Assyrian empire rose to become the most powerful of the new states and expanded to absorb the kingdoms of Syria-Palestine. This was also the time of the expansion of the trade networks of the Phoenician city-states, a phenomenon which was in part an attempt to meet the new demands of the Assyrians. Phoenician colonization spread along the coast of northwest Africa, Sicily, Sardinia and Spain. Greek colonization in the west followed the southern coast of Italy, Sicily and Corsica to the south coast of France. It also stretched along the coast of the north Aegean and into the Black Sea.

Cyprus was one of the most important points of contact between the Greek world and western Asia. The northern part of the island had been settled from mainland Greece and Crete following the collapse of the Mycenaean civilization and the southern part was occupied by the Phoenicians. Amongst the most important Cypriot centres, Kition had been built over an earlier Mycenaean settlement. The kings of Cyprus paid tribute to the Assyrian kings. One of the earliest Greek trading centres of this new phase, al Mina, was established on the mainland, at the mouth of the Orontes river. The evidence from al Mina suggests that Greeks began trading there in the later 9th century and continued to flourish until about 600 (around the time of the collapse of the Assyrian empire).

The rapid inclusion of Greece into the newly expanding trade networks is revealed by finds at many sites from the 9th to 7th centuries. Syrian,

"Commerce could even win a man prestige, because it gave the merchant familiarity with barbarous countries and gained him the friendship of foreign rulers and a wide experience of affairs. Some merchants even became the founders of great cities, such as Protis, for example, who won the friendship of the Gauls living along the Rhone and founded Massalia. It is said that both Thales and Hippokrates the mathematician engaged in trade, and Plato paid for the expenses of his stay in Egypt by selling oil. "
Plutarch, *Life of Solon*

Mesopotamian and Cilician seals have been found at Pithekoussai, Olympia, Samos and Delos. On Euboea, Syrian and Egyptian-style amulets were found at Lefkandi and a burial at Eretria had a Phoenician scarab in a gold setting. Phoenician bronze and silver bowls are even more widely distributed, from Cyprus, mainland Greece (Athens, Olympia and Delphi) to Italy (Praeneste and Falerii). Large tripod cauldrons and other metalwork from Syria, and perhaps Urartu (Armenia) appears in Greece from the 8th century. Such cauldrons, usually with attached figures or heads, often of griffins, were soon copied in Greece. Eastern influences spread rapidly and some bronze plaques from Crete have distinctly Assyrian motifs. Technology as well as style was also influenced by these foreign contacts. Ivory working is found in Greece once again, and there were faience workshops on Rhodes and Samos.

At Athens oriental motifs such as sphinxes were added to the geometric vase decoration, but in Corinth a new style developed, with incised decoration, painted in black on a white ground (called protocorinthian). This, along with Euboean imitations of it, became one of the commonest exports of the period and is found from al Mina and Naukratis in the east, to Italy and Carthage in the west.

Contacts with Egypt intensified in the 7th century, even more so after the founding of the trading town at Naukratis. The tradition recorded by Herodotos attributes the foundation of the town to the reign of the pharaoh Amasis (570—526), but the archaeological evidence suggests a somewhat earlier date, about 630. The influence of the Egyptian style had already been felt through art and objects exported by the Phoenicians, but now there were direct contacts. Egyptian influence is particularly notable in the development of the *kouros* figures of the Archaic period. Naukratis itself remained a flourishing centre and was visited by many of the leading Greek thinkers and politicians of the day, such as Thales and Solon. The town was also renowned for its beautiful prostitutes.

The greatest of the Greek colonizers were the Euboeans and many of the major colonies in south Italy and Sicily were founded by Eretria and Chalkis. Corinth also played a significant role as a trading city in this phase. Although the Corinthian foundations were fewer than those of Euboea, she was the mother-city of the richest of the Sicilian cities, Syracuse. Syracuse itself founded further cities (as did other colonies) and came to dominate the eastern part of the island.

The 8th and 7th centuries, the time of the great phases of colonization, was also a time of rapid cultural and political development in Greece itself. The alphabet was introduced through contacts with western Asia and wealth undoubtedly increased through the foreign trade ventures. The emergence of the city-states was soon followed by the codification of the laws.

Political Life and the Formation of the City-States

The best-known constitutions of Classical Greece are those of Athens and Sparta. They were the most powerful of the states of southern Greece and in many ways the history of the 5th to 4th centuries is that of their developing rivalry. Following the Persian Wars they were recognized both by themselves and by the other Greek states as the leaders of Greece. But they were not the only powerful states in Greece.

As Greece emerged from the Dark Age, Corinth established herself as one of the most important city-states. It was in a good position, having access through the Gulf to the Ionian Sea and to the Aegean across the isthmus. The surrounding region was fertile and wine and olives were cultivated. Under the rule of the tyrants Kypselos and Periander, the economy was developed, with pottery exports predominating. The vessels, small but perfectly formed, were decorated in the Orientalizing style. Incised and painted in black on white, they incorporate motifs from the repertoire of western Asia: sphinxes, griffins, the tree of life and friezes of palmette and lotus. It was not to be a significant political centre in the Classical period, but Corinth became a rich merchant city.

Another Peloponnesian city of enormous prestige was Argos, reputedly the oldest of the Greek cities. It achieved prominence under the rule of the tyrant Pheidon and was the first mainland city to introduce coinage. Later it suffered at the hands of Sparta, and was to become her inveterate enemy. In the Classical period it was most notable for its artistic talents; both Polykleitos, creator of some of the most copied of Greek sculptures, and his Athenian contemporary, Pheidias, were trained there.

In central Greece the most powerful of the cities was Thebes. Like its neighbour, and rival, Orchomenos, it was of Mycenaean origin. Ultimately, Thebes came to challenge Sparta for the hegemony of Greece, but most of its history was dominated by its struggle to control the Boiotian League.

The development of the democratic system in Athens was viewed, even as early as Aristotle, as an evolution from kingship through aristocracy and tyranny. Tradition attributed the unification of Attica and the rejection of kingship to the mythical Theseus. The kingship was replaced by elected officials, the *archons*. There was certainly a period when the landed aristocratic families were vying for control, and the legislator Drakon may have been responsible for curbing their power. The first leader to codify the Athenian laws (*c.* 624/621), Drakon has become proverbial for his severity, but the claim that he "wrote his laws in blood" is a misconception. Undoubtedly his laws were in some respects harsh, and may have caused the problems (particularly that of debt slavery) which Solon later tried to alleviate. They were not, however, without understanding, as is shown in the legislation on murder, the only part to survive (having been enshrined in Solon's code). Drakon was the first to make the important distinction between murder and manslaughter, the punishment for the latter being banishment, not death.

The next great Athenian reformer was Solon, and many later laws have been attributed to him. Elected *archon* for 594—593, his first, and one of his most important moves, was the cancellation of debts (*seisachtheia*) and the abolition of debt slavery. Debtors who had been sold as slaves abroad were repatriated. Solon was also responsible for the imposition of other important economic regulations. Up to this time, landowners had been able to sell their surplus produce abroad, but Solon recognized that the agricultural production of Attica was insufficient for its needs, with the exception of olive oil. While the export of olive oil was permitted that of other commodities, particularly corn, was prohibited. Realizing that the prosperity of Attica required trade and crafts Solon is supposed to have stipulated that a father should ensure that his sons learnt a craft and an increase of trade (particularly in pottery) does seem to belong to this period.

To some extent Solon's reforms limited the power of the aristocratic families (the *eupatrids*), and instead based control upon wealth. The newly established social groups were the "knights" (*hippeis*), the *hoplites* (*zeugitai*) and the *thetes*. The *archons* and treasurers came from the richest of the *hippeis*, the *pentakosiomedimnoi*, and other offices from the top two classes. In effect the

change was relatively minor since the richest were usually from the *eupatrid* families, but it did open the way to a "democratization" based upon wealth.

Solon's other legislation was particularly strong on family law and moral values. He ensured the rights of heiresses and legislated on adoption, in order to prevent families (particularly aristocratic ones) from dying out. Other laws were concerned with adultery and the prostitution of boys. He also prohibited overly ostentatious funerals.

The reforms of Kleisthenes (508) bound Attica together constitutionally and attempted to give political equality to all citizens. Attica was divided into political units, *demes,* each of which had a local assembly, a treasury and an official. All citizens were attached to a *deme* and their descendants retained the link whether resident or not. An artificial grouping of three *demes,* one from each of the regions of Attica—coastal, inland and city—made up a tribe (*phylai*). This restructuring broke the regional control of the aristocratic families. The officials were still elected from the top economic class, but Kleisthenes restricted the power of the *Areopagus* (the council of ex-*archons*) with the creation of a new council, the *Boule*. This was made up of 50 councillors from each of the ten tribes, each group (*prytaneis*) serving for one-tenth of the year. The concentration of power was thus in the hands of the *Boule* and the *Ecclesia*, the people's assembly.

Another important innovation of Kleisthenes' was *ostracism*. Intended as a curb on individual power and as a guard against tyranny, this was a method by which a citizen could be sent into exile for ten years, but without losing either citizenship or property. A ballot of all citizens would decide the matter: the name was written on a sherd of pottery (*ostrakon*) and the sherds then counted. The quorum needed was 6000, and a high number of those votes had to be cast against the individual in question before *ostracism* took place. It was later used, with varying degrees of success, against many notable Athenians, including Themistokles, Kimon, and Alkibiades.

Although these reforms established Athenian democracy before the commencement of the Persian Wars, there were some later refinements. In 451 Athens introduced the requirement that both parents of a citizen should be Athenian. Previously citizenship had only been demanded of the father and a number of notable Athenians had "foreign" mothers: Kleisthenes, Themistokles, Kimon and Thucydides. This legislation was probably intended as another curb on the aristocracy, with their international connections, and it reflects a vital aspect of Athenian democracy, its strict limitations. Although foreigners did eventually acquire some rights and a chance to achieve citizenship, women and slaves always remained outside the system.

Whilst the development of the constitution of Athens was achieved by a series of reforms over a long period, in Sparta the constitution was attributed to a single individual, Lykourgos. The date of Lykourgos' legislation and its significance are matters of scholastic dispute. The basis of the reforms was the *rhetra*, which may have been oracular in origin. Lykourgos may be a mythical figure and the ancient Greeks themselves had little solid information about him, calculating the reforms to dates between (in modern terms) 1100 and 776. Today, even the lowest of these is regarded as being too high, and the years around 650 are considered to be more realistic.

Sparta alone of the southern Greek states retained its kingship throughout the Classical period. It was invested in two houses, the Agiads and Eurypontids, which never intermarried. They were leaders in war and religion, as well as judges. Real power was held by the *Gerousia*, a council of thirty, including the two kings. Membership was restricted to a group of aristocratic families and limited to men over sixty years old. Once elected a man remained a member of the *Gerousia* until his death. There was a sovereign assembly (*Apella*) of the citizens which annually chose the five magistrates (*ephors*). The *ephors* formed a check on the power of the kings, swearing an oath to support them, but only if the kings kept the constitution. The political system meant that in foreign affairs Sparta generally supported oligarchies rather than either democracies or tyrannies.

The citizens, or Spartiates, were a relatively small group, perhaps numbering some 9,000 men. They were forbidden to be traders or manual workers, instead they were full-time warriors. At birth, each was given an allotment of state land (*klaros*) sufficient for his support (hence the term *homoioi* "equals"). This land was worked by the *helots* owned by the state. The *helots* were the population of Laconia and Messenia conquered during the expansion of Spartan power in the mid-8th century. The *perioikoi* were the citizens of subject towns which had not been enslaved. They had citizenship rights in their own towns, and were permitted to follow any occupation but they were obliged to supply troops to Sparta in time of war.

The general perception of Sparta in modern literature has tended to be negative, especially when its society is compared with that of Athens. There has undoubtedly been a lack of sympathy with the Spartan militaristic system. Athens has been lauded, as the supposed ancestor of democracy and for its culture (although this was more a product of its imperial ambitions than its democracy). Whilst the Spartan political system can hardly be described as a democracy, even in the Athenian sense, equality of the citizens seems to have been achieved there first. But that equality was not liberty. Nevertheless the Spartan system was highly regarded by many ancient Greeks, and Athens always had influential pro-Spartan groups.

Sparta, was not, however, a cultural wasteland. It was celebrated in early times for its choirs and music. Music and dance were both useful in military training. Although never notable for its architecture or sculpture, Spartan bronze-working was almost unparalleled in the Archaic period. The largest and finest of all Archaic bronze *kraters*, excavated at Vix in France, is the work of a Spartan craftsman (*c.* 530). Standing 1.64-metres high and weighing 208-kilogrammes it is decorated around the neck with a cast frieze of warriors and chariots and elaborate handles with Gorgon's heads. The body of the vase is plain. Herodotos describes a very similar bronze vesssel which the Spartans sent as a gift to Kroisos, king of Lydia (*c.* 550) when the king wished to enter into alliance with them. Sparta was, even at this early date, recognized as the most powerful of the Greek states.

Men and Women, Men and Men

As they emerged from the Dark Age, the city-states of Greece developed their own identities, but whether oligarchies or democracies, they shared a number of institutions and attitudes. Greece was generally a sex-segregated society, hence the hostility of other Greeks to the freedom of Spartan women who frequently appeared, and worse, did athletic exercise, in public. The role of women in Athens was the complete opposite. There it was inappropriate to speak about female relatives, or even mention their names, when in the company of unrelated men. The women had their own apartments in a house and were rarely seen in public. Nor was there any formal education for girls. This, of course, depended on wealth and class: for poorer women work was doubtless a necessity. Nor does it necessarily give a real impression of the society. Women were powerful within the home, and in many other cultures a lack of formal education has not prevented literacy. Women played an important role in religion: the festival of Demeter in Athens (the *Thesmophoria*) was closed to men, and one of the highest offices of the state, the priesthood of Athena Polias, was held by a woman. Interestingly, Greek literature provides the very antithesis of idealized Greek womanhood in the Amazon—whose existence and society is debated in detail by both Herodotos and earlier writers. The Amazon was neither a male nor a citizen, she was, however, a warrior eschewing the domestic virtues practised by Greek women. There were of course groups of women who did not conform to the ideal, but were still within society, such as the courtesans (*hetairai*). Such women are often depicted attending at (male) parties, and were accomplished musicians. Amongst the most noted was Aspasia, who came from

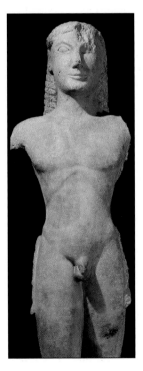

The style of the Kouros, *a standing athletic youth, usually naked, is clearly derived from Egyptian art. The stiff posture, left leg forward, broad shoulders and narrow waist are all conventional features of Egyptian statuary. The earliest large-scale sculptures of the Archaic Period, these figures are usually life-size and they were originally brightly painted. The female versions (*kore*) are all clothed. They are mostly carved in Greece's finest stone, marble, although some were cast in bronze.* Kouroi *were set up as funerary images or as dedications in temples. The later figures became more detailed in treatment of musculature and their poses were relaxed, opening the way to the Classical style.*

Miletos and became the mistress of Perikles, one of her chief attractions being her political wisdom. It should be emphasised that such an open alliance, between a leading aristocrat and a *hetaira*, was far from conventional and Perikles was made to suffer at the hands of Athens' comedians.

The attitude to women and segregation of the sexes was surely a contributory factor to one of the most striking developments of Greek society, its homosexual emphasis. It was a feature of most Greek city-states and was institutionalized in some of their armies, notably those of Elis, Sparta and Thebes.

Much literature, particularly the philosophical, emphasises the educational aspect of the relationship between an older man and a youth. The younger was to see in the older a model to be emulated, the older would admire the younger for his beauty which was identified with his physical strength as a young warrior. It was supposed to be a question of love of character, rather than physical attraction. Despite the tendency in much Greek literature to emphasise an ideal chaste relationship (and to censure consummation), literary anecdotes and paintings (of a quite explicit nature) on pottery rather suggest that the ideal remained, in many cases, just that. However, Greek society generally did not tolerate the same relationship between two adult men or the continuance of a relationship beyond a youth's maturity (he then assumed the elder role to a younger man). It should also be noted that while the practice was widespread and generally similar, the manners and customs of one city state might offend the propriety of another. In Athens, where the official emphasis was on a chaste relationship, jokes could be made about the outrageous moral laxity of the Spartans. The Thebans were particularly noted for their indulgence in homosexuality, to the extent that a Theban hero, Laios, was supposed to have invented the practice. It was in the Theban "Sacred Band" that homosexuality was deliberately used to great military effect: lovers were placed side by side in battle because it was believed that this would encourage them to greater feats of valour.

The Greek world which developed in the Archaic period shared much in common in terms of customs, language and culture. But it was also deeply divided, particularly politically. The threat of conquest by Persia briefly brought unity of purpose to some of the states, but it also sowed the seeds of a rivalry which would last even longer. The political composition of Greece — its fragmentation into city-states — inevitably led to a state of almost continuous warfare. The equation of citizenship with military service was found in most city-states, hence there was a considerable emphasis on military training and young men were prized for their worth as fighters. In Sparta and Crete all society was "subordinated" to military necessity.

Oracles and Games

One of the unifying forces of the Greek world was religion, and the Archaic period saw the development of a number of important local and pan-Hellenic centres. Dodona, reputed to be the oldest oracle of Zeus, had as its focus a sacred oak tree. Situated in the Pindos mountains of Epirus, it was remote from most of the major centres of the Classical period, and although the evidence indicates its origins in the Bronze Age, it was not richly endowed with monuments until the Hellenistic period. By contrast, the oracle of Apollo at Delphi near his sacred mountain, Parnassos, gained in importance in the late Archaic period and was to become one of the most revered of shrines. From an early date the oracle's advice was regularly sought, and it received rich gifts from foreign rulers, such as Kroisos of

Lydia. In the Classical period it continued to be consulted and was sometimes bribed. Its enigmatic pronouncements gave it considerable influence in Greek politics, playing a particularly important role during the years of overseas colonization. The control of Delphi was in the hands of the Amphictyonic Council, which was in turn usually dominated by Thessaly. Delphi was the site of the pan-Hellenic Pythian Games which were accompanied by an interstate truce. The most famous games of the ancient world were those held at Olympia in Elis. The Olympic Games, traditionally founded in 776, were held every four years and the span of the Olympiads was used as a method of dating throughout the Greek world. Gradually, Olympia's shrines were enlarged and in 430 Pheidias' colossal gold and ivory statue of Zeus was installed in the sanctuary.

One of the earliest of the religious unions was in Asia. The cities of the Ionian coast joined together to form the Panionion, with its temple of Poseidon at Mycale. Delos, birthplace of Apollo, also became an important centre for the Ionians at an early date. Initially dominated by Naxos, the Athenians soon gained a controlling influence on the island and it was later used by them as the focus of the anti-Persian defensive Delian League.

This figure of an archer was created on the island of Sardinia where bronze-working was a flourishing craft. Many such figures, representing warriors, musicians and women, were deposited as offerings in sacred wells. The dating of such pieces is controversial, but most are ascribed to the 9th—7th centuries, the period at which contemporary Greece was emerging from the Dark Age and commencing its most intense colonial activity. Although the Greeks founded many colonies in Italy and on Sicily, the Phoenicians appear to have been more active on Sardinia. The sparcity of evidence for Greek colonization of the island during this period does not necessarily negate the possibility of earlier contacts. Many of these bronze warriors bear a distinct resemblance to those shown on Egyptian reliefs depicting the Shardana. The Phoenicians called Sardinia Shardan and a connection is generally assumed. Most historians had thought that the island took the name from the Shardana who settled there in the Dark Age, but it has recently been suggested that the Shardana were the indigenous population who, as mercenaries and pirates, left the island and became one of the groups which brought about the collapse of the Mycenaean civilization.

Dark Age Greece

With the collapse of the Mycenaean civilization the face of life in Greece changed dramatically with the loss of both literacy and narrative art.

Following the collapse of the Mycenaean kingdoms around 1200/1180 BC, Greece entered a long Dark Age. There is still much archaeological material from the period, but it shows an economic recession and rapid decline of overseas contacts. There are, however, many continuities into the Geometric and Archaic periods. The Dark Age is one of the most controversial phases in Greek history and numerous theories and explanations of the evidence have been proposed.

The production of pottery continued, and following the fall of Mycenae it has been divided into twelve phases. The development from the two phases of Mycenaean Late Helladic IIIC through Submycenaean, Early, Middle and Late Protogeometric, to Early, Middle and Late Geometric (each with two phases) is the key to understanding all the other archaeological material from the Dark Age. Many influences from Mycenaean pottery are found in the decoration of Geometric pottery (late 9th-8th centuries) showing that there was some sort of continuity.

Although pottery production continued the earlier traditions, there are many striking differences with Mycenaean civilization. There is hardly any new construction in stone or brick, and certainly nothing like the cyclopean walls of Mycenae and Tiryns. Many crafts including ivory and bronze working either declined or ceased altogether. Literacy also came to an end. This can be explained by the breakdown of the centralized, bureaucratic, palace-centred kingdoms, and their replacement by a scattered agricultural population which had no need for writing. Writing reappears in the 8th century, and using a new alphabet instead of the Linear B script of the Mycenaeans. The Syro-Palestinian model for this new Greek Alphabet is now widely recognized as of 11th century date, although no examples of writing from the Aegean can be dated earlier than the 8th century. The use of the chariot, too, seems to disappear, to be reintroduced later. This could, like writing, be associated with the end of a powerful elite.

The archaeological record suggests that following the Mycenaean collapse there was a much smaller population, some estimate that there was only one tenth of that of Mycenaean times. The lack of archaeological evidence for settlements has been explained in a number of ways: that the population was dispersed in small villages and farms which are difficult to identify in the archaeological record, or that they were all gathered in a few larger settlements. Instead of the stone and brick-built buildings of the earlier period, perhaps the houses of this period were built of perishable materials, such as wood. A more radical change in the lives of the peoples has been suggested as another explanation: instead of agriculture, there was a greater reliance on pastoralism, and hence fewer permanent settlements. The most radical solution of the problems of the archaeology of Dark Age and Geometric Greece goes even further, challenging the accepted chronology of the Late Bronze Age of the whole Near East. It claims that the chronology, derived from Egyptian synchronisms, is too high by as much as 250 years. Lowering the dates would mean that the fall of Mycenaean civilization would have taken place around 950 BC instead of 1200. Although some specialists on the Greek Dark Age have accepted that this reduction would explain some of the problems, this solution has, so far, met with little enthusiasm.

A finely decorated Geometric vase from Attica, dating to around 740—720 BC. With the disappearance of the Mycenaean palace civilization visual narrative art was abandoned by the Greek potters and they turned instead to the creation of complex and frequently beautiful abstract patterns.

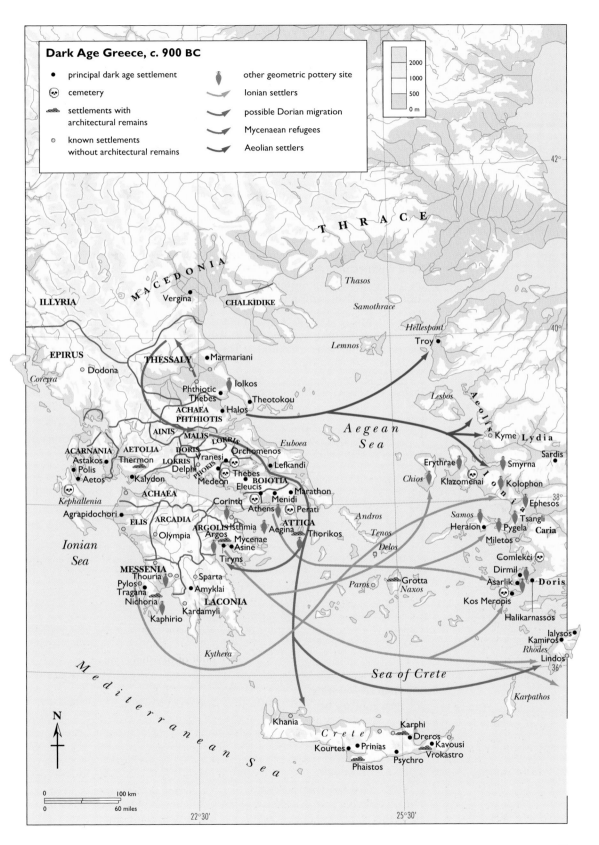

Dark Age Greece, c. 900 BC

- principal dark age settlement
- cemetery
- settlements with architectural remains
- known settlements without architectural remains
- other geometric pottery site
- Ionian settlers
- possible Dorian migration
- Mycenaean refugees
- Aeolian settlers

Rise of the City-States

The 8th century BC witnessed Greece's emergence from the Dark Age and a simultaneous growth in prestige of the Greek cities which would come to dominate political life and regional administration.

"Theseus conceived a wonderful and far-fetched plan, which was nothing less than to concentrate the inhabitants of Attica into a capital. In this way he transformed them into one people belonging to one city, whereas until then they had lived in widely scattered communities ... he proposed a constitution without a king: there was to be a democracy, in which ... everyone would be on an equal footing."
Plutarch, *Life of Theseus*

The *Polis*, or city-state, perhaps developed first on the Greek coast of Asia Minor, in centres such as Smyrna. The situation of the cities, surrounded by non-Greeks would naturally focus on the urban centres, walled for defence.

On the Greek mainland many of the cities were former Mycenaean strongholds (a notable exception being Sparta, deliberately built away from the older site). Most focussed on the citadel (*akropolis*) which was the temple area and a place of refuge in times of trouble. But the *polis* was more than simply the buildings, it was the citizenship, those resident in the town and surrounding countryside. The early development of the classical *polis* is unclear, but it has been assumed that there was a period of strife between the elite families who were the main landholders, and other social groups such as the peasantry and owners of smaller farms. The attraction of the population to the urban centres is clearly significant, but undocumented.

The 8th and 7th centuries were a period of changing political structures in which kingship gave way (in most *poleis*) to elected officials. In a number of states, tyrannies were established. These tyrannies tended to encourage the

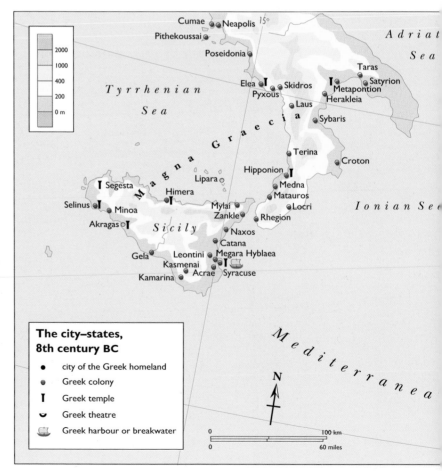

The city–states, 8th century BC

- ● city of the Greek homeland
- ● Greek colony
- Ⲧ Greek temple
- ⌣ Greek theatre
- 🛶 Greek harbour or breakwater

ultimate development of democracy rather than aristocratic rule. The kingship was usually broken down into religious, military and judicial offices (particularly notable at Athens where the three *archons* exercised those functions). Some states, such as Sparta, retained the monarchy, although its power was tempered by elected officials. In the new system, the city god replaced the king. In a number of cities with Mycenaean traditions, such as Athens, Mycenae itself and Tiryns, the temple was built on the site of the former palace (which itself had had a religious function). Even in design these temples harked back to the Mycenaean *megaron*. At Athens the religious function of the kings was transferred to the *archon basileus*.

The towns increased their importance as the places where political and economic power were concentrated, and as centres of the state. As the states formed around the cities, disputes over borders were inevitable. Of the early wars, the Lelantine war between Chalkis and Eretria in Euboea (late 8th century) was the most significant apparently attracting coalitions on each side.

Some Greek sanctuaries now became pan-hellenic, or ethnic, centres. In Asia a confederacy of cities (the Ionian League) had a common cult centre in the temple of Poseidon at Mycale. Olympia, the centre of the worship of Zeus, was a focus for Dorian states, but even before the foundation of the Olympic Games (traditionally 776), it had pan-hellenic prestige. Other temples noted for their oracles, such as those of Zeus at Dodona and of Apollo at Delphi were consulted by all Greek states and by "barbarians".

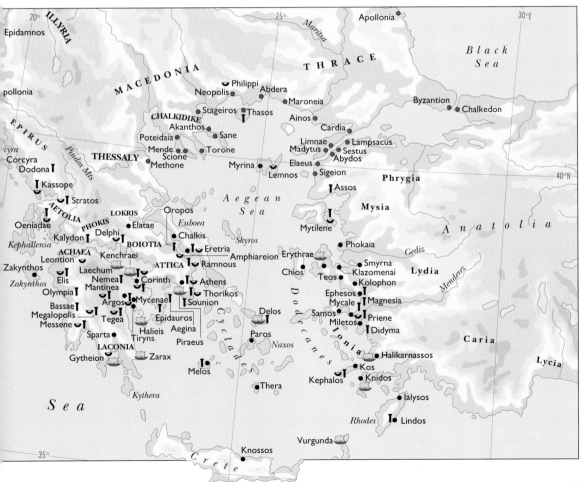

Migration and Colonization

Various factors encouraged the Greeks to found colonies throughout the Mediterranean and Black Sea regions and the two centuries between 750 and 550 BC witnessed extensive colonial activities.

"The voyage round Sicily takes rather under eight days in a merchant ship, yet, in spite of the size of the island, it is separated from the mainland by only two miles of sea ... After the fall of Troy, some of the Trojans escaped from the Achaeans and came in ships to Sicily, where they settled."

Thucydides, *The Peloponnesian War, Book VI*

There is evidence for Mycenaean migration to Cyprus following the crisis of 1200 and for later Dark Age migrations to western Asia Minor. The major phases of migration and colonization, however, belong to the period 750—550 BC. Many dates for the foundations of colonies are derived from the work of Thucydides, confirmed (or confused) by the pottery evidence.

Undoubtedly pressures upon the land caused by population growth and state formation were important, but may not have been the prime factor, as often claimed by historians. Political unrest (as with the Spartan founders of Taras) also provided motivation, but trade was undoubedly a major, if not the most significant, cause for expansion. In the eastern Mediterranean, where colonization was limited by the city-states and empires, trading cities were

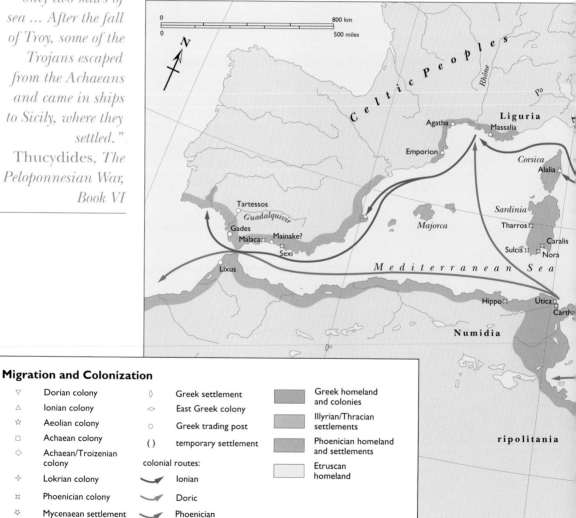

Migration and Colonization

▽	Dorian colony	◊	Greek settlement
△	Ionian colony	⬦	East Greek colony
☆	Aeolian colony	○	Greek trading post
□	Achaean colony	( )	temporary settlement
◇	Achaean/Troizenian colony		
✥	Lokrian colony	colonial routes:	
¤	Phoenician colony	⟍	Ionian
✿	Mycenaean settlement	⟍	Doric
		⟍	Phoenician

- Greek homeland and colonies
- Illyrian/Thracian settlements
- Phoenician homeland and settlements
- Etruscan homeland

established. The earliest was at al-Mina in Syria and later Naukratis in Egypt. Trade must have provided the information on which colonization was built. The search for raw materials, particularly metals, was important. Foundations at Massalia (modern Marseille) and in Etruria were able to exploit the tin route from the north. Phoenician colonists in the west had also been involved in metal mining, notably silver from Spain. Around the Black Sea, the corn trade provided the incentive for colonies from Miletos and later from Megara. The corn from these foundations, and control of the sea routes to them, was to be of increasing importance, particularly to Athens.

The founder of a colony remained a citizen of the mother city, but other peoples could join. Ties with the mother-city continued, and these could lead to problems, as during the Peloponnesian War. The mother-city also provided the model for constitution and cult. The cities were not simply trading entreports and agricultural land was as important as good harbours. This could lead to conflict with indigenous peoples. Conflict also broke out with other powers, such as Carthage over its influence in Sicily, or with other colonies, usually of a different origin.

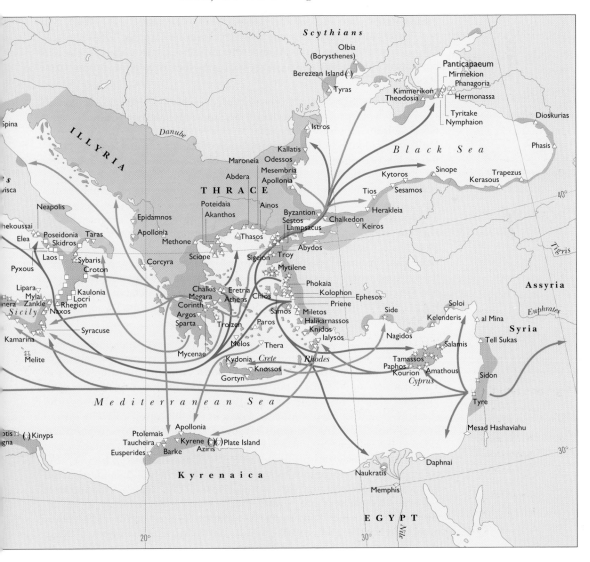

Egypt and Kyrenaica

Early contact between Egypt and Greece resulted in the establishment of Greek colonies and a cultural interchange which would profoundly influence the Greek world.

"When King Psamatichos came to Elephantine, this they wrote, who sailed with Psamatichos son of Theokles. They went beyond Kerkis, as far as the river let them; Potasimto led the foreigners and Amasis the Egyptians. And Archon, son of Amoibichos, and Peleqos, son of Endamos, wrote us."

Greek graffiti, dating from c. 593 BC, discovered on the colossi of Ramesses II at Abu Simbel

Connections between the Geometric Greek world and Egypt began during the 8th—7th centuries, probably through the activities of Phoenician traders. A variety of Egyptian objects have been found all around the Mediterranean from Spain and Carthage, Etruria and Sicily to the Greek islands. More direct contacts between the Greeks and Egypt in the late 8th or 7th century might be indicated by bronzes found on Crete and at Samos. These increased with the accession of the Egyptian pharaoh Psamtik I (664—610 BC) who employed Carian and Ionian mercenaries. Such mercenaries continued to play an important role in the Egyptian army and a contingent was included in the army which Psamtik II sent against the kingdom of Kush (Nubia) in 593 BC. Some of the Greek soldiers carved inscriptions on the colossi of the temple of Abu Simbel. Carians and Ionians, supposedly numbering 30,000 were also employed in the army of Haaibre (Apries, 589—570 BC), which was defeated by the usurper Ahmose (Amasis, 570—526 BC). Herodotos states that it was Amasis who gave Naukratis to the Greeks as a commercial base; but archaeology indicates that it is older, dating from about 620 BC.

Lying 50 miles from the Mediterranean coast, but only 10 miles from Sais (Sau) the dynasty's capital, Naukratis became a melting pot of Egyptian and Greek culture, and most of the influences seem to have been on the Greeks. Unlike the colonies in Italy, the population of Naukratis came from many different places, largely East Greek, such as Chios, Samos and Miletos. It also differed from the other colonies in that it was a trading and manufacturing centre rather then having any agricultural base. One of the principal exports was Egyptian corn, exchanged for olive oil, wine and silver. There were many influential Greek visitors to Naukratis, such as the Athenian law-giver, Solon, and the philosopher Thales of Miletos, and of course, the historian, Herodotos. Naukratis was important in opening up Egypt to the Greeks at a significant historical moment. Through these visitors and traders, Egypt's thought and institutions, its art and technology had a profound influence on the development of classical Greece. Following the Persian conquest of Egypt in 525 BC, the city remained prosperous, but was eventually superseded by Alexandria.

Naukratis' primary activity was trade, but the other principal Greek city in north Africa, Kyrene, was a more typical colony, its site being chosen for agriculture. Kyrene was founded about 630 BC by colonists from the island of Thera, which could not support its growing population. Other cities were founded shortly afterwards at Apollonia (Kyrene's port), Euesperides (Benghazi) and Taucheira (Tocra). Later, in the 6th century, Kyrene invited new colonists from the Peloponnese and Dorian islands. Kyrene itself was ruled by a royal family, the Battiads, and the Egyptian pharaoh Amasis is said to have taken one of its princesses as a wife. The relationship between the colonies and the indigenous Libyan population is not well documented and there was certainly not the cultural interaction which characterizes Naukratis. Kyrene sent envoys when the Persians conquered Egypt in 525 BC, and was later included in the Persian empire. Kyrene continued to enjoy prosperity in the Hellenstic period, but lost its independence, being absorbed into the Ptolemaic possessions.

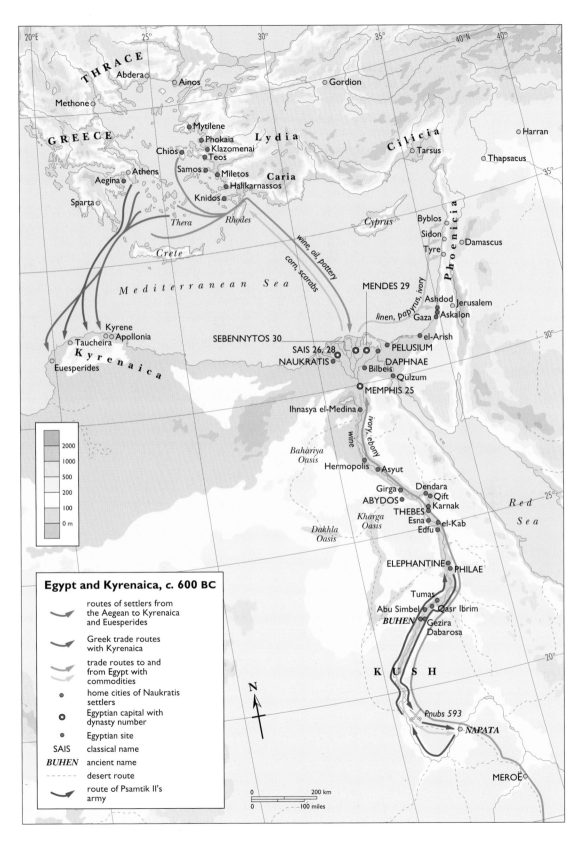

20°E 25° 30° 35° 40°N 40°

THRACE
Abdera
Ainos
Gordion
Harran
Methone

GREECE
Lydia
Cilicia
Mytilene
Phokaia
Klazomenai
Chios
Teos
Tarsus
Thapsacus
Samos
Miletos
Caria
Athens
Halikarnassos
Aegina
Knidos
Sparta
Thera *Rhodes*
Cyprus
Byblos
Sidon
Phoenicia
Tyre
Damascus
Crete

Mediterranean Sea

wine, oil, pottery
corn, scarabs

MENDES 29
Ashdod Jerusalem
linen, papyrus, ivory
Gaza Askalon

Kyrene
Apollonia
Taucheira
el-Arish
Kyrenaica
SEBENNYTOS 30
PELUSIUM
Euesperides
SAIS 26, 28
NAUKRATIS DAPHNAE
Bilbeis
Qulzum

MEMPHIS 25

Ihnasya el-Medina

wine
Bahariya Oasis
ivory, ebony
Hermopolis Asyut

Girga Dendara
ABYDOS Qift
Kharga Oasis Karnak
THEBES
Red Sea
Esna el-Kab
Dakhla Oasis Edfu

ELEPHANTINE PHILAE

Tumas
Abu Simbel Qasr Ibrim
BUHEN Gezira
Dabarosa

KUSH

N

Pnubs 593
NAPATA

MEROË

2000
1000
500
200
100
0 m

Egypt and Kyrenaica, c. 600 BC

- routes of settlers from the Aegean to Kyrenaica and Euesperides
- Greek trade routes with Kyrenaica
- trade routes to and from Egypt with commodities
- home cities of Naukratis settlers
- Egyptian capital with dynasty number
- Egyptian site
- SAIS classical name
- *BUHEN* ancient name
- desert route
- route of Psamtik II's army

0   200 km
0   100 miles

The Greeks in Italy

The Greek colonization of Italy and Sicily was of fundamental importance in the transmission of Greek culture to the Etruscans and the emergent Roman state.

"Zankle was originally founded by pirates who came from Cumae, the Chalkidian city in Opicia, but later a large number of people came from Chalkis and the rest of Euboea and joined in settling the place."
Thucydides, *The Peloponnesian War, Book VI*

The earliest Greek foundation in Italy was by the Euboeans at Pithekoussai on Ischia. This was probably a centre for iron working, the ores being brought from the island of Elba. The cemeteries have yielded Egyptian scarabs and faience, and Syrian pottery, indicating wide-ranging contacts. The site was probably abandoned in favour of Cumae on the mainland. Cumae itself became the mother-city of Naples.

There were important Achaean foundations along the southern coast. Sybaris, with its rich agricultural hinterland, became proverbial for luxury. It was also the main centre for trade between Miletos and the Etruscans. It was destroyed by its rival and neighbour, Croton in 510. Later, in 443, the Athenians founded Thurii near the site of Sybaris. It is best remembered as the city where the historian Herodotos would eventually settle after his extensive travels around the Mediterranean and Asia Minor. Croton and the Spartan foundation of Taras (modern Tarento) also had excellent ports as well as good land for growing corn. Enormous amounts of pottery were imported from Greece to Italy, but soon native schools developed, initially modelling their decoration on that of imported vessels.

The orientalizing phase in Etruscan culture begins in the late 8th century. Euboean and Corinthian vases were imported and are also found at Rome (in tradition, founded by Romulus in 754 BC) in contexts of around 700. Corinthian imports continue through 7th century along with those from the East Greek cities, but by the 6th century Athenian vases were supplanting the Corinthian. There is some evidence for Greek settlements in Etruria, including the report that a Corinthian nobleman, Demaratos, settled at Tarquinii married an Etruscan woman and was father of Tarquinius Priscus fifth king of Rome. Demaratos is supposed to have brought potters with him, who were responsible for the development of clay statuary in Etruria. Gravisca, the port of Tarquinii had a Greek quarter from 6th century, and Caere was partly Greek. Pottery from cemeteries at Vulci and Visentium might be the products of Euboean artists working in Etruria, but local artists were soon copying the styles. Etruscan metalwork has been found in Greece, and according to Pausanias, an Etruscan king was the first foreigner to make a dedication at Olympia. Despite these exchanges relations were not always amicable. An allied Etruscan and Carthaginian fleet attacked the Phokian colony of Alalia in Corsica (535), its survivors fleeing to Rhegion. A later Etruscan attack on Cumae was defeated (524).

The Temple of Hera, built at Poseidonia during the 6th century BC. Poseidonia was founded by the Achaean colonists who had settled at Sybaris in southern Italy. The impetus behind the foundation may well have been the desire to extend trade links. The site was flooded in the middle ages and later notorious for its malaria and these factors deterred stone-robbers, thus contributing to the survival of a particularly fine series of early temples.

In Sicily the first colonisers were the Euboeans of Eretria and Chalkis. The Rhodians and Cretans founded Gela in 688, which itself later founded Akragas (580). Syracuse, a Corinthian foundation (734), had the best harbour on the east coast. It was generally hostile to the other cities and to the indigenous population, expanding its influence in the 7th century, to gain control of the southeast of the island. Carthage established a permanent presence in the west of the island, as defender of the Phoenician colonies. There were conflicts between Carthage and the rising powers of Theron, tyrant of Akragas, and Gelon, tyrant of Syracuse. The Greek cities on Syracuse mostly owed their wealth to agriculture, but also at times good economic relations with Carthage.

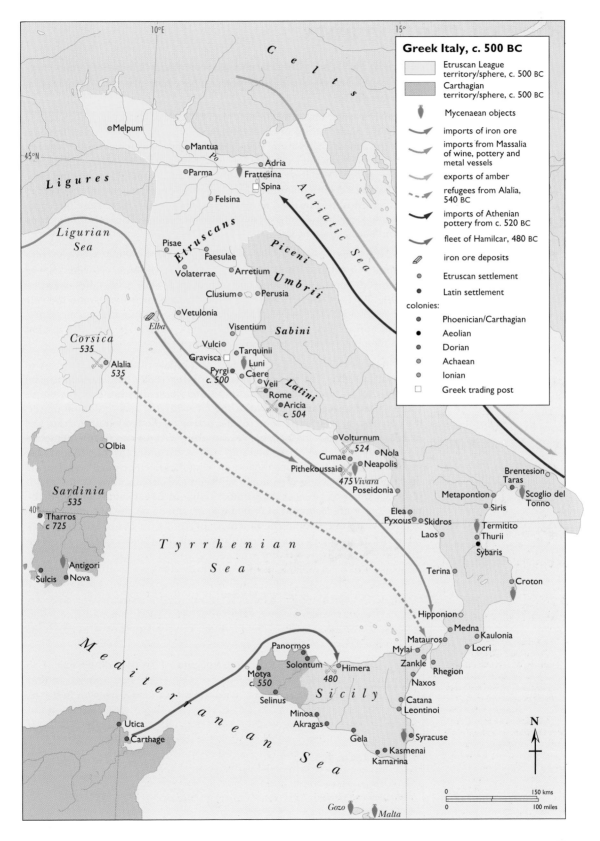

Greek Italy, c. 500 BC

Etruscan League territory/sphere, c. 500 BC

Carthagian territory/sphere, c. 500 BC

Mycenaean objects

imports of iron ore

imports from Massalia of wine, pottery and metal vessels

exports of amber

refugees from Alalia, 540 BC

imports of Athenian pottery from c. 520 BC

fleet of Hamilcar, 480 BC

iron ore deposits

Etruscan settlement

Latin settlement

colonies:

Phoenician/Carthagian

Aeolian

Dorian

Achaean

Ionian

Greek trading post

Celts

Melpum

Mantua

Po

Adria

Parma

Frattesina

Spina

Felsina

Ligures

Ligurian Sea

Piceni

Adriatic Sea

Pisae

Etruscans

Faesulae

Volaterrae

Arretium

Umbrii

Clusium

Perusia

Vetulonia

Elba

Visentium

Sabini

Corsica 535

Vulci

Alalia 535

Tarquinii

Gravisca

Luni

Pyrgi c. 500

Caere

Veii

Latini

Rome

Aricia c. 504

Volturnum

524

Nola

Cumae

Neapolis

Pithekoussai

475 Vivara

Poseidonia

Brentesion

Taras

Metapontion

Scoglio del Tonno

Siris

Olbia

Elea

Pyxous

Skidros

Sardinia 535

Laos

Termitito

Thurii

40°

Tharros c 725

Sybaris

Tyrrhenian Sea

Terina

Croton

Antigori

Nova

Sulcis

Hipponion

Medna

Kaulonia

Matauros

Mylai

Locri

Mediterranean Sea

Panormos

Zankle

Solontum

Himera

Rhegion

Motya c. 550

480

Naxos

Selinus

Sicily

Minoa

Catana

Akragas

Leontinoi

Utica

Gela

Syracuse

Carthage

Kasmenai

Kamarina

N

0   150 kms

0   100 miles

Gozo

Malta

45°N

10°E

15°

Rise of the Tyrants

Although the reigns of some tyrants were marked by the use of foreign mercinaries and bribery to maintain power others were generally thought of as being beneficent.

"The longest tyranny was the Sikyonian, that of Orthagoras and his sons: it lasted a hundred years. These monarchs owed their long innings to the fact that they treated their subjects with moderation and in many matters subjected themselves to the rule of law ... In general they drew the people towards them by repeated acts of care for them."
Aristotle, *Politics,* Book V

Tyranny was an almost constant feature of Greek political life. On mainland Greece the main period of the tyrannies was the 7th-6th centuries. In some states it formed a transition from kingship and aristocracy to democracy. During the Persian wars, the Persians tried to reinstate tyrants (as at Athens), as more amenable to their rule. Tyrants frequently came from the elite families. They seized power, but usually ruled with popular assent and mercenary assistance. Most tyrants tried to establish dynasties, and there were intermarriages amongst their families. Opposition was initially from other elite families, and later caused by the actions of the successors.

The tyrants were generally noted for their lavish building works, as with Peisistratos at Athens. They were also noted for economic reforms. One of the earliest tyrants was Pheidon ruler of Argos (*c* 660), sometimes regarded as a king. Pheidon introduced regular weights and measures. Under the rule of the Kypselidai (*c* 657—585) Corinth came to be dominant in pottery production and export, art and trade. Under Periander, the son of Kypselos, Corinthian colonization and expansion increased.

In Athens, a young aristocrat, Kylon, son-in-law of Theagenes tyrant of Megara, failed in his attempt to seize power (632), and Solon refused absolute power. But tyranny came to Athens when after two failed attempts (560) Peisistratos gained control of the city with Thracian gold and mercenary troops. In restricting some of the power of the landed aristocrats and increasing privileges for farmers, Peisistratos paved the way for the democratic reforms to come. His rule was viewed as generally beneficent. He increased olive and vine production on what had been grazing land. During his reign Attic black-figured wares replaced Corinthian wares as the major pottery export of Greece. Peisistratos' religious benefactions included the building or embellishment of the temple of Athena on the Akropolis, building at Eleusis and work in the sanctuary of Apollo on Delos. He also elaborated the Panathenaic festival and transferred the Dionysia to the city. This

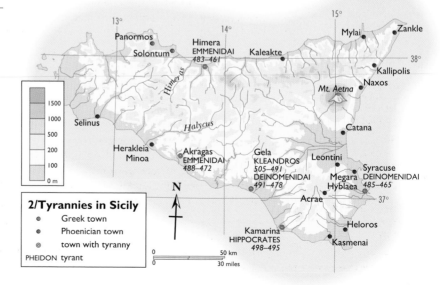

2/Tyrannies in Sicily
- ● Greek town
- ● Phoenician town
- ◎ town with tyranny

PHEIDON tyrant

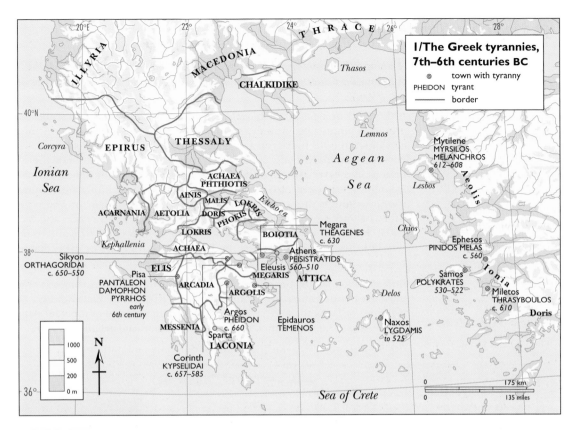

1/The Greek tyrannies, 7th–6th centuries BC

◎　　town with tyranny
PHEIDON　tyrant
──────　border

The ruins of the fine Temple of Apollo at Corinth. One of the first Greek city-states to fall under the sway of a tyrant, Corinth was controlled by the Kypselidai for around 72 years. The dynasty's founder, Kypselos, was popular with the people and never employed a bodyguard. His son, Periander, reigned for 44 years and was counted amongst the "Seven Wise Men" of his era. Periander never enjoyed his father's popularity and shortly after his death authority was passed to a more moderate bourgeois government.

last was an important move, as the festival was essentially rural. Its transfer bound the city and country more closely, part of the centralization of Attica. The festival was also to become the focus of theatre, one of Athens' most enduring contributions to Greek culture. Peisistratos' sons Hippias and Hipparchos succeeded him. Hipparchos was murdered by two young aristocratic lovers, Harmodios and Aristogeiton in 514. This act later became a symbol of liberation. Hippias' rule became oppressive and he employed foreign mercenaries, imposing further taxes to pay for them. Intervention by Sparta and the Alkmaionid clan ousted Hippias. There were still pro-Peisistratid (or anti-Alkmaionid) factions in Athens, and Hippias guided the Persian army to Marathon, in the hope of restoration.

There were tyrants in Ionia and the Aegean islands. One of the most notable was Polykrates, who established himself as ruler of Samos (530—522). He entered into treaty with the Egyptian pharaoh Amasis and adopted an anti-Persian policy. Successful through war and piracy, Polykrates made Samos a flourishing centre. He was another renowned builder. His large fleet enabled him to expand his power, capturing islands and some mainland towns. He defeated the Lesbian fleet which had gone to the aid of Miletos. Sparta and Corinth both sent help to aid Samian opposition to Polykrates. It was unsuccessful. Polykrates' fate was tied to Persian expansion. Cambyses invaded Egypt (525) shortly after Amasis' death, and Polykrates attempted to change sides. He was lured to Asia where he was murdered by the satrap.

Many of the colonies in Sicily also came under the rule of tyrants, and although these were replaced by the mid-5th century, there was a return to tyranny at the end of the century, when Dionysios I gained power in Syracuse. The rule of his son continued tyranny into the Hellenistic period.

Athens Ascendant

Taking full advantage of their secure position and access to the sea, the Athenians gradually expanded their power-base until they were masters of all of Attica.

"How splendid a thing is political equality; the Athenians under the tyrants were no better soldiers than their neighbours, but once they were rid of them they were far the best."
Herodotos,
Histories

Although not a particularly rich agricultural land, Attica had some geographical advantages. Athens was protected by mountains from land attack and the Akropolis had its own water supply, invaluable in time of siege. The city also benefited from good harbours. Phaleron was the first, but the Piraeus, the best harbour, only became safe after Athens gained control of Salamis. There were other good harbours apart from those near Athens itself. Although there was arable production in the plain of Marathon, Athens always needed to import grain from the Black Sea region and from Egypt. It was, however, a great producer and exporter of olive oil and its pottery industry was important in the 9th-8th centuries. Of its other natural resources, the silver mines of Laurion were the most important.

Attica was not simply the city of Athens with its territory and subjects; other *poleis* were important, particularly Eleusis and Rhamnous. Eleusis, where the mysteries of Demeter were celebrated, was made a symbol of unity for Attica by Peisistratos, and remained one of its most significant religious centres.

Athens was probably a starting point for the Ionian migrations. It was during

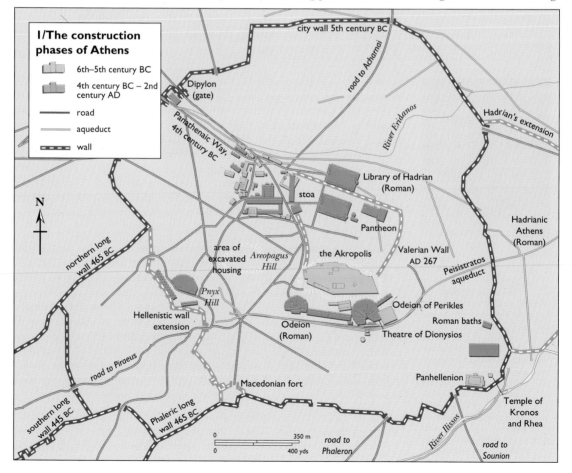

I/The construction phases of Athens

- 6th–5th century BC
- 4th century BC – 2nd century AD
- road
- aqueduct
- wall

N

city wall 5th century BC
road to Acharnai
River Eridanos
Hadrian's extension
Dipylon (gate)
Panathenaic Way, 4th century BC
Library of Hadrian (Roman)
stoa
Pantheon
Hadrianic Athens (Roman)
northern long wall 465 BC
area of excavated housing
Areopagus Hill
the Akropolis
Valerian Wall AD 267
Peisistratos aqueduct
Pnyx Hill
Hellenistic wall extension
Odeion (Roman)
Odeion of Perikles
Roman baths
Theatre of Dionysios
southern long wall 445 BC
Phaleric long wall 465 BC
road to Piraeus
Macedonian fort
Panhellenion
Temple of Kronos and Rhea
River Ilissos
road to Phaleron
road to Sounion

0   350 m
0   400 yds

An Athenian gold coin carries the impression of an owl, the bird of Athena, the patron goddess of Athens. Athena's importance to the city would later be symbolized by the colossal gold and ivory statue of the goddess which stood within the Parthenon.

the 9th-8th centuries that Athens probably absorbed the other cities of Attica, culminating with the seizure of Eleusis. In myth the process is ascribed to Theseus. Athenian development is generally viewed (as it was by Aristotle) as constitutional progress from kingship, through aristocracy and tyranny to democracy. Drakon (*c* 624) codified the laws, although he was probably not as harsh as later tradition claimed. The next major reforms were those of Solon (*archon* 594—593) who freed debtors and their land and abolished debt slavery. He also introduced important economic reforms, banning the export of natural produce except olive oil. Democratic development was furthered by the tyranny of the Peisistratids (546—510), which began the centralization of Attica and turned Athens into a major city. The actions of Peisistratos increased the influence and economic security of the farmers and traders, whilst reducing the power of the landed nobles. The reforms of Kleisthenes carried this further and completely reorganised citizenship. Nevertheless, Athenian democracy was limited to free male adult citizens; it excluded slaves, women and allies.

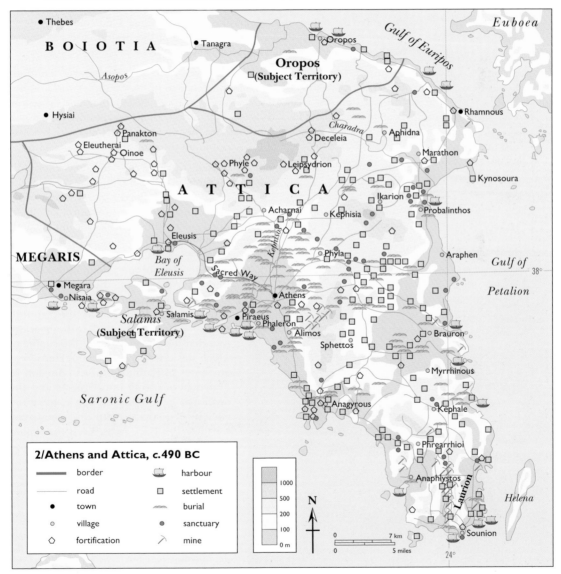

2/Athens and Attica, *c.*490 BC

border	harbour
road	settlement
town	burial
village	sanctuary
fortification	mine

The Classical Myths

The ancient Greek myths have proved to be a seemingly inexhaustible treasure-house of legends and characters, and for millennia artists and writers have plundered them for inspiration.

"The gods ... had sat down for a conference with Zeus in the Hall of the Golden Floor. The lady Hebe, acting as their cupbearer, served them with nectar and they drank each other's health from tankards of gold as they looked at the city of Troy."
Homer, *The Iliad, Book IV*

The myths of ancient Greece have been a great influence on the literature and art of western Europe, and were once an integral part of education. The myths were also extensively used by the dramatists and historians of ancient Greece. Episodes from them decorated pottery, or formed the sculptural decoration of temples. In their surviving forms many of them are of quite late date, often in the works or writers who have moulded them, rationalized them and interpreted them for themselves. Nevertheless the fundamental story, characters and purpose remain clear.

The myths were a way of explaining how things came to be. They justified or warned about certain phenomena, or they set examples of behaviour. Myths explained the names and origins of places and things. They could provide an historical basis for social cohesion, explaining the origins of the city-state. Myth was also concerned with the relationship between gods and humans.

In the myth of the fertility goddess Demeter, Demeter's daughter Persephone is abducted by Hades and carried off to the underworld. In her distress, Demeter roams the world in search of her daughter, and crops fail, bringing famine. The satisfactory resolution, that Persephone spends half the year on earth with her mother and the remainder in Hades with her husband, explains the cycle of the seasons and the growth of crops.

One myth seems to contain an allusion to the Asiatic influences on early Greek culture. Europa was the daughter of the king of Tyre, on the Phoenician coast. Zeus desired her and transformed himself into a white bull, appearing when Europa was with her friends on the shore. Gradually overcoming her fear, Europa climbed on the bull's back. He immediately plunged into the waves and carried her over the sea to Crete, where she gave birth to Minos. Her brother Kadmos was sent to find her. Whilst roving through Boiotia, he killed a giant serpent and at Athena's instigation sowed its teeth in the ground. Warriors sprang up and with these he founded the city of Thebes (the citadel of which was called the *Kadmeia*). Herodotos attributes to Kadmos the introduction of Phoenician writing into Greece, and the myth may be a veiled allusion of the influence of Phoenician culture on the Greek world of the Dark Ages. Even the names seem to have a Phoenician origin: Kadmos

A Roman mosaic dating from the 3rd century AD illustrates the myth of Zeus and Ganymede, and further reveals how the mythology of ancient Greece continued to be a source of inspiration to artists and craftsmen throughout the ages. Ganymede was a boy of remarkable beauty, the son of the Trojan prince Tros. Zeus sent an eagle to convey the boy to Olympus where he was employed as cup-bearer to the gods. To compensate Tros for the loss of his son, Zeus granted him a stud of exceptional horses.

Right: An Athenian four-drachma coin bears the impression of the owl, the symbol of Athena, the city's patron. To the bird's left can be seen a representation of Athena herself, carrying in her right hand a miniature figure of Nike, the goddess of victory.

can be equated with the semitic word *qedem* ("east") and Europa derives from a semitic word for sunset (ie "west"). The influence of western Asia on Archaic Greek culture is now widely recognized, and in addition to the visual arts, strong parallels can be found in some of the myths with episodes in Mesopotamian epics.

Some other myths were much simpler. The metamorphosis of various of Apollo's lovers explained the origin and form of certain plants. Daphne, when pursued by the god, turned into a bay tree, which he made his sacred plant. When Hyacinth was killed by a discus thrown by Apollo, the flower which carries his name sprang from the blood. Cyparissus who died of grief when he accidentally killed his favourite stag, was turned by Apollo into the perpetually mourning tree. The tale of Narcissus and Echo is of a similar type.

Whether simple stories about the origin of plants or more complex explanations for the universe, Greek myths appeal to the imagination and to the emotions. Perhaps their popularity is due largely to the very "humanity" and fallibility of the Greek immortals — but, whatever its cause, the fact remains that the names of the Greek gods and heroes remain in everyday usage.

In a scene from the east frieze of the Siphnian Treasury at Delphi, Aphrodite and Artemis lean forward eagerly to learn from Apollo the latest news from Troy. As the minister of Destiny Zeus remained neutral in the Trojan War, but the lesser gods were not above taking sides and actively interfered in the affairs of their favourites.

III: The Persian Rival

The meteoric rise of the Persians, from minor kings on the periphery of the Assyrian empire to masters of western Asia, Anatolia and Egypt would have a profound influence on centuries of Greek history.

"... the rest of the Athenians supposed that the Persian defeat at Marathon meant the end of the war. Themistokles, however, believed that it was only the prelude to a far greater struggle, and he prepared, as it were, to anoint himself for this and come forward as the champion of all Greece: in fact he sensed the danger while it was still far away, and put his city into training to meet it. "
Plutarch, *Life of Themistokles*

The Persian empire dominated the international political scene for the three hundred years from the mid–6th century until its conquest by Alexander of Macedon. Its influence was to be found, not only in the foreign policies of the Greek states, but frequently in their own internal disputes. The formation of the Delian League, and its metamorphosis into the Athenian empire, was a direct result of the conflict with Persia and the new war against Persia, proposed by Philip of Macedon and carried out by Alexander, was claimed to be an act of revenge for the aggression of Xerxes. The invasions of Greece by Darius and Xerxes form the subject of, or the background to, some of the most celebrated works of Greek literature, such as the *Histories* of Herodotos and some of the plays of Aischylos. Similarly, some of the greatest Athenian monuments, such as the Parthenon, were built as memorials to that conflict. The importance of the relationship between Greece and the Persian empire at the height of the Classical period cannot be overemphasized.

Persia is usually characterized as a typical "oriental" despotic monarchy, its history bedevilled by palace intrigues and "harem" conspiracies. This view, developed partly as an 18th and 19th century western European response to what constituted "oriental", was modelled very largely (if not very accurately) on the Ottoman Empire. But it is also a view presented by the Greek sources such as Herodotos and Ktesias. Herodotos' *Histories* chronicled the rise of Persia and the conflict with the Greek states, and contrasted the despotic Persian kingdom with the democratic Greek states. Ktesias of Knidos was physician to Artaxerxes I and wrote a history of Persia in 23 books. It survives in fragments, mostly abridgements, in later writers. Ktesias, as a member of the Persian court, could claim an intimate knowledge of its intrigues and his gossipy "history" has doubtless been largely responsible for the image of a eunuch-dominated and intrigue-ridden society. Although much Greek literature displays anti-Persian sentiment, it did not generally portray the Persians as inferior; it did, however, emphasize their "otherness".

Recent reassessments of the history of Persia under the Achaemenid dynasty have radically changed our perceptions, and help to explain how the old cultures of Egypt, Mesopotamia and Anatolia were absorbed and adapted into the new empire. They have also emphasized the complexity of the Greek-Persian relationship. Although anti-Persian sentiment was a "correct" political stance in many states, the reality was much more ambivalent.

Many Greeks worked for the Persian Great King or his satraps, and a number of political figures, including some whose policies had been strongly anti-Persian, eventually found refuge at the Persian court. Amongst the earliest Greeks to enter Persian service were craftsmen who worked on the tomb of Cyrus at Pasargadai. Greek work and architectural influence is also to be found in the great palace complex at Persepolis. It was not only East Greeks who were employed at the Persian court. The physician, Democedes, who had previously been in the service of the satrap of Sardis, was retained by Darius, but eventually escaped to return to his native city of Croton in Italy. Greek physicians were highly respected and Artaxerxes employed two: Apolionides of Kos and, later, the "historian", Ktesias.

The Rise of Persia

Between 750—550 BC western Asia was dominated by the Assyrian empire, its territory extending from Mesopotamia to the Mediterranean. Also subjected were parts of Anatolia and, for a time, Egypt. To the east, beyond the Zagros mountains, Persia was one of two new kingdoms forming on the Iranian plateau, the other being that of the Medes. In biblical and Greek sources, the Medes and Persians are almost inseparable (the Greek term for pro-Persian was "medising"). The Persians spoke an Indo-European language related to that of the Medes and had established their kingdom around the city of Anshan to the northwest of Susa and Pasargadai further to the east. One of its kings, Kurash (Cyrus) submitted to the Assyrian ruler Assurbanipal in 647, but the names of others are known only from the later sources.

There were direct contacts between the Greeks and the Assyrians through the trading emporium at al Mina, and through Cyprus, but also through the increasing numbers of mercenary soldiers who served in foreign armies. The major power in Anatolia neighbouring the Greek cities of the coast, was Lydia. Herodotos begins his narrative with a history of Lydia, so important was its role in the story of the conflict of Greeks and Persians. Gyges, king of Lydia (c.680—c.650) was reputedly the first foreign king to send gifts to the temple of Apollo at Delphi. Gyges supplied Carian and Ionian troops to the Egyptian pharaoh Psamtik I to aid him in his suppression of opposition in the Nile delta. Such mercenaries continued to play an important role in the armies of succeeding pharaohs. Psamtik I also opened Egypt to Greek traders with the foundation of Naukratis. Around the same time (c.630), Greek colonists founded Kyrene further along the north African coast.

Lydian power was temporarily eclipsed when Gyges' kingdom was overrun by Cimmerian tribes which continued to ravage the country for much of the next hundred years. Greater political changes soon followed. With the fall of Nineveh to the armies of Babylon and the Medes (612), the Assyrian empire in western Asia was divided between the victors. For the next hundred years Babylon was the dominant power, controlling Mesopotamia and Syria-Palestine. The Medes added north Syria and eastern Anatolia to their territories which now stretched to the Indus. Despite its great extent, little is yet known about the Median empire because its capital city of Hangmatana (later Ekbatana) has not been excavated.

Alyattes, a descendant of Gyges, defeated the Cimmerians and began to rebuild the Lydian kingdom. This brought him into conflict with the Medes, but by a peace treaty in 585, sealed by royal marriage, the Lydian border was established at the Halys river. Lydia was a rich country with extensive gold supplies. It is credited with the invention of stamped coinage, and, in the reign of Kroisos, with introducing both gold and silver coin. The expansion of Lydia under the rule of Kroisos absorbed the Greek cities of the coast. Kroisos' wealth was proverbial, and he gave lavish gifts to the shrine at Delphi and to others on the Ionian coast, such as Ephesos and Branchidai. Legend claimed that an Athenian, Alkmaion, the founder of one of the city's most powerful families, derived his vast wealth from stuffing his clothes and mouth with so much gold dust from the king's treasury that he could hardly walk. The court of Kroisos attracted other influential Greek figures, amongst them the Athenian statesman Solon.

In 559 BC, another Cyrus ascended the Persian throne and rapidly turned Persia into a major power. According to one account, Cyrus defeated the

Median king Astyages in battle at Pasargadai (*c.*550). He thus came to rule the whole Median empire which stretched from the borders of the Lydian kingdom to the Indus. Cyrus soon directed his attention to the west, and confronted the army of Kroisos at Hattusas. Neither side won and having retreated to Sardis, where he was besieged by Cyrus, Kroisos was reputed to have taken his own life (547). In the succeeding years Median generals brought the coastal cities of Ionia, Caria and Lycia under Persian rule. Following the fall of Lydia, Sparta sent an envoy to warn the Persian Great King that it would not allow the Greeks to become his subjects. In 539 Cyrus moved against the Babylonian empire, stretching through Mesopotamia, Syria and Palestine to the borders of Egypt. With its conquest, Cyrus became the ruler of the largest empire the world had yet seen.

Cyrus was killed on campaign in central Asia (530), and was succeeded by his son Cambyses (529—522), who had been officiating as ruler in Babylon. In 525, Cambyses conquered Egypt and soon after, the cities of Kyrene and Barce sent their submission. In the reign of Darius, Kyrenaica became a satrapy and the Persians gave their support to its kings, the Battiads.

Whilst Cambyses was in Egypt, his brother Bardiya (Smerdis) rebelled and seized the throne (the official account, written by Darius, alleged that Cambyses had murdered Bardiya secretly, and that an usurper, claiming to be Bardiya, had set himself up as king). He was murdered by a group of nobles, including Darius, a member of the royal Achaemenid family, although not in the line of succession. On his return to Pasargadai, Cambyses died or was himself murdered. Darius ascended the throne, legitimizing his accession by marrying two daughters of Cyrus and a daughter of Bardiya.

Darius (521—486) set about reorganizing the empire, using the Assyrian provincial system as his blueprint. The new provinces were ruled by satraps, who were virtually kings in their own territory. As a check on the satraps some officials, notably the commander of the garrison, reported directly to the Great King. Darius also improved communications between the regions of his vast empire. In this too he was building on an Assyrian inheritance. Notable was the royal road between Sardis and Susa. He also standardized weights and measures throughout the empire, regular taxation was introduced and there were other economic reforms, although the use of coin was still not widespread.

Throughout this period geographical and ethnographical knowledge was increasing. The Phoenican activities in the western Mediterranean, followed by those of the Greeks, had opened up whole new regions. In the east, the Carian, Skylax of Karyanda, explored the Indus and the route to the Red Sea for Darius. Phoenician ships circumnavigated Africa at the request of the pharaoh Nekau (*c.*600) and other fleets sailed around the west coast of Africa from .Carthage. This expansion of horizons was reflected in the literature of the Ionian coast, where Hecateus of Miletos was the first to weld history, ethnography and geography into a coherent whole. Although Herodotos' purpose was much more than to simply gather ethnographic information, his digressions (particularly those on Scythia and Egypt) were a development upon the approach of earlier writers such as Hecateus.

The First Conflict

Having established his authority throughout the empire, Darius turned his attention towards the Black Sea and Europe. His intention was to attack the

A panoramic view of the Persian capital at Persepolis. Located on a spur at the foot of a mountain, the palace of Persepolis was built on an enormous terrace on three different levels. Construction was commenced during the reign of Darius the Great, shortly after the suppression of a revolt in one of the satrapies. It may be conjectured that the magnificent scale of the palace with its 18-metre high columns was designed specifically with the intention of cowing into submission any other would-be rebels.

Scythians. Their territories stretched over the steppes of central Asia, from the east of the Caspian Sea. They had already posed a threat to the northern and eastern frontiers of the Assyrian empire, and their southward movements had been the cause of the Cimmerian migration into Lydia. The satrap of Cappadocia had made an expedition to the northern shore of the Black Sea to prepare for an attack on the European Scythians. It may be that Darius, unaware of the vast distances involved, thought that he could attack the Scythians of Asia from the north.

This campaign brought Darius' army to Thrace and the borders of Macedonia. The rulers of Macedonia claimed Greek descent and their language was certainly a dialect of Greek. The kingdom's political life was however very different from that emerging in the city-states of southern Greece, being largely feudal. Macedonia stood on the main overland routes from Thrace to Thessaly and then into central Greece. Not suprisingly, in the events to come, its rulers acknowledged Persian might—but they had little choice with the vast Persian armies marching through their territory. Macedonian kings usually aided the Persians, simply to get them on their way as quickly as possible. At the same time, they usually claimed to be defending the interests of the Greek states, particularly Athens.

In 513 Darius crossed the Bosporos and marched northwards to the Danube. His fleet sailed along the coast of the Black Sea to the mouth of the Danube where they met. From here he launched an attack on the Scythians. The campaign is reported by Herodotos but much remains obscure. Darius withdrew to Sestos, and crossed back to Asia, leaving the satrap of Daskylion, Megabazos, to bring Thrace under Persian control. The activities of Megabazos resulted in a new Persian satrapy, Skudra, stretching from the Black Sea coast to the borders of Macedonia. Amyntas, the king of Macedonia, submitted to Persian authority and his daughter later married Megabazos' son. Amyntas benefitted from this Persian campaign, making territorial gains in Paionia.

With Megabazos ruling over the newly acquired territory in Thrace, Darius appointed a new satrap, Otanes, in Daskylion, and installed his own brother, Artaphrenes, as satrap of Sardis. Otanes swiftly brought Byzantion, Chalkedon, Antandros, Lamponian and the islands of Lemnos and Imbros under direct Persian control, thereby gaining command of the corn route from the Black Sea through the straits, although they do not seem to have interfered with it.

In 505 the tyrant Hippias, expelled from Athens, arrived in Sardis and appealed to Artaphrenes to restore him. An Athenian embassy soon followed, with the opposite intention. Artaphrenes decided to support Hippias, thereby making an enemy of Athens. The repercussions were felt a few years later. On Naxos, a democratic revolt expelled its aristocratic rulers, and Aristagoras, the tyrant of Miletos, persuaded the satrap Artaphrenes to launch a naval expedition against the island, which, if captured would make a good Persian base in the Cyclades. The expedition ended in failure and Aristagoras, in a desperate attempt to save the situation, encouraged cities of the Ionian coast to revolt. He declared democratic rule in Miletos and abandoned his role as tyrant. He then appealed to Sparta and Athens for aid. It was in Athens that Aristagoras found support, the city fearing the return of Hippias. Twenty Athenian and Eretrian ships were sent to aid the rebellion.

In 499 a Greek attack was launched on Sardis, and the city was burned, but the Greek forces were defeated soon after at Ephesos and the Athenian ships withdrew. Darius was incensed and swore vengeance on Athens for its part in the revolt. He ordered that every time he sat down at the table, a servant was to repeat three times "Master, remember the Athenians". Byzantion, with other cities on the Hellespont and most of Cyprus, now joined the rebellion (498—7). The revolt dragged on: Persia regained control of Cyprus and eventually Miletos itself was besieged. The Ionian fleet was sent to Lade nearby, but was outnumbered and defeated (494). Miletos was captured, its males deported and remainder of the population enslaved. Meanwhile, Aristagoras had fled to Thrace, where he was killed in battle.

The Ionian Revolt began, not as a nationalist reaction to Persian rule, but as the result of the intrigues of individual rulers. The tyrants had proved too fickle for Persian liking and, as a response to the revolt, Mardonios, a son-in-law of Darius, was sent to declare democracy in many of the Ionian cities (492). Meanwhile his fleet sailed around the coast and a large army made for the Hellespont. They crossed into Thrace. Herodotos claims that he intended to march against Athens and Eretria to punish them for aiding the Ionian Revolt, but the fleet came to grief off Mount Athos and the army was defeated by the tribe of the Brygi. Seriously wounded, Mardonios retreated.

The First Invasion

The following year, Darius sent to the Greek states demanding submission: many complied, especially the islands, but in Sparta and Athens his ambassadors were summarily executed, a flagrant breach of custom. Darius launched an attack on Athens and Eretria for their involvement in the Ionian Revolt. This time the Persians avoided the northern route and sent the fleet, under the command of Datis, directly across the Aegean. It progressed slowly, but without opposition. The elderly Hippias accompanied the fleet, still seeking his reinstatement in Athens.

The army landed on Euboea. Karystos, then Eretria, fell. After a few days rest to recuperate and resupply, the Persians sailed for Attica. The bay of

Marathon was chosen for a landing place, perhaps at Hippias' suggestion. It had the advantage of drawing any Athenian force away from the city, thus allowing any pro-Persian (or pro-Hippias) faction to initiate a coup d'état.

The victory at Marathon, won by a predominantly Athenian army over vastly superior numbers, was to become the symbol of Greek and Athenian liberation. The Persian retreat was swift.

Various internal problems and aristocratic disputes in Athens were followed by further democratic reforms (486). These years saw the increasing political

The Gate of Xerxes at Persepolis is guarded by two winged bulls. Between such activities as the invasion of Greece (480 BC) and the sack of Babylon (478 BC) Xerxes still managed to find time to make considerable additions to the palace, although the credit for the origination of the plans for the 13-hectare site is generally attributed to his father, Darius.

prominence of Themistokles. One of his ambitions was to create a strong Athenian navy. Following the victory of Marathon, Persia was no longer regarded as a threat by the majority of Athenians, so Themistokles invoked the much lesser, but more immediate, possibility of war with neighbouring Aegina. In 483 a rich new vein of silver was found in the state-owned mines at Laurion. The surplus was normally divided amongst the citizens, but was now, at Themistokles' instigation, voted to build a new fleet of triremes. The creation of a navy was to change the course of Athenian history.

The Invasion of Xerxes

The elderly Darius died without making any further attempts on Greece. His successor, Xerxes (485—465), although a younger son, had been appointed Crown Prince, and for over a decade had been officiating as viceroy in Babylon. Xerxes united both royal lines, his mother, Atossa, being a daughter of Cyrus.

Xerxes began his reign by putting down rebellions in Egypt and Babylonia, but he soon turned his attention towards Greece. A canal was cut through the Mount Athos peninsula, bridges built across the Hellespont and the river Strymon and supply depots set up for the enormous army and its support.

The Greeks met in conference on the isthmus of Corinth in the summer of 481. A general truce was established (so the war between Athens and Aegina was ended for the time) and an alliance of states.

The Persian army overwintered in Asia and then, early in 480, crossed into Europe. The army on land moved slowly through Thrace, rejoining the fleet in Thessaly. The leading family of Thessaly, the Aleuadai, seems to have already acknowledged Persian authority in 492.

Thermopylai was the best point of defence in central Greece. Leonidas, king of Sparta led an army there, and a fleet of Athenian and Peloponnesian ships gathered nearby at Cape Artemision. Xerxes' superior numbers were of no help in the pass and the initial attacks failed. Then, apprised of a mountain route, he despatched a group of "the Immortals" to attack the Greek rear. Leonidas dismissed many of the non-Spartan troops, leaving 300 Spartiates, their helots, and small forces of Thespians and Thebans to defend the pass. Their desperate stand inflicted heavy casualties on the Persians, and protected the retreating Greeks. The fleets clashed at Artemision on the same day, the Persians losing many ships. News of the Persian land victory reached the Greek fleet that evening and it set sail immediately.

Xerxes, faced with little resistance, marched his army into central Greece. In Attica, the evacuation of the people was underway, the women and children being removed to Troizen and Aegina and the men joining the fleet at Salamis. The Athenian Akropolis was besieged and eventually stormed, its temples burnt. The armies of the Peloponnese were defending the isthmus. The Persian ships sailed to Salamis, where, unable to manoevre in the confined waters, they were destroyed.

Xerxes watched the defeat of his fleet from a throne set up at the foot of mount Aigaleos. After a day's bloody conflict, the Persians retreated to Phaleron and sailed for Asia. Xerxes returned to Asia overland. The bulk of the Persian army, under the command of Mardonios retired to Thessaly, where it overwintered.

The following year, a revolt in Chalkidike was suppressed before Mardonios again led the Persian army south, into Attica. A large force of Spartiates and their allies marched from the Peloponnese and the Persians withdrew to

Boiotia, where they relied on their Theban allies. The Athenians joined the army which advanced to confront the Persians. The battle was a series of skirmishes culminating in the confrontation at Plataiai. The Persians were defeated, Mardonios was killed and the army routed.

Whilst the war on mainland Greece continued, the Greek fleet had sailed across the Aegean to Delos, where it received appeals from Samos and Chios to liberate Ionia. The Persian fleet beached at Mycale near Miletos, but the Greeks broke through their defences and burned the ships. The victorious Greek fleet then sailed for the Hellespont, where the war ended with the capture of the Persian base at Sestos. The following year 478, a fleet was sent under the command of Pausanias, regent of Sparta, to continue the offensive on the Ionian coast. Cyprus was captured, and, more importantly, Byzantion which controlled the access to the Black Sea corn route. Shortly after, the satrapy of Skudra was disbanded, to the profit of Alexander of Macedon who expanded his kingdom eastwards to the river Strymon.

Return to Disunity

The invasions of Darius and Xerxes had briefly united some of the Greek states against Persia, but only a minority. In the succeeding decades, the internal conflicts of the Greek states were to play an important role in attitudes towards Persia. Within many states there were pro-Persian groups, even if official policy was hostile. Persia continued to provide a refuge for exiles and some notable anti-Persians, ironically, ended their careers in the court or service of the Great King. Amongst them was Themistokles, the architect of Athenian naval supremacy, who fell victim to his city's political vagaries and the hostility of the aristocratic families. He was ostracized and was eventually forced to flee to Persia, ending his life as governor of Magnesia.

The divisions in Greek political unity soon reappeared. Athens began to refortify the city and, at Themistokles' instigation, the Piraeus, which was a better harbour than the open bay of Phaleron. Sparta opposed these moves. Even more importantly, Athens began to establish her position as defender of Ionia, based upon her larger naval capability.

A controversial figure both in his own day and subsequently, Themistokles was a brilliant politician and a military leader of undisputed genius. Having fought at Marathon, Themistokles never underestimated the Persian threat and he was responsible for the fortification of the Piraeus and the development of the Athenian fleet which demolished the Persians at the decisive battle of Salamis.

For a short period, Sparta lost full control of the Peloponnese and Argos regained some former cities; Elis and Mantinea established democracies. Sparta had nominally been in naval command, but failed to turn herself into a real naval power. At the same time, she failed to exert control on land in the medising states of central Greece, most notably Thessaly and Boiotia. The Spartan regent Pausanias returned to Byzantion and began to intrigue with the Persians for his own ends. He is supposed to have possessed a bodyguard of Egyptians and Persians, to have adopted Persian dress and to have sought the hand of Xerxes' daughter.

The Athenian defeat of Persian forces at the battle of the river Eurymedon, on the coast of Pamphylia (early 460s), marks the end of this phase of the conflict and the rise of Athenian naval power in the Aegean. The fleet was led by Kimon, the son of Miltiades, victor of Marathon. In 465 Xerxes was assassinated, his eldest son, Darius, was accused (although not responsible) and murdered by his younger brother, who succeeded as Artaxerxes I (464—425). Direct Persian intervention in the Aegean ceased for some time, but Greek intervention in the Persian empire increased.

Persia and the West

The history of western Asia between the 7th and 5th centuries BC is one of rivalry, warfare and annexation. Gradually it was the Persians who achieved supremacy over their neighbours.

"It now plainly appeared that Aristagoras of Miletos was, after all, but a poor-spirited creature: himself responsible for setting Ionia by the ears and all the subsequent trouble, nevertheless, when he saw these towns falling one after another, and realized that he had no chance against Darius, he began to look around for means of escape."
Herodotos,
Histories

The years of Greek migration and colonization had been coincident with that of the Phoenicians at the height of the late Assyrian empire; events in western Asia were now to model the history of Greece for the next 200 years. The first crisis came with the fall of the Assyrian capital Nineveh to an alliance of the Medes and Babylonians (612). A rump Assyrian state continued to resist with Egyptian support, but following defeat at a battle near Hama (605), Assyria was completely absorbed into the Babylonian kingdom. The Medes expanded their territory to the north of the new Babylonian empire into eastern Anatolia, where they confronted another rising power, the kingdom of Lydia. Peace was concluded between the Medes and Lydians in 585. The expansion of Lydia under the rule of Kroisos absorbed the Greek cities of the Ionian coast. Meanwhile further east, in Iran, Cyrus the king of Anshan (559—530) conquered the Median empire in 550. This brought the whole of the, now extensive, Median empire under Cyrus' rule. At the news of this defeat, Kroisos decided to move eastwards into the former Median territories of Anatolia. He sought the advice of the Delphic Oracle, to be told that he would destroy a great kingdom. He assumed that Persia was meant and crossed the Halys River. Cyrus himself led his armies into battle. The confrontation at Hattusas ended in stalemate, and Kroisos retreated to Sardis, where he was besieged (547). Following the defeat of Kroisos, Median generals brought the coastal cities under Persian rule and satraps were installed. Ruling from Sardis and Daskylion, these satraps were to be influential players in the politics of Greece. The Greek cities had their own rulers. Essentially tyrants, they retained their independence so long as they paid taxes and sent contingents to the Persian army.

Persian expansion continued. Babylon fell in 539. Cyrus' successor Cambyses (529—522) brought Egypt into the empire (525) and in

Top right: *An enthroned Darius gives audience in the Persian capital at Persepolis. Heir to the vast empire created by the expansionist policies of Cyrus and Cambyses, Darius, above all else, was concerned with establishing administrative order throughout his realm. Activities such as the suppression of the Ionian Revolt and the subsequent invasion of mainland Greece were undertaken with a view to attaining this primary goal.*

EGYPT
◊ 525 BC
Egypt conquered
by Cambyses

512 Darius (521—486) crossed the Hellespont and invaded Thrace, campaigning against the Scythians. Macedonia recognized the Persian power.

Revolt in Ionia led ultimately to Darius' invasion of Greece. Rather than a wave of anti-Persian feeling, it was personal ambitions of some of the tyrants of the Greek cities that initiated the crisis. Aristagoras of Miletos persuaded the satrap to mount a naval expedition against Naxos (499). Its failure prompted Aristagoras to rebel. The tyrants were ejected from many cities, Aristagoras himself laying aside his powers. Aristagoras went to Greece for help for the cities. Sparta refused aid, but the new democracy in Athens, fearing the return of the tyrant Hippias who had Persian support, sent a fleet. The Athenians withdrew after early defeats but the revolt lasted six years before, with the capture and sack of Miletos, Persian authority was restored over the Ionian coast (493). The satrap installed democracies in place of the tyrants in many of the cities. Many Ionians fought on the Persian side in subsequent conflicts.

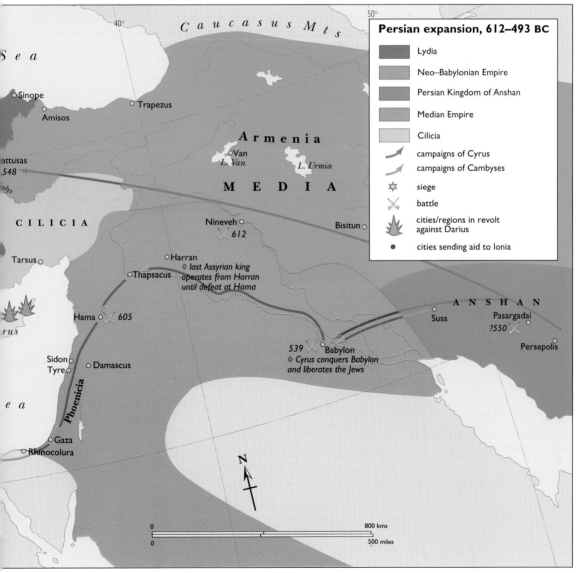

Persian expansion, 612–493 BC

- Lydia
- Neo–Babylonian Empire
- Persian Kingdom of Anshan
- Median Empire
- Cilicia
- campaigns of Cyrus
- campaigns of Cambyses
- siege
- battle
- cities/regions in revolt against Darius
- cities sending aid to Ionia

Kingdom of Macedonia

The history of Macedonia between 650–436 BC is one of gradual expansion marked by political duplicity which involved maintaining relations with both the Greeks and Persians.

"Darius wrote to Megabazos, whom he had left in command in Thrace, instructing him to turn the Paionians, men, women, and children, out of their homes and bring them to him … the result of the campaign was that a number of Paionian tribes were transferred bodily to Asia. The tribes in the neighbourhood of Mount Pangaion and Lake Prasias were not subjected by Megabazos – though he did attempt the conquest of the latter."
Herodotos,
Histories, Book V

In the years of Macedonian expansion under Philip II (359—336 BC) the Athenian orator Demosthenes referred to Greece's northern neighbours as "barbarians", claiming that they had only recently ceased to be shepherds. Certainly the Thracians and Illyrians were non-Greek speakers, but in the northwest, the peoples of Molossis, Orestis and Lynkestis spoke West Greek. It is also now accepted that the Macedonians spoke a dialect of Greek and although they absorbed other groups into their territory, they were essentially "Greeks". The main difference between Macedonia and the city states of the south was that it was ruled by a king and powerful nobility.

The Macedonian kingdom emerged around 650 BC and the throne was held by the Argead family, which claimed an origin in Argos. This claim to Greek ancestry was apparently recognized when the future Alexander I wished to compete in the Olympic games (*c.* 506). Later Macedonian princes also competed in the games. The earliest centres of power were around Aigai, with its royal burial ground at Vergina.

There were centres of South Greek settlement in the region from the 8th century, and these were to be the source of future conflict between Macedonia and the southern states, particularly Athens. Methone was founded *c.* 730, by Eretrians from Euboea, who perhaps were also founders of Pydna. Other Euboean colonies led by Eretria and Chalkis were established on the three peninsulas of Chalkidike.

Rather little is known of the first century and a half of the Macedonian kingdom. It is with the Persian invasions that information increases (principally from Herodotos). These were significant years in the development of Macedonia. Darius led an army into Europe in 512 and campaigned against the Scythians, north of the Danube. The Persians then attacked the Paionians, and the Macedonian King Amyntas I (died *c.* 496) aided Persian victory by attacking the Paionian rear. Amyntas then annexed (or was given) Amphaxitis and a coastal strip of the Thermaic Gulf. He offered refuge to the Athenian tyrant Hippias in 506, and perhaps supplied Athens with timber for ships.

Macedonian expansion is attributed to Amyntas' son Alexander I (*c.* 497—*c.* 454) who absorbed the rich agricultural lands of Pieria, and

Bottiaia as far as Pella. The Persians were again active in Thrace in 492 and Alexander maintained good relations with them, marrying his sister to the son of the satrap Megabazos. With the main Persian invasion, Alexander smoothed the Persian progress through Thessaly and after Salamis, attempted to split the Greek alliance. He encouraged Athens to accept an advantageous capitulation offer. Athens refused. Following the Persian withdrawal from Greece in 479, and the disbanding of the satrapy of Skudra (Thrace), Alexander was able to take over territories between Amphaxitis and the Strymon which included the silver deposits of Mount Dysoron. Despite his assistance to the Persians, Alexander spread propaganda about his noble intentions towards the Greek city states.

The mineral resources of Mount Pangaion had been exploited by the Thracians, but the island city of Thasos was also active in the region. Athenian expansion into the northern Aegean forced Thasos to relinquish gold mines and territory on the Thracian coast. Athens continued to be active in an attempt to gain control of the gold mines at Nigrita and the Bisaltic silver mines.

In Macedonia, internal instability followed the death of Alexander I. Perdikkas II (c. 454—413) signed a treaty with Athens, but this was terminated by the Athenians before 433 when they were supporting opposition to the king. Athenian expansion increased with the foundation of Amphipolis, on the Strymon, in 436. Athenian control of the north Aegean trade had a severe impact on the economy of the Balkans. The region thus became one of the important arenas during the Peloponnesian War.

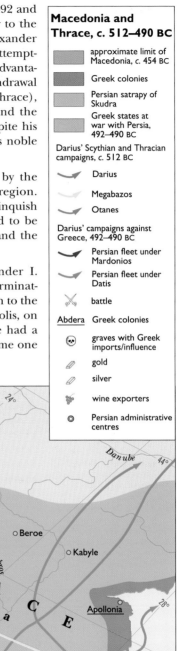

Macedonia and Thrace, c. 512–490 BC

- approximate limit of Macedonia, c. 454 BC
- Greek colonies
- Persian satrapy of Skudra
- Greek states at war with Persia, 492–490 BC

Darius' Scythian and Thracian campaigns, c. 512 BC

- Darius
- Megabazos
- Otanes

Darius' campaigns against Greece, 492–490 BC

- Persian fleet under Mardonios
- Persian fleet under Datis
- ✕ battle
- Abdera — Greek colonies
- graves with Greek imports/influence
- gold
- silver
- wine exporters
- Persian administrative centres

Persian Campaigns I

In 492 BC and again in 490, Darius launched attacks on Greece, but a combination of adverse elements and Athenian tactical genius was to result in defeat and withdrawal.

Having crushed the Ionian revolt, Darius began preparations for his attack on Greece. The first Persian invasion came in 492 when Mardonios led the army across the Hellespont and into Thrace and Macedonia. Athens and Eretria are assumed to have been Mardonios' ultimate target, but they escaped when much of the Persian fleet was destroyed by storms while sailing around the Mount Athos peninsula. His forces decimated, Mardonios withdrew. The next assault same in 490 BC when Darius sent a fleet under Datis. The Athenian exile, Hippias, son of the tyrant Peisistratos, accompanied it; he may well have had allies in Athens. The fleet sailed directly across the Aegean. First it attacked Naxos: its city was burnt. Then Eretria in Euboea was sacked, and its population deported. Sailing south, the Persian fleet moored at Marathon. The Athenians sent the runner, Pheidippides, to Sparta for assistance, but the city was celebrating a festival and troops were unable to attend before it ended. A small contingent of Plataians did, however, arrive. The Athenians had the more favourable position on the plain, but were greatly outnumbered by the Persian infantry and cavalry. Datis kept the army at Marathon for several days without engaging, but sent part of the fleet against the undefended town. The Athenian commander, Miltiades, decided to attack. He stretched his troops to balance the larger Persian force. The Persians broke through the weak Athenian centre which gave way, but the wings put their Persian opposites to flight. Reforming as one unit, the Athenians confronted the Persian centre. Great losses were suffered by the Persians with reputedly almost 7000 killed. Only 192 Athenians (Plataians and slaves excluded) died. The Athenian army immediately returned to Athens and was able to confront the Persian fleet when it arrived at Phaleron. Rather than risk a second confrontation, Datis sailed for Asia.

Much of our knowledge of the Persian campaigns is founded upon the works of the Greek historian Herodotos (c. 485—425 BC). Called by Cicero 'the father of history', Herodotos based much of his great narrative account on materials gathered during his extensive travels in Asia Minor and the Middle East. After spending many years in the Athens of Perikles—where he may have enjoyed the friendship of the playwright Sophokles—the great historian finally settled in the west, at the colony of Thurii.

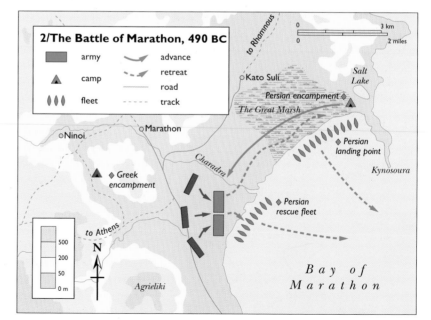

2/The Battle of Marathon, 490 BC

army
camp
fleet
advance
retreat
road
track

to Rhamnous
0   3 km
0   2 miles

Kato Suli
Salt Lake
Persian encampment
The Great Marsh

Ninoi
Marathon
Persian landing point
Kynosoura
Charadra
Greek encampment
Persian rescue fleet

to Athens
N

500
200
50
0 m

Agrieliki

B a y   o f   M a r a t h o n

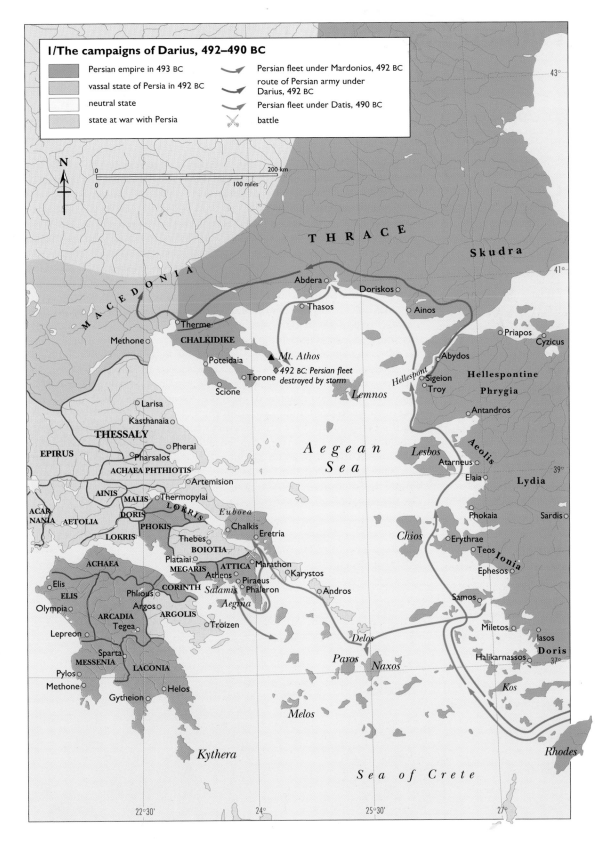

Persian Campaigns II

Undeterred by his father's failure, Xerxes launched a further invasion of Greece in 480 BC. The issue of the conflict would decide forever the question of Greece's inclusion in the Persian Empire.

A harsh and temperamental task-master, Xerxes (here portrayed in a frieze at Persepolis) frequently revealed his willingness to drive his army and its commanders to the utmost of their abilities.

The Persian army of Darius' heir, Xerxes, wintered in Asia Minor (480), then moved towards the Hellespont. The ancient sources number this vast army at over 5 million but it is more likely that a mere 150,000 combatants were actually involved. When Thessaly and the north were lost to the advancing Persians, a Greek army of 6—7000 men, under the command of the Spartan King Leonidas, went to defend the pass of Thermopylai. An Athenian–Peloponnesian fleet of less than 300 ships sailed to Artemision, close-by. The Persian fleet suffered severe losses through storm, and from skirmishes with Greek vessels. Xerxes launched two unsuccessful assaults on Thermopylai. Informed of the mountain path, he sent his crack troops, "the Immortals", to cut off the Greek rear. The defenders retreated in front of the Persians who were thus able to move on the main army. Realizing the hopelessness of his position and wishing to preserve the bulk of his army, Leonidas quickly dismissed most of the Peloponnesian troops, retaining only a small force of about 1000, mainly Spartan. They were all slain, although they inflicted heavy losses and prevented the destruction of the remainder of the retreating Greek force. On the same day the fleets met in battle, both suffering losses. That night the Greek fleet withdrew to Salamis. The Persian fleet soon followed. The Persian army now advanced on Athens (most of its population had been evacuated), and the Akropolis was burnt. The Greek fleet once again prepared to confront the Persians. A bloody battle ensued and the Persians withdrew, sailing directly for Asia. Xerxes withdrew rapidly by land, but a Persian force remained under the command of Mardonios. The largest Greek army so far assembled, 35,000 men, now marched in pursuit. They confronted the Persians and their Theban allies at Plataiai in Boiotia the following year (479). Mardonios was slain and, the Persians fled. The war in mainland Greece was over.

2/The Battle of Salamis, 480 BC

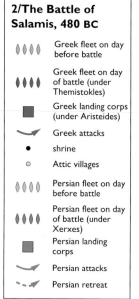

◊◊◊◊	Greek fleet on day before battle
◊◊◊◊	Greek fleet on day of battle (under Themistokles)
▪	Greek landing corps (under Aristeides)
⌒	Greek attacks
●	shrine
○	Attic villages
◊◊◊◊	Persian fleet on day before battle
◊◊◊◊	Persian fleet on day of battle (under Xerxes)
▪	Persian landing corps
⌒	Persian attacks
⌐⌐►	Persian retreat

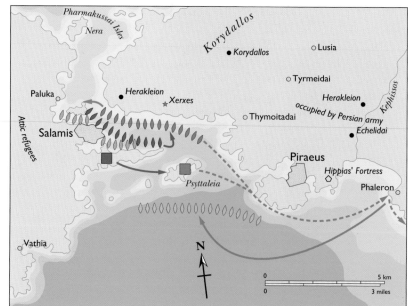

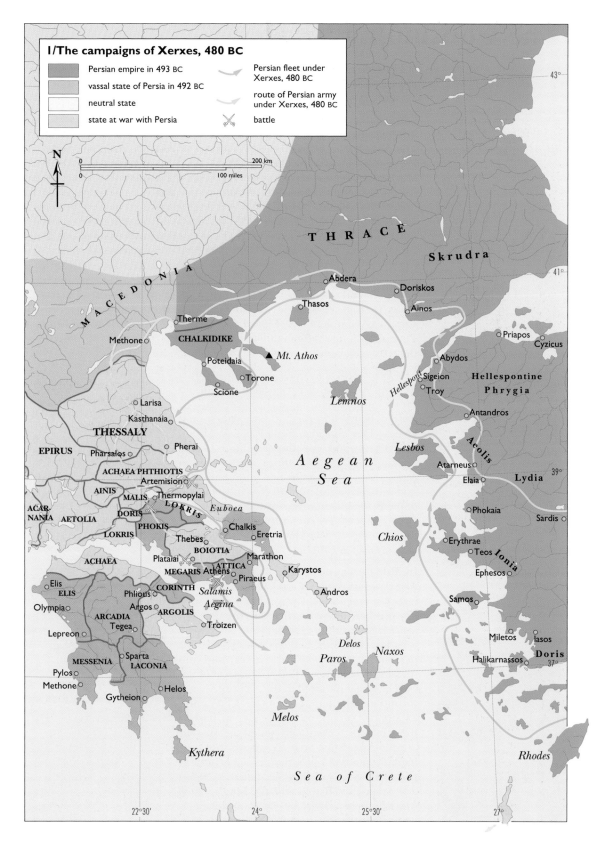

I/The campaigns of Xerxes, 480 BC

- Persian empire in 493 BC
- vassal state of Persia in 492 BC
- neutral state
- state at war with Persia
- Persian fleet under Xerxes, 480 BC
- route of Persian army under Xerxes, 480 BC
- battle

N

0   200 km
0   100 miles

THRACE

Skrudra

MACEDONIA

Abdera
Doriskos
Thasos
Ainos
Therme
Methone
CHALKIDIKE
Priapos
Cyzicus
Poteidaia
Mt. Athos
Abydos
Hellespontine Phrygia
Torone
Sigeion
Scione
Troy
Lemnos
Antandros
Larisa
Kasthanaia
THESSALY
Lesbos
Aeolis
Pherai
Atarneus
Lydia
EPIRUS
Pharsalos
Aegean Sea
Elaia
ACHAEA PHTHIOTIS
Artemision
AINIS
Thermopylai
Phokaia
ACAR-
NANIA
MALIS
DORIS
LOKRIS
Sardis
Euboea
AETOLIA
PHOKIS
Chios
Erythrae
LOKRIS
Chalkis
Teos
Ionia
Thebes
Eretria
BOIOTIA
Ephesos
Plataiai
Marathon
ACHAEA
ATTICA
MEGARIS
Athens
Karystos
Elis
Piraeus
ELIS
CORINTH
Salamis
Andros
Samos
Olympia
Phlious
Aegina
Argos
ARGOLIS
ARCADIA
Lepreon
Tegea
Troizen
Delos
Miletos
Iasos
MESSENIA
Sparta
Naxos
Halikarnassos
Doris
Pylos
LACONIA
Paros
Methone
Helos
Gytheion
Melos

Kythera

Rhodes

Sea of Crete

Hellespont

43°
41°
39°
37°

22°30'
24°
25°30'
27°

The Continuing Rivalry

The battle of Plataiai did not end the rivalry between Persia and Greece. For another century a tangled skein of diplomacy and plotting would continue to be woven.

"They make no cult statues or temples or altars, and think those who do this foolish ... When he sacrifices, no man may pray for himself alone; but he prays that it may be well for all the Persians, and for the King."
Herodotos, *The Histories*

Only at the time of the invasions of Darius and Xerxes did the states of southern Greece present anything like a united resistance to the Persian empire. The relationship between the Greek cities of Asia, the mainland states and Persia was tempered by internal factors and political expediency. The death of a Great King was always a time of crisis in the empire: rival claimants and rebellion usually followed. Both Athens and Sparta aided such revolts for their own purposes and these foreign interventions inevitably had political repercussions at home. From 459 BC, Athens involved herself in a costly rebellion which broke out in Egypt in the last years of Xerxes' reign. At first successful, the leader Inaros defeated and killed the satrap. He then sought Athenian aid, perhaps in exchange for corn. The new Great King, Artaxerxes I, attempted to divert Athens by inciting Sparta to invade Attica: but Sparta did not oblige. The tide turned when the Persian army arrived in Egypt (perhaps 456). The war dragged on and the Athenian fleet of 250 ships was completely destroyed two years later (454). In the words of Thucydides', "few out of many returned home". Those that did, escaped via the coast to Kyrene.

The Peace of Kallias (449) ended the conflict between Athens and Persia for a period, but the Peloponnesian war was to see renewed conflict between Persia and both Athens and Sparta. This time the arena was Asia Minor. Athen's support for the rebellion of the Lydian Satrap Pissouthnes and his son Amorges (413) brought her into confrontation with Persia and also affected the outcome of the Peloponnesian War. The Persian prince Cyrus, who was given control of the whole of the satrapies of Asia Minor, gave his support to Sparta against Athens.

In 401, Cyrus revolted against his brother, Artaxerxes II. With an army including 13,000 Greek mercenaries, Cyrus marched against his brother. They confronted the Persian army at Kunaxa north of Babylon. The Greek wing was victorious, but Cyrus was killed after personally wounding Artaxerxes, and the remainder of his army fled. The retreat of the Greek force is narrated in the *Anabasis*, one of the most celebrated works of Greek literature: its author, Xenophon, was leader of part of the army which eventually joined the Spartan army in Asia Minor. Sparta's support for Cyrus had now put it at war with Persia. Attempts at peace, firstly by Sparta in 392, failed. In 387—386 Artaxerxes II imposed the King's Peace which limited activity by the states of mainland Greece for the next half century.

The ruins of the Apadana, or audience-hall, of the Persian capital, Persepolis. One of the most distinctive features of Persian architecture was the use of extremely tall stone columns to support highly-decorated wooden ceilings. The columns of the Apadana are over 18-metres high and are surmounted by ornate capitals which contribute to the top-heavy appearance.

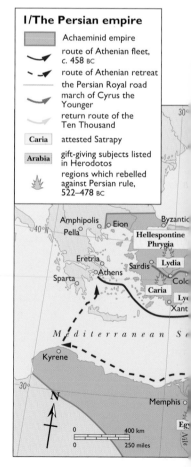

I/The Persian empire

- Achaeminid empire
- route of Athenian fleet, c. 458 BC
- route of Athenian retreat
- the Persian Royal road
- march of Cyrus the Younger
- return route of the Ten Thousand
- **Caria** attested Satrapy
- **Arabia** gift-giving subjects listed in Herodotos
- regions which rebelled against Persian rule, 522–478 BC

Amphipolis
Pella
Eion
Byzantic
Hellespontine Phrygia
Eretria
Sardis
Lydia
Sparta
Athens
Caria
Col
Ly
Xant
Mediterranean Se
Kyrene
Memphis
Eg
Nile
0   400 km
0   250 miles

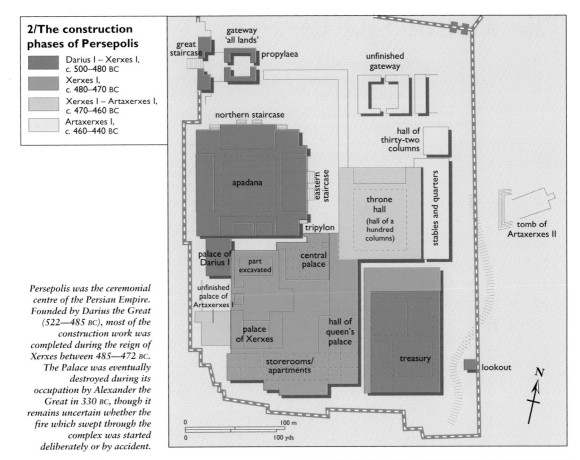

2/The construction phases of Persepolis

- Darius I – Xerxes I, *c.* 500–480 BC
- Xerxes I, *c.* 480–470 BC
- Xerxes I – Artaxerxes I, *c.* 470–460 BC
- Artaxerxes I, *c.* 460–440 BC

great staircase

gateway 'all lands'

propylaea

unfinished gateway

northern staircase

hall of thirty-two columns

apadana

eastern staircase

tripylon

throne hall (hall of a hundred columns)

stables and quarters

tomb of Artaxerxes II

palace of Darius I

part excavated

central palace

unfinished palace of Artaxerxes I

palace of Xerxes

hall of queen's palace

treasury

storerooms/ apartments

lookout

N

Persepolis was the ceremonial centre of the Persian Empire. Founded by Darius the Great (522—485 BC), most of the construction work was completed during the reign of Xerxes between 485—472 BC. The Palace was eventually destroyed during its occupation by Alexander the Great in 330 BC, though it remains uncertain whether the fire which swept through the complex was started deliberately or by accident.

0   100 m
0   100 yds

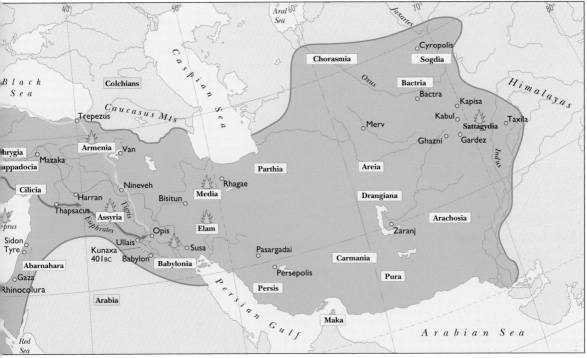

Aral Sea

Caspian Sea

Jaxartes

Cyropolis

Chorasmia

Sogdia

Black Sea

Colchians

Oxus

Bactria

Bactra

Himalayas

Caucasus Mts

Trepezus

Kapisa

Kabul

Taxila

Merv

Sattagydia

Ghazni

Gardez

Indus

Armenia

Van

Phrygia

Mazaka

Cappadocia

Parthia

Areia

Cilicia

Nineveh

Rhagae

Harran

Bisitun

Media

Drangiana

Thapsacus

Assyria

Arachosia

Euphrates

Tigris

Opis

Elam

Zaranj

Cyprus

Sidon

Tyre

Ullais

Kunaxa 401 BC

Babylon

Babylonia

Susa

Pasargadai

Carmania

Pura

Abarnahara

Gaza

Rhinocolura

Persepolis

Persis

Arabia

Persian Gulf

Maka

Arabian Sea

Red Sea

The Rise of Sparta

Sparta's aggressive expansionist policies would bring her into conflict with many of her neighbours and resulted in the development of an increasingly militaristic culture.

"The whole structure of their society is directed to securing one part only of virtue, military prowess, as being valuable in the acquisition of power. Hence the Spartans prospered while at war but began to decline once they reached a position of supremacy; they did not understand what being at peace meant and never attached any importance to any other kind of training than training for war."
Aristotle, *The Politics, Book II.*

Sparta's position in the Eurotas valley allowed its expansion in all directions. To the east, her principal rival was Argos, but the richest territory lay to the west, in Messenia. Sparta's early conquests are attributed to the kings of the 9th and 8th centuries. Some conquered towns remained largely autonomous but were required to provide Sparta with troops. Sparta's southward expansion began with the subjection of Geronthrai and Amyklai (by 750 BC) and continued to the coast. Following the capture of Helos (740—700), an Argive-backed city on the gulf, a new policy towards the population was adopted. No longer were towns allowed to remain autonomous, but the population was reduced to *helot* status, becoming slaves of the Spartan state. This policy was applied with particular force in Messenia, which became subject after a long struggle lasting from 735 to 715. The repercussions of Sparta's actions in Messenia were to dominate its policy for the next 350 years.

Sparta was involved in the foundation of some colonies in the period of the great migration, but only one is known later, at Taras (708). In this case the colonists were a specific group called the Partheniai, who had revolted and Sparta's solution was to establish the colony.

Spartan aggression against Argos ended in disaster in 669 when her army was defeated at Hysai. The king of Argos extended his power across the Peloponnese to Olympia, and this prompted a Messenian rebellion (660). Spartan failures to secure other territories led to a change in policy and the increase of influence through the Peloponnesian League, "the Lacedaemonians and their allies", a loose confederation of states which retained their autonomy. Elis, Arcadia, Corinth and Megara were usually allies. Argos always remained hostile and Achaea, separated from the south Peloponnese by mountains, was usually independent. By the beginning of the Peloponnesian War, the Spartan alliance also included Boiotia.

Top right: Although the origins of this 5th-century bronze warrior are uncertain it seems probable that he is Spartan in manufacture. The style and modelling of the cloak-shrouded figure are unique and represent an entirely new direction in Archaic sculpture. As a whole, the piece brilliantly symbolizes the austere militarism which the Spartans so prized.

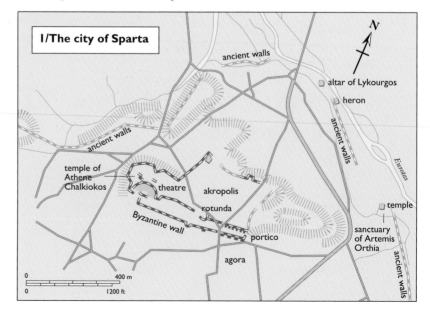

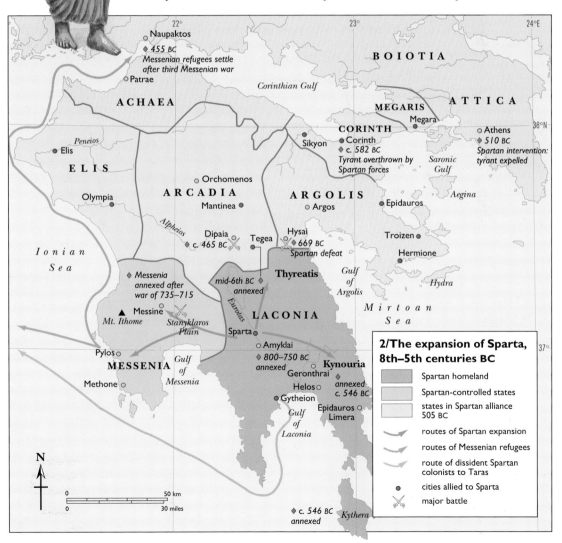

In 546, Kroisos of Lydia sought the help of Sparta against Persia, but Sparta was engaged in a war with Argos for control of the Thyreatis and did not lend aid. Kroisos' kingdom fell to the Persians. Sparta, however, was successful and absorbed Thyreatis, the coastal strip of Kynouria and the island of Kythera. Sparta eventually came to take a lead against Persian advances on Greece, but it is uncertain whether the part she played in evicting the tyrants was due to the pro-Persian stance many of them adopted. Sparta may have played a role in the fall of the Kypselids in Corinth (582) and certainly did attack Lygdamis of Naxos (525 or 515) and Polykrates of Samos (525) and Hippias of Athens (510).

Following the Persian Wars, there was a challenge to Sparta's hegemony in the Peloponnese. In 470, Elis, the majority of the Arcadian cities and Argos were in alliance against Sparta. The Arcadians were defeated at Tegea and Dipaia (465) but a massive earthquake devastated Laconia and the *helots* seized the opportunity to revolt (3rd Messenian War). Following a battle in the Stanyklaros plain, the helots retreated to mount Ithome. Sparta's allies now came to her aid, as did Athens. The *helots* on Ithome were forced to capitulate in 460 and Athens helped them to settle at Naupaktos.

Naupaktos
◆ 455 BC
Messenian refugees settle
after third Messenian war
Patrae

BOIOTIA

Corinthian Gulf

ACHAEA

MEGARIS   ATTICA
Megara

CORINTH
Sikyon   Corinth   Athens   38°N
◆ c. 582 BC   ◆ 510 BC
Tyrant overthrown by   Spartan intervention:
Spartan forces   Saronic   tyrant expelled
Gulf

Peneios
Elis   Orchomenos

Aegina

ELIS   ARCADIA   ARGOLIS
Olympia   Mantinea   Argos   Epidauros

Alpheios
Dipaia   Tegea   Hysai   Troizen
◆ c. 465 BC   ◆ 669 BC
Spartan defeat   Hermione

Ionian   Gulf
Sea   Messenia   mid-6th BC   Thyreatis   of
annexed after   annexed   Argolis   Hydra
war of 735–715

Mirtoan
Messine   Sea
Mt. Ithome   Stanyklaros   LACONIA
Plain   Sparta

Pylos
Gulf   Amyklai
MESSENIA   of   ◆ 800–750 BC   Kynouria
Messenia   annexed   annexed
Methone   Geronthrai   c. 546 BC
Helos
Gytheion   Epidauros
Gulf   Limera
of
Laconia

N

0   50 km
0   30 miles

◆ c. 546 BC   Kythera
annexed

2/The expansion of Sparta, 8th–5th centuries BC

Spartan homeland
Spartan-controlled states
states in Spartan alliance 505 BC
routes of Spartan expansion
routes of Messenian refugees
route of dissident Spartan colonists to Taras
cities allied to Sparta
major battle

Ancient Explorers

*As the peoples of the ancient world established colonies and sought oppor-
tunities for increased trade their knowledge of the surrounding world grew
ever more detailed.*

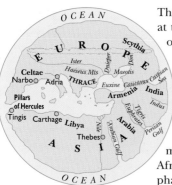

The early Greeks, in common with many ancient peoples, placed themselves
at the centre of a world of concentric circles of decreasing knowledge, the
outer being occupied by mythic creatures and semi-mythic peoples (the
Scythians, Aithiopians and Indians). This world view reflected a range of
experience dominated by contact with Egypt and the empires of western
Asia; Italy and western Europe were largely unknown.

The early first millenium was the era of Phoenician colonization in
north Africa and the western Mediterranean. This reached its peak at
the time of the Assyrian empire when the Phoenicians exploited the silver
mines of Spain and sailed to Britain for tin. Their activities on the coast of
Africa also increased; a Phoenician circumnavigation of Africa for the
pharaoh Nekau II (*c.* 600) is reported, as is a later journey by Hanno (*c.* 525)
from Carthage around the coast of west Africa perhaps as far as Cameroon.
Greeks too, occasionally made long journeys. Aristeas of Prokonessos (7th
century) went to the northern shores of the Black Sea and eastwards almost
as far as the Hindu Kush.

*The first map of the world
was produced by the
Babylonians but the Greeks
were soon developing their
own cartographic skills. The
map above is based upon one
designed by Hecateus and was
intended to aid political
decision-making. According to
Herodotos it was engraved
upon a bronze tablet and was
carried to Sparta by
Aristagoras of Miletos during
the revolt of the Ionian cities
against Persian rule in
499–494 BC.*

The age of Greek migration and colonization followed upon that of the
Phoenicians and some of the new colonies were able to exploit the land
routes which already existed throughout Europe, Asia and Africa. The 7th to
9th centuries were also a time when Greek mercenaries were employed by
the eastern powers. The Greek and Carian soldiers of the Egyptian pharaoh
Psamtik II were sent against the Kushite kingdom of Napata.

Greek contact and conflict with the Persian empire greatly increased experience of "barbarian" peoples, through the troops of the empire sent to
Greece. Many Greeks were employed as soldiers and officials in the empire,
such as Skylax of Karyanda, who sailed down the Indus and around Arabia
for Darius (*c.* 518). These contacts increased geographical knowledge and
had a deep influence in literature and art. The peoples who had occupied
the outer circle, the Aithiopians and Scythians, were now known through
direct contact. Charon of Lampsakos (fl. 469—400) wrote on Aithiopia and

Demokritos of Abdera (born *c.* 460)
was supposed to have visited Meroë,
Babylon, Persia and India.

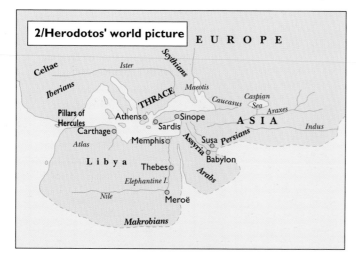

The Hellenistic period saw further
expansion. Ptolemy II of Egypt sent
expeditions up the Nile, renewing
trade with the Kushite kingdom
based on Meroë, and also opened
the Red Sea routes. This enabled the
king to bring elephants for use in his
wars, but also led to the development
of the Red Sea route to India which
was operating by the Augustan period. The expansion of the Seleukid
empire and the Greek kingdom of
Bactria into northern India opened
the silk route from China.

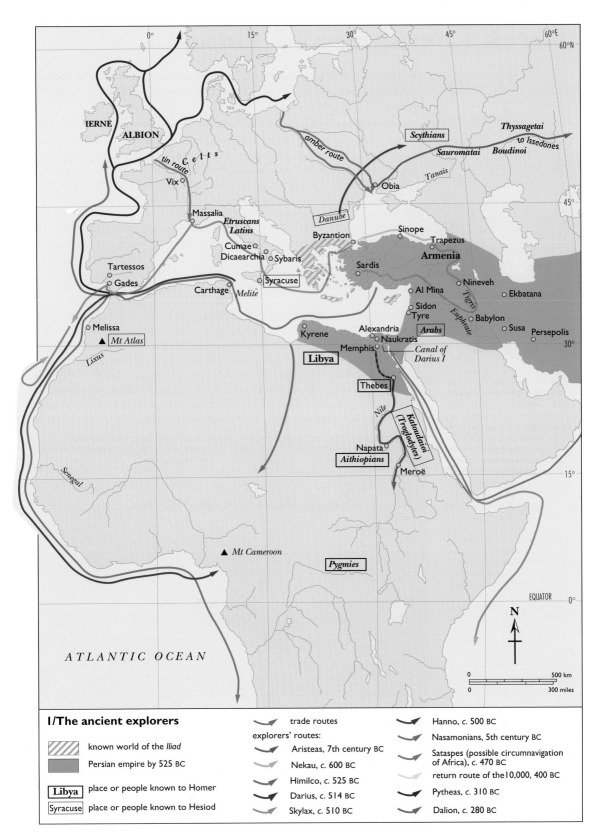

IERNE

ALBION

Celts

tin route

Vix

Massalia

Etruscans
Latins

Cumae
Dicaearchia ○ Sybaris

Tartessos

○ Gades

Carthage ○ *Melite*

amber route

Byzantion

Scythians

Thyssagetai

Sauromatai *Boudinoi* to Issedones

Tanais

Obia

Danube

Sinope

Trapezus

Armenia

Sardis

Nineveh

Al Mina

Ekbatana

Sidon
Tyre

Tigris

Euphrate

Babylon

Arabs

Susa

Persepolis

Melissa

▲ Mt Atlas

Lixus

Kyrene

Alexandria
Naukratis

Libya

Memphis

Canal of
Darius I

Thebes

Nile

Katondaioi
(Troglodytes)

Senegal

Napata

Aithiopians

Meroë

▲ Mt Cameroon

Pygmies

EQUATOR

N

0°

0   500 km

0   300 miles

ATLANTIC OCEAN

I/The ancient explorers

//// known world of the *Iliad*

▓ Persian empire by 525 BC

Libya place or people known to Homer

Syracuse place or people known to Hesiod

⌇ trade routes

explorers' routes:

⌇ Aristeas, 7th century BC

⌇ Nekau, *c.* 600 BC

⌇ Himilco, *c.* 525 BC

⌇ Darius, *c.* 514 BC

⌇ Skylax, *c.* 510 BC

⌇ Hanno, *c.* 500 BC

⌇ Nasamonians, 5th century BC

⌇ Sataspes (possible circumnavigation
of Africa), *c.* 470 BC

⌇ return route of the 10,000, 400 BC

⌇ Pytheas, *c.* 310 BC

⌇ Dalion, *c.* 280 BC

Greek Literature and Thought

Ancient Greece became a centre of intellectual activity, producing philosophers, historians, scientists and dramatists many of whose works would remain not only influential but unchallenged for centuries.

The earliest surviving Greek literature is epic poetry. The Homeric epics (probably 8th century), originally oral, were written down only in the 6th century. Hesiod developed the form further, but using non-heroic themes such as operations of the farming year. There are some indications that Homer may have been an Ionian and it was Ionia which remained the intellectual centre of Greece until the Persian Wars. The two most notable poets of the early sixth century, Sappho and Alkaios, both came from the island of Lesbos. The increasing Greek involvement in Egypt and western Asia was certainly an important stimulus to intellectual development at this time; Sappho's brother was a trader at Naukratis and Alkaios' brother a mercenary at Babylon. Thales of Miletos (fl. 585) also visited Egypt, where he was supposed to have learnt some important mathematical principles. He was the first to ask "What is the primary substance of which the universe is made", his answer was water. Thales thus opened the path to the development of philosophical speculation. Pythagoras (fl. 530), expelled from his native Samos by the tyrant Polykrates also travelled in Egypt and Babylonia. He was drawn to the study of mathematics through trying to establish fixed relations between notes of the musical scale. He eventually settled at Croton in southern Italy, and may (or may not) have discovered the geometrical theorem which bears his name. Geography and ethnography also flourished in Ionia. Hecateus of Miletos

Above: The greatest narrative account of the Peloponnesian War was written by Thucydides (c. 460—400 BC) during his 20 years of exile from Athens. Ironically, it was a charge of military incompetence which resulted in the banishment of this greatest of military historians. In 422 BC, having been made a general, Thucydides was tasked with the protection of Amphipolis from the onslaught of the Spartan commander Brasidas. Although his squadron of ships arrived too late to save the Athenian colony, Thucydides was able to secure the port of Eion and to defend it against repeated Spartan attacks. Unfortunately, this limited success was not sufficient to protect the historian from the exigencies of Athenian political life.

Right: Sokrates (469—399 BC) is portrayed in a mural from a Roman villa at Ephesos. An Athenian by birth, Socrates spent a large portion of his life in attempting to convince his fellow citizens of their own moral lassitude through the use of ironical debate and rhetorical questioning.

Above: The Athenian philosopher Plato (c. 429—347 BC) was originally a disciple of Socrates. Having travelled widely he founded his own academy in Athens where he developed his famous theory of forms. The basis of his system is a belief in the existence of immutable universal forms, the understanding of which should be the primary aim of all philosophy.

Right: By birth a Thracian, Aristotle (384—322 BC) spent 20 years at Plato's academy in Athens, before visiting Macedonia at the invitation of Philip II. Having acted as tutor to Alexander the Great for some three years, he founded his own school in Athens but was eventually forced to flee to Euboea in the face of increasingly anti-Macedonian sentiment. He died at Chalkis.

Far right: Aischylos (c. 525—456 BC) was one of the greatest of Greece's tragic dramatists. Born at Eleusis in Attica, he fought with the Athenians during the Persian invasion of 490 BC and was wounded at Marathon. Although he is believed to have written around 60 plays only seven have survived, the most important being the trilogy Oresteia.

(c. 500) wrote the first prose history and geography, and the nature of his work was undoubtedly an influence on the work of Herodotos, himself of Carian ancestry. From his birthplace of Halikarnassos Herodotos moved to Athens, which by mid–5th century had emerged as the leading intellectual city of Greece.

The great contribution of Athens to literature in the Classical period was in the field of drama. Dramatic productions developed from Dionysiac rites and were performed only at two times of the year, in late winter and early spring. Tragedy came to be the dominant form in Greek literature of the 5th century. It could be based on recent history, but most usually it retold myth or heroic epic. The trials of the house of Agamemnon or the royal house of Thebes were favoured subjects: Aischylos (525—456), Sophokles (c. 496—406) and Euripides (c. 484—406?) all wrote versions of the tragedies of Orestes and Elektra, and Oedipus. Comedy derived from fertility rituals and always retained its bawdy aspect. The plots usually involved, and satirized, contemporary figures and events. The leading exponent, Aristophanes (c. 448—388), wrote his best plays during the stressful years of the Peloponnesian War.

Although Athenian drama has been an important influence on western literature, the legacy of its philosophy is even greater. Sokrates (c. 469—399) was not a teacher in the conventional sense, nor did he write, he was, however, enormously influential and his ideas can be found in the earlier works of his student Plato (429—347). Plato travelled to Egypt and Kyrene and to Sicily and southern Italy. He addressed the nature of the state and of justice, in *The Republic,* and again in the less utopian, *The Laws.* Plato's influence on the development of philosophy was not only through his written works, but also through the foundation of the Academy at Athens, which drew students from all over the Greek speaking world. Aristotle (384—322), born in Thrace studied at the Academy in Athens and later became tutor to Alexander the Great. Astonishingly versatile, he wrote in all fields of philosophy—politics, ethics, logic, metaphysics and on natural science, and next to Plato his work has been the most enduring. Athens was also important in the development of the three great philosophical movements of the Hellenistic world: the Cynics, the Epicureans and the Stoics. All of them continued to flourish into the later Roman empire and had wide appeal.

IV: Perikles to Philip

The fifty years following Xerxes' invasion saw both the flowering of Classical culture and the growth of resentments between Athens and Sparta which would result in war, weakness and the rise to power of Macedonia.

Athens and the Delian League

Whilst Sparta suffered temporary political setbacks in the Peloponnese, and had yet to decide her direction, Athens rapidly established herself as the leading naval power in Greece, and the defender of the East Greek states against the Persian threat. The early members of the Delian League were the large eastern islands; Samos, Chios and Lesbos, Delos (where the league's treasury was held), and many of the Cyclades. Some cities of Chalkidike soon joined (by 478) with Rhodes and perhaps some of the cities on Cyprus.

The purpose of the League was defence against Persian aggression. The members swore to have the same friends and the same enemies, but they were discouraged from forming alliances amongst themselves. At first, Athens was the leader but did not totally dominate the League: in the League assembly Athens and the allies all had the same number of votes. League members provided ships for the fleet, but some gave money instead and increasingly, payment replaced ships. Eventually only the islands of Chios and Lesbos kept their own fleets. This was a considerable advantage to Athens, since it built-up Athenian naval power and meant that, ultimately, when the members rebelled they had neither fleets nor experience.

In Athens, Kimon, son of Miltiades the victor of Marathon, was the leading political figure. He soon began military activities, capturing the Persian base of Eion, at the mouth of the river Strymon, and the island of Skyros (476/5). Athenian *cleruchies* were established in both. *Cleruchies* differed from ordinary colonies in that they retained Athenian citizenship. They were to be imposed with increasing frequency on rebellious League members and became one of the principal grievances against Athens.

Rebellions amongst the allies began quite early. The first was on Naxos (*c.*469/8) after which Athens became more aggressive in policing the League. Following the suppression of the rebellion on Naxos, the Athenian fleet defeated the Persians in battle at the river Eurymedon in Pamphylia. This was celebrated as a great victory, and brought more members to the League from the regions of Caria.

Returning from the victory, Kimon moved to suppress a revolt on the island of Thasos (465), which had control of important silver mines. The Thasians appealed to Sparta, which offered to invade Attica, but a devastating earthquake in the Peloponnese led to a helot revolt and Sparta could not act. Sparta now sought help from Athens—and it was sent, but the 4000 hoplites, led by Kimon, were summarily dismissed. Having been slighted, the pro-Spartans, such as Kimon, lost power and Athens returned to its anti-Spartan policy, forging new alliances with Argos and Thessaly. Meanwhile, Thasos was defeated, her fleet forfeited and the city walls pulled down.

Athens' increasing power made other states wary. Corinth had maintained good relations with Athens, but when Megara left the Peloponnesian League and joined Athens (460), the situation changed. The first Peloponnesian War (460—446)) opened with a battle between Corinthian and Athenian forces at Halieis, followed by a sea-battle off Aegina. The Spartan army now moved into central Greece and Boiotia became the battlegound. A Spartan

"After Athens' final defeat in the Peloponnesian War, the Spartans made a show of treating the Thebans as friends and allies, but the truth was that they were suspicious of the city's power and of her ambitious spirit: above all they hated the party ... to which Pelopidas belonged, which was believed to be devoted to the cause of liberty and of government by the people."
Plutarch, *Life of Pelopidas*

The Parthenon and, to the left, the Erechtheion with its caryatid porch. Just under 70 by 30-metres in plan, the Parthenon was designed by the architect Iktinos, who worked with Athens' master-builder Kallikrates. This beautiful building stood intact with all its sculptures until 1687 when a Turkish powder-magazine within its walls was ignited by a shell fired by a Venetian artillery battery besieging the city.

victory at Tanagra was swiftly followed by an Athenian one at Oinophyta (457). Athens' old rival, Aegina, fell in 456 and became a tributary of the League. Following these successes, and with control of Boiotia, Athens became the most powerful land and sea power in Greece. A truce with Sparta soon followed (451).

At the same time as the war in the Peloponnese, Athens became increasingly involved in events overseas, not always successfully. From 459 Athens supported the revolt of Inaros in Egypt. The motivation is a little obscure, but perhaps Athens wished to secure supplies of Egyptian corn: political changes in the north Black Sea (round Panticapaeum) may have necessitated new sources. Activities in Sicily about the same time (457) also brought new corn supplies. The rebellion began successfully: the satrap Achaimenes, brother of Xerxes, was killed and the Persian garrison besieged in Memphis. Artaxerxes tried to persuade Sparta to intervene on mainland Greece, but was refused. A Persian army was despatched to Egypt, and forced the rebels into the Delta marshes. In 454 an Athenian fleet of 250 ships, sent to Egypt in 459, was destroyed. The survivors eventually limped home via Kyrene. There is no evidence that the rebellion had been supported by the Battiad kings of Kyrene, who were usually pro-Persian, but their monarchy collapsed shortly after in an ostensibly "democratic" revolution.

The transition from confederacy to empire was gradual. In 454 the League treasury was moved from Delos to Athens for reasons of safety and by the 440s inscriptions refer to "the cities which the Athenians rule", rather than by the original name of the League "the Athenians and their allies".

This final phase of Athenian imperialism coincided with the political dominance of Perikles, whose mother belonged to the powerful Alkmaionid family. It had been agreed that the temples destroyed in the invasion of Xerxes should be left as monuments to Persian aggression, but the conclusion of peace with Persia (the Peace of Kallias 449) gave Perikles the opportunity to rescind the agreement and pursue his vision of a grand civil plan. Perikles used the League's spare cash for a lavish building programme. The Parthenon itself glorifies the conflict and triumph over Persia, the frieze, with its 192 horsemen, alluding to the 192 Athenian heroes of Marathon.

Rebellions against Athens continued. Control of Boiotia was lost after the defeat at Koroneia (446), sparking further revolts in Euboea and Megara.

The Spartan king invaded Attica but inexplicably withdrew (and went into self-imposed exile). Shortly after, the Thiry Years Peace was agreed between Athens and Sparta. Athens ceded some territories and Sparta finally acknowledged Athenian naval supremacy.

The Peloponnesian War

The 27 year long war between the alliances of Athens and Sparta falls into two distinct phases and had several arenas of confrontation. In the first phase, Archidamos II, king of Sparta, annually marched his army into Attica destroying the harvests. This caused severe problems, but achieved little militarily. The invasions of Archidamos forced the people to seek refuge in the city and between the Long Walls connecting Athens with the Piraeus. With something approaching 300,000 people crowded into the city, plague broke out in 430; one of its victims being Perikles (d.429). Another outbreak (427/6) may have killed as much as one quarter of the entire population.

Perikles' death saw the emergence of Kleon, a radical demagogue, as the leading, and belligerent, voice in Athenian politics. In 427, following the collapse of an anti-Athenian rebellion in Mytilene on Lesbos, Kleon called for the execution of all adult males and the enslavement of all women and children. A heated debate in the assembly followed and a trireme was dispatched to carry out its wishes. The Athenians had second thoughts, and sent a second trireme to countermand the decree. It arrived just in time, but a ruthless new tendancy in Athenian imperialism was revealed.

Following Archidamos' death, the general Brasidas used the Spartan army far more effectively, choosing Chalkidike as his arena. Brasidas occupied Megara, than marched rapidly through Thessaly to capture Amphipolis. This city, a constant goal of Athenian ambitions, was in a position to control the important timber and gold production around Mount Pangaion. In an attempt to recapture Amphipolis, an Athenian fleet was sent to Chalkidike under the command of Kleon. Both Kleon and Brasidas were killed in the battles for the city. With the deaths of the two most pugnacious leaders, there were moves for peace. The shortlived Peace of Nikias was agreed in 421.

The second phase of the war began in 417 with an Athenian attack on Melos. The island was blockaded and eventually surrendered. This time Athens did carry out the genocide earlier threatened to the rebellious Lesbians: all adult men were killed, the women and children enslaved; 500 Athenian colonists were sent. Sparta did not intervene.

With the recommencement of hostilities, new leaders emerged. In Athens, the most notable was Perikles' relative and protégé, Alkibiades. Descended from the Alkmaionidai, Alkibiades was renowned for his good looks, extravagant lifestyle and pronounced lisp. His political career had great successes, and some notable changes of allegiance. Sicily now became a main centre of confrontation. There are indications that Perikles had ambitions in Sicily which were never fulfilled, and the first Athenian force was sent to aid Leontini against Syracuse during the Archidamian War (427—424). The major conflict (415—413) was a direct, but ultimately disastrous, attack upon Syracuse itself. Appointed as one of the leaders of the second expedition to Sicily, Alkibiades was accused by his enemies of profaning the Eleusinian mysteries. He was recalled to face trial, but instead fled to Sparta. He served with the Spartan fleet before another change of career, speaking Persian and wearing Persian dress, as advisor to the Persian satrap Tissaphernes. From neutral, he became pro-Athenian, and had some notable successes before his second exile from his home city.

The final phase of war, 413—404, began with the Spartan occupation of Deceleia (a strategy suggested by Alkibiades) which prevented Athenian exploitation of the silver mines at Laurion and caused economic problems.

The Persian satraps of Asia Minor now became involved in the war. Artaxerxes I had died in 424 and after some dynastic struggle his son, Darius II, ascended the throne. Pissouthnes, the satrap of Sardis, revolted (413 or earlier) and the Persian general Tissaphernes was sent against him. A number of cities again paid their taxes to Persia, not to Athens, and received Persian garrisons. Although Pissouthnes was defeated and sent to his death at Susa, his son Amorges continued the rebellion in Caria with Athenian aid. Tissaphernes was installed as satrap of Sardis and Alkibiades became his advisor. They encouraged an oligarchic revolt in Athens (411). The Athenians hoped this would gain them Persian support, and Alkibiades hoped it would enable him to return to Athens. The rule of "the 400" lasted only four months. Shortly after, a victory at Cyzicus (410) restored Athenian morale and allowed them to regain some cities which had already ousted their Persian garrisons. Alkibiades was one of the successful generals, and briefly returned to Athens before the disaster at Notion (407/406) once again forced him into exile.

Cyrus, a younger son of Darius, was sent as commander of most of Lydia, Phrygia and Cappadocia, restricting the, understandably, resentful Tissaphernes to Caria (407). Cyrus was to aid Sparta and finance the Spartan fleet. Nevertheless there was Athenian victory at Arginusai (406) before the final Spartan victory at Aigospotami. This battle brought the war to a close by cutting off the corn supply to Athens (404).

The Parthenon's most exceptional feature was the brilliantly-sculptured frieze which ran along the top of the wall within the outer colonade. The frieze's subject matter was the annual Panathenaic procession and this detail shows the riders of the procession, young men of military age in the pride of life. The master-sculptor who directed the work on the Parthenon was Pheidias, the friend of Perikles. It was Pheidias who executed the colossal statue of Athena which stood within the building, 12-metres high in ivory and gold.

Kingdoms of Northen Greece

By Philip II's time, Macedonia was heavily influenced by Greek culture and its cities were modelled on Greek lines, but there was also a strongly tribal tradition, with an important and powerful military elite. The succession to the Macedonian kingship was nearly always violent, and kings were frequently murdered. Perdikkas II (*c.*454—413) played a significant role in the events of the Peloponnesian War. Initially an ally of Athens, he later sought the aid of the Spartan general Brasidas and his army against Arrhibaios king of the Lynkestrians, but did not allow Sparta to build up a power-base in the region. Wishing to maintain a balance of power between the South Greek states, Perdikkas' son, Archelaos (413—399), later favoured Athenian interests. Problems struck the region in the following decades, with both internal dynastic struggles and invasion from the northwest. The Illyrian ruler, Bardylis, expanded his power and invaded Macedonia on several occasions. Meanwhile, on the southern borders, Thessaly became a threat.

Thessaly was a rich agricultural region long-renowned for horse-breeding. On the route to Macedon and the Hellespont, it was strategically important, and had a good harbour at Pagasai. It also had a religious influence, since the Thessalians traditionally controlled the Amphictyonic Council based upon Delphi. Like Macedon and Epirus, it was viewed somewhat askance by the southern Greek states, not having developed in the same way politically. Unlike Macedon, Thessaly was not under the rule of kings, but a number of important families were constantly vying for power. At times they achieved something approaching a kingship (called locally, *tagos*) but never permanently. The most influential of the families was the Aleuadai of Larisa.

The architectural sculptures on the exterior of the Parthenon depicted scenes from mythology such as the birth of Athena from the head of Zeus and her contest with the Sea-God for the patronship of Athens. This badly damaged sculpture from the west pediment portrays Iris, the messenger of the gods.

During the early phase of the Persian Wars, the Aleuadai had submitted to Persia but at the time of Xerxes' invasion they had sought help from Sparta. A joint Spartan and Athenian force, with Themistokles as one of its commanders, had gone to defend the Vale of Tempe, the direct access from Macedonia. Alexander of Macedon wanted the Persians to advance through his territory as swiftly as possible, and for some reason, the joint Greek force withdrew, opening Thessaly to Persian invasion. Inevitably, it medised. Following the Persian defeat, Leotychidas attempted to break the hegemony of the Aleuadai (476), continuing Spartan ambitions in the region which had begun in the reign of Kleomenes I (*c.*500). Later, Thessaly allied itself with Athens, although there was strong anti-Athenian feeling in some quarters by the outbreak of the Peloponnesian War. During the Archidamian War the Spartans managed to establish a colony at Heraclea (426), close to Thermopylai, which was to become a valuable strategic base on the Thessalian border. They later established a garrison at Pharsalos (by 395).

Spartan Hegemony

The end of the Peloponnesian War and the defeat of Athens left Sparta as the dominant power, but did not bring lasting peace. Sparta's activities in a number of different regions were an increasing cause of concern to the other leading Greek states. In Thessaly the Spartans now entered into an alliance with Lykophron of Pherai and encouraged Larisa in its dispute with Macedonia over the territory of Perrhaibia. With the colony at Heraclea, and the garrison at Pharsalos, these activities could be seen as a direct threat by the Boiotians. Furthermore, Spartan policy was now dominated by Agesilaos II (399—360) who saw Thebes, rather than Athens, as the new threat to Spartan hegemony. In Sicily, Sparta supported the tyranny of Dionysios I of Syracuse (406—367), which may have antagonized both Athens and Corinth (Syracuse was a Corinthian colony). Dionysios would continue friendly relations with Sparta and received Spartan aid in his war with Carthage (396).

In Asia, Spartan activities had continued since the defeat of Athens. Darius, alerted by Tissaphernes, recalled Cyrus on suspicion of plotting rebellion. Darius, already ill, died in Babylon (404) and was succeeded by his eldest son Artaxerxes II. Although suspicion still lay on Cyrus, he was sent back to his post. Alkibiades, learning that Sparta intended to deal with Cyrus rather than the newly crowned king, made to inform Artaxerxes, but he was murdered before he could act and Cyrus launched his rebellion (401). With his army, including some 10,000 Greek mercenaries, Cyrus marched to defeat at Kunaxa near Babylon. After their long march back to Ionia (the subject of Xenophon's *Anabasis*) these soldiers became involved in the Spartan war to liberate the coastal cities from Persian rule. Following his accession, Agesilaos II invaded Asia where his resounding victory at Sardis resulted in the fall and execution of Tissaphernes.

Corinth, allied with Argos, Boiotia and Athens moved to break Sparta's rising power. The Corinthian War started in Boiotia (395) and saw conflict on mainland Greece and in the Aegean, mainly around Rhodes and the Hellespont. The Spartan garrison at Pharsalos was massacred and Thebes took Heraclea. Sparta sought peace with Persia and conferences were held at Sardis and Sparta (392), but Artaxerxes was still hostile to Sparta, and agreement was not reached. After changes of heart, Artaxerxes eventually directed his general to support Sparta in the Aegean war against Athens. Sparta took the Hellespont, aided by Persia and a contribution of twenty ships from Syracuse. The conflict came to an end with the King's Peace (387/6). By this, Heraclea was returned to Spartan control; many of the Asiatic cities came once again under Persian rule; Athens may have been forced to disband her navy and remove the gates to the Piraeus. Persian control over Cyprus was reasserted. Athens had been active there and had made an alliance with Evagoras of Salamis.

Following the treaty there was relatively little interference by the mainland Greek states in Asia until the reigns of Philip and Alexander. Both Athens and Sparta did, however, support opposition to Persia in Egypt. The pharaoh Hakor (393—380) had allied himself with Evagoras (389), and also with Athens. Artaxerxes sent an army to regain Egypt (385—383), but it was repulsed by Hakor and a mercenary force under the command of the Athenian general Chabrias.

Theban Ascendancy

The Corinthian War had temporarily ended Spartan activities in Thessaly, and Boiotia established a series of alliances there. In Chalkidike the city of Olynthos came to prominence and in a territorial dispute, the cities of Akanthos and Apollonia and Amyntas, king of Macedon sought help from Sparta against it (382). Thebes and Athens were prepared to aid Olynthos. Crisis again loomed. The Spartan general, Phoibidas, marched north and, en route, aided a coup at Thebes. Acting purely out of Spartan self-interest, Phoibidas left a number of troops to garrison the Theban citadel, the Kadmeia. The Olynthian campaign eventually went Sparta's way and Sparta was, for the moment (380), pre-eminent in Greece.

Soon the tables were turned. With Athenian assistance, Pelopidas and some other Theban exiles liberated the Kadmeia and slew the tyrants (winter 379/8). Athens knew that in aiding Thebes, she had antagonized Sparta, and therefore sought defensive alliances with some of the Aegean islands (the origin of the Second Athenian Confederacy). In response there were invasions of Boiotia by the Spartan kings Kleombrotos I (in 379) and Agesilaos (378 and 377), but these were successfully resisted by the joint Athenian and Theban army. Real Theban success began with the victory of the "Sacred Band" at Tegyra (375), but it was the triumph of the battle of Leuctra (371) which ushered in the years of Theban ascendancy.

Spartan influence in central Greece was further eroded by the rise of Jason of Pherai who had become *tagos* of all Thessaly. Jason destroyed the stronghold of Heraclea and annexed the disputed territory of Perrhaibia on the borders of Macedonia. He extended his influence into Epirus where the Molossians had formed a state which combined kingship with elected offices and a "senate". Jason had made himself master of central Greece but was assassinated (370) before he could display his power at the Amphictyonic Council. It was Thebes which ultimately gained control of the Amphictyony.

Following Leuctra, Spartan power was eclipsed, and Theban actions were to ensure it could not recover. Through its military training and society Sparta had for long maintained the foremost army in Greece. But the number of Spartiates had been decreasing for some time. Leuctra was a decisive blow; of the 700 Spartiates who took part, 400 were killed. Sparta was no longer the only state in which military training was important. In Thebes, homosexuality in the army was institutionalized: the Theban "Sacred Band" comprized three hundred men, pairs of lovers who fought side by side. Originally the Sacred Band had been distributed among the front ranks of the phalanx, but at Tegyra, Pelopidas had employed it as a separate formation. From that point it became one of the most effective military machines in Greece and was not defeated until it confronted the army of Philip of Macedon at the battle of Chaironeia in 338.

The two architects of Theban greatness were Epaminondas and Pelopidas. Pelopidas was active in central and northern Greece, against Jason of Pherai's successor, Alexander, and Alexander of Macedon, while for three years in succession (369—367), Epaminondas led the Theban armies into the Peloponnese. The result was the liberation of Messenia from Spartan rule. Athenian and Theban interests had frequently coincided, but Theban supremacy, and particularly the domination of Boiotia, saw Athens forming alliances with Sparta. A peace conference held at Delphi (368) failed because Sparta refused to recognize an independent Messenia. Another conference was held the following year (367) at Susa. Pelopidas, again sought Spartan agreement to the loss of Messenia and asked for the Athenian fleet to be beached. There was still no agreement, even though Persia supported the Theban proposals. Finally, following the Theban seizure of Oropos, a King's Peace (366/5) achieved some agreement between Thebes and Athens. In 364 Pelopidas was killed at Kynoskephalai, but the battle was a Theban victory and forced Macedonia to join the Boiotian League. By 362, Thebes had achieved an extensive network of alliances in the Peloponnese and central Greece, but that same year Epaminondas was killed at the battle of Mantinea and, with the loss of both its leaders, Theban power was broken.

There was increasing discontent amongst the members of the Athenian Confederacy, caused largely by the old problems of imperial ambition and the imposition of *cleruchies*. Some members seceded, allying themselves with Thebes, others came under the influence of Persia and of the Carian satrap,

Mausolos who had established his new capital at Halikarnassos in 377.

The Revolt of the Satraps, affected many of the western provinces of the Persian empire. It began with the rebellion of Ariobarzanes, which was soon followed by those of Mausolos, Autophradates of Lydia, Orontes of Armenia and Datames. Both Athens and Sparta actively supported individual rebels and sent military aid to the Egyptian pharaoh Djeho (in Greek, *Tachos*). The elderly Spartan king, Agesilaos, landed in Egypt with 1000 hoplites and the Athenian, Chabrias, was put in charge of the fleet (361). Advancing on Phoenicia, there was a rebellion against Djeho, and his cousin Nekhthorheb (*Nectanebis*) was proclaimed king. Nekhthorheb sought the help of Agesilaos, eventually received it and Djeho fled to Persia. Agesilaos died whilst returning to Greece.

Philip of Macedon

Mausolos of Caria was seen as the major threat to the Greeks, but the real threat came from Macedonia. In 359, Philip II ascended the throne of Macedon. In the same year, Athenian and mercenary forces landed at Methone in an attempt to install Argaios as king. There was no revolt in support of the pretender, and returning to the coast the army encountered Philip, who defeated them. The victorious Philip then offered terms which the Athenians were unable to refuse. He now approached the Athenian Assembly seeking an alliance. In 358 he defeated the Illyrian Bardylis. Moving into the Strymon basin he acquired the Bisaltic silver mines, and attacked Amphipolis. The city appealed to Athens, but her activities in Euboea and the Chersonese prevented intervention. Philip sent envoys to Athens to allay fears, offering to give Amphipolis (which he was still besieging) to Athens in exchange for Pydna. The cities of Chalkidike, led by Olynthos, now appealed to Athens, but, with the outbreak of the Social War (357), Athenian action was impossible. Philip captured Amphipolis and declared the city independent. He promptly laid siege to Pydna and Athens declared war. In 356, having entered into alliance with Chalkidike, Philip laid siege to Poteidaia. Athenian help was too late, the Poteidaians were sold into slavery and the city given to Chalkidike.

This exquisitely-carved ivory head of Philip II of Macedon was discovered at Vergina, site of the Macedonian royal tombs. The carving is a little over three centimetres in height and its fine craftsmanship belies Demosthenes' claim that the Macedonians were "barbarians". Philip's interest in Greece exceeded mere territorial ambitions and he employed many Greeks at his court, including the philosopher Aristotle who acted as tutor to Alexander the Great.

Philip's success was due in large part to his own character, but also to the weakness of, and divisions amongst, the states of Greece. Spartan power had been greatly reduced by the events of the preceding years, and the loss of Messenia; Athens was similarly weakened by the "Social War" with her allies (357—355). It was the "Sacred War" (355—346) between Phokis and the allies of Thebes that drew Philip into central Greece. Philip first gained control of Thessaly, invited by the Aleuadai to depose the house of Pherai. This gave Philip the control of the majority of votes in the Amphictyonic Council; but it was some time before he was able to exercise that authority.

In his youth, Philip had been taken as a hostage to Thebes by Pelopidas. Whilst there he seems to have been deeply influenced by Epaminondas and came to appreciate the Theban's efficiency in war and command. On his return, he built up the Macedonian army and turned it into the most efficient military machine of its day. Philip expanded the Macedonian kingdom, fighting in Thrace and Illyria. The invasion of Persia was halted by his assassination, but the plans had been laid. It was on this foundation that Alexander's successes were built, and with it the transformation of the Persian empire into a Greek one.

Perikles and the Athenian Empire

As Athens' imperial ambitions grew, her attitude towards both colonies and neighbours became increasingly belligerent, resulting in hostility and open revolt.

"Perikles, because of his postion, his intelligence, and his known integrity, could respect the liberty of the people and at the same time hold them in check. It was he who led them, rather than they who led him, and, since he never sought power from any wrong motive, he was under no necessity of flattering them."
Thucydides, *Book II, The Peloponnesian War*

The years immediately following the Persian wars had seen the formation of the Athenian, or Delian, League. Its purpose was defensive and anti-Persian, but with rebellions amongst its allies Athens became more aggressive. The key figure during this phase was Kimon, son of Miltiades (the victor of Marathon). The transition from "league" to "empire" was gradual, one of the defining moments being the transfer of the League treasury from Delos to Athens in 454.

From 459, Athens was involved in the revolt of Inaros in Egypt. It was a costly conflict which dragged on until 454. During the same period there were activities closer to home. Megara, in a border dispute with Corinth, deserted the Peloponnesian League and joined Athens. Aegina too, was secured for Athens, but through military means (by the general Tolmides in 456). These years were renowned for the great building activities which they witnessed, notably the construction of the Parthenon (begun 447), but of greater military significance were the Long Walls connecting the city with its harbours at the Piraeus and Phaleron.

Exactly when Perikles emerged as the political leader in Athens is a little uncertain. It was after the death of Kimon in 451, although he was politically active as early as 462. The Peace of Kallias (449) between Persia and the Greek states meant that the continuance of the League was no longer necessary to preserve the freedom of the islands. The League, however, was not disbanded: revolts against Athens were put down with increasing severity and taxes were increased. On the mainland, a rebellion in Boiotia was supported by exiles from Euboea. The Athenian forces were defeated at the Battle of Koroneia (447/446) and control of Boiotia was lost. Euboea itself rebelled next and whilst Perikles was leading an expedition there, Megara revolted and Sparta invaded Attica. Shortly afterwards Athens signed the Thirty Years Peace with Sparta. This saw the end of any Athenian land empire, but acknowledged her hegemony at sea.

A famine in Athens in 445 was relieved only by shipments of corn from Egypt. Threat of famine and a surplus population must have been motives for the Athenian cleruchies and colonies which were regularly sent out in these years. In southern Italy, Sybaris was refounded, as Thurii (443). In the north Aegean, where some Greek cities of the coast were already members of the Delian League, new colonies were established at Brea (440s) and Amphipolis (437) in order to gain control of the mineral wealth of the hinterland. Perikles led an expedition to the Black Sea to ensure Athenian control of the corn route.

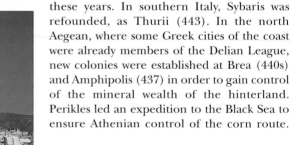

Perhaps the single greatest architectural symbol of the Athenian Golden Age under Perikles is the Parthenon which surmounts the Akropolis. In its design and execution the Parthenon is a classic Doric temple, veering away from tradition only in its possession of an exquisitely-carved frieze which ran along the top of the wall within the outer colonnade.

A member of the aristocratic Alkmaionid family, Perikles was a convinced democrat who, as a result of his influence on Athenian politics and brilliant oratory, was known facetiously as "Zeus".

This region was also the centre of tensions which led to the outbreak of war in the late 430s. The crisis came in 433 when a quarrel between Athens, Corinth and the Corinthian colonies in northwest Greece brought the first open clash between Athenian and Peloponnesian League ships. In the same year, Athens demanded that Poteidaia in Chalkidike, another Corinthian colony which paid tribute to Athens, should pull down part of its walls and send the Corinthian magistrates away. Corinth sent aid. Athens besieged Poteidaia. An Athenian trade embargo on Megara (433) was followed by constant diplomatic activity, but Perikles refused to compromise. In 431 Athens and the Peloponnesian League went to war.

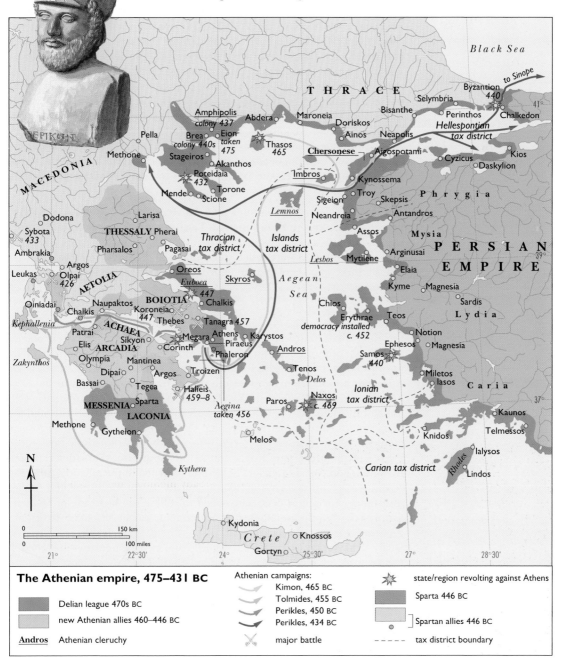

The Athenian empire, 475–431 BC

- Delian league 470s BC
- new Athenian allies 460–446 BC
- <u>Andros</u> Athenian cleruchy

Athenian campaigns:
- Kimon, 465 BC
- Tolmides, 455 BC
- Perikles, 450 BC
- Perikles, 434 BC
- ✕ major battle

- ✸ state/region revolting against Athens
- Sparta 446 BC
- Spartan allies 446 BC
- - - - - tax district boundary

Peloponnesian War – the Aegean

For over 25 years Athens and Sparta were embroiled in a costly war, which would set the Aegean ablaze and spread as far west as Sicily.

"I began my history at the very outbreak of war, in the belief that it was going to be a great war and more worth writing about than any of those which had taken place in the past ... The two sides were at the very height of their power, and ... the rest of the Hellenic world was committed to one side or the other ... This was the greatest disturbance in the history of the Hellenes, affecting also a large part of the non-Hellenic world, and indeed, I might almost say, the whole of mankind."

Thucydides, *History of the Peloponnesian War, Book I*

The first phase of the long struggle between Sparta and Athens and their respective allies, the Archidamian War, lasted from 431—421. In southern Greece, the war was dominated by Sparta's annual incursions into Attica. In the west, a bloody civil war in Corcyra (Corfu) broke out in 427, but both Athenian and Peloponnesian attempts to intervene failed. The first Athenian expedition to Sicily (427—424) was also fruitless. Athenian successes began with the capture of 120 Spartiate warriors at Sphakteria in 425, and the virtual blockade of the Peloponnese. The theatre of war moved north when the Spartan general Brasidas occupied Megara, then marched through Thessaly and Thrace to capture Amphipolis. The same year (424) saw an Athenian defeat by Boiotian forces at Delion, the only real land battle of the war. A one-year truce followed. In 422, the aggressive Athenian leader Kleon conducted a campaign to the Chalkidike. At the battle to recapture Amphipolis, the Athenians were defeated and Kleon was killed. Brasidas too was killed and with the deaths of the two most belligerent leaders, the way to peace was open. In 421, the Peace of Nikias was concluded for fifty years: it lasted for two.

The Spartan victory at Mantinea over Athenian-backed Argive forces (418) helped to restore the Peloponnesian League. Athens became more aggressive and in 417 attacked the neutral island of Melos. Following its surrender (415) all adult men were killed, the women and children enslaved. Sparta did not intervene. An Athenian expedition was sent to Sicily in 415, ending disastrously, in 413.

The final phase of the war 413—404, began with the Spartan occupation of Deceleia in Attica. The Persian satraps of Asia Minor now became involved in the war. Athens built a new fleet, despite economic and manpower problems and Sparta ordered her own allies to build a fleet. The Peloponnesian fleet was not large, but active in Ionian waters. There were revolts amongst the Athenian allies. Athens gained the upper hand after the naval battle at Kynossema in the Hellespont. Two battles at Abydus (411) and Cyzicus (410) also saw the defeat of the Peloponnesians and secured the route through the Bosporos for Athens. Sparta now sought peace, but the democractic government in Athens refused the terms offered. The Spartans now recaptured Pylos and the Megarians Nisaia, but in the Bosporos, Alkibiades captured Byzantion and Chalkedon, and Selymbria returned to the alliance. Athenian resurgence continued, and in 406, Archelaos of Macedon provided Athens with timber for a new fleet. This sailed to relieve the blockade of Mytilene and met the Peloponnesian fleet at Arginusai. It was an Athenian victory, but there were serious losses on both sides. Athens again became involved in Sicily. A further confrontation at Aigospotami in the Chersonese resulted in the capture of most of the Athenian fleet. The fall of Byzantion and Chalkedon to the Peloponnesians was followed by a general revolt of Athens' allies. Athens was now under siege by land and sea and famine threatened. There were calls by other Greek cities for the vengeance meted out by Athens herself: massacre and enslavement. Sparta resisted these. Eventually Athens agreed the terms of peace; the Long Walls and those of the Piraeus, were pulled down and almost all of the fleet was surrendered.

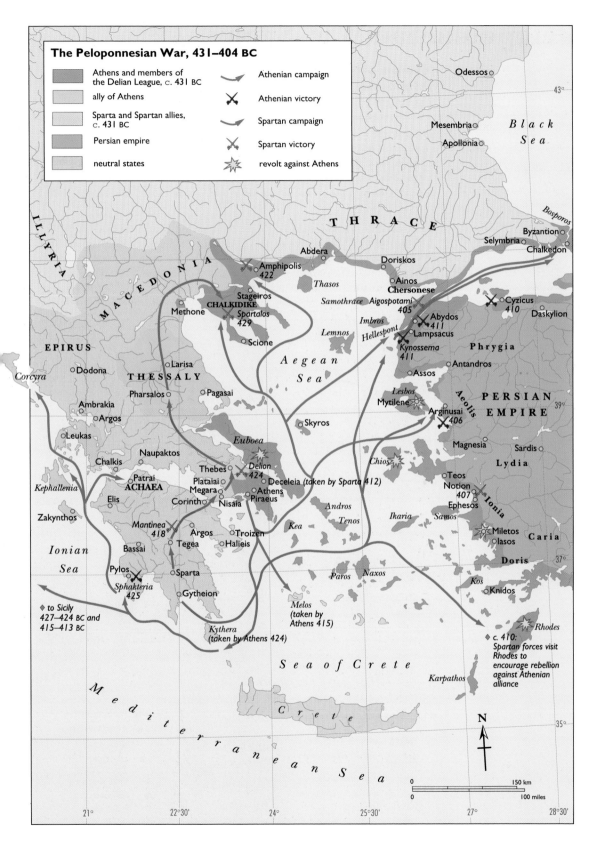

The Peloponnesian War, 431–404 BC

- Athens and members of the Delian League, c. 431 BC
- ally of Athens
- Sparta and Spartan allies, c. 431 BC
- Persian empire
- neutral states
- ⟍ Athenian campaign
- ✕ Athenian victory
- ⟍ Spartan campaign
- ✕ Spartan victory
- ✳ revolt against Athens

Odessos

Black Sea

Mesembria
Apollonia

T H R A C E

Bosporos

Byzantion
Selymbria
Chalkedon

Abdera
Doriskos

Amphipolis
422

Thasos

Ainos
Chersonese

Stageiros
CHALKIDIKE
Spartalos
429

Methone

Scione

Samothrace Aigospotami
405

Imbros
Lemnos

Abydos
411
Lampsacus

Hellespont

Kynossema
411

Assos

Antandros

Phrygia

M A C E D O N I A

I L L Y R I A

E P I R U S

Larisa

Corcyra

Dodona

THESSALY

Pharsalos
Pagasai

Aegean Sea

Skyros

Lesbos
Mytilene

Arginusai
406

Aeolis

P E R S I A N EMPIRE

Magnesia

Sardis

Lydia

Ambrakia
Argos
Leukas

Euboea

Chalkis
Naupaktos

Thebes
Plataiai
Megara

Delion
424

Deceleia *(taken by Sparta 412)*

Athens
Piraeus

Chios

Teos
Notion
407
Ephesos

Ionia

Kephallenia

Patrai
ACHAEA
Corinth
Nisaia

Andros

Tenos

Ikaria

Samos

Miletos
Iasos

Caria

Elis

Zakynthos

Mantinea
418
Tegea

Argos
Troizen
Halieis

Kea

Doris

Ionian Sea

Bassai

Pylos
Sparta

Sphakteria
425

Gytheion

Paros *Naxos*

Melos
(taken by Athens 415)

Kos
Knidos

◆ to Sicily
427–424 BC and
415–413 BC

Kythera
(taken by Athens 424)

Rhodes

◆ c. 410:
Spartan forces visit
Rhodes to
encourage rebellion
against Athenian
alliance

Karpathos

S e a   o f   C r e t e

C r e t e

M e d i t e r r a n e a n   S e a

N

0   150 km
0   100 miles

43°
39°
37°
35°

21°   22°30'   24°   25°30'   27°   28°30'

Peloponnesian War–Sicily

Athenian activity in Sicily would reach its climax during the Peloponnesian War when her expedition to Syracuse ended in defeat and the slaughter of her troops.

"This was the greatest Hellenic action that took place during this war, and, in my opinion, the greatest action that we know of in Hellenic history – to the victors the most brilliant of successes, to the vanquished the most calamitous of defeats; for they were utterly and entirely defeated; their sufferings were on an enormous scale; their losses were, as they say, total... So ended the events in Sicily."

Thucydides, *History of the Peloponnesian War*

Foreign domination of Sicily and its population was divided between the Phoenician towns in the western part of the island, which were under the protection of Carthage, and the Greek colonies, some ruled by tyrants, in the eastern part. When the tyrannies fell, Akragas in 472 and Syracuse in 467, a form of democracy was established. Athens became involved in Sicily at quite an early date, making alliances with the Greek cities, the earliest being Segesta (457).

As a result of internal island conflict, Athens and Sparta clashed on Sicilian soil during the Peloponnesian War. Segesta began a war with neighbouring Selinus, which called upon Syracuse for help. Thucydides claims that the Athenians wished to conquer Sicily and that a delegation from Segesta merely served as the pretext for action. The Segesteans argued that if Syracuse conquered the whole of Sicily it would then come to the aid of Dorians in

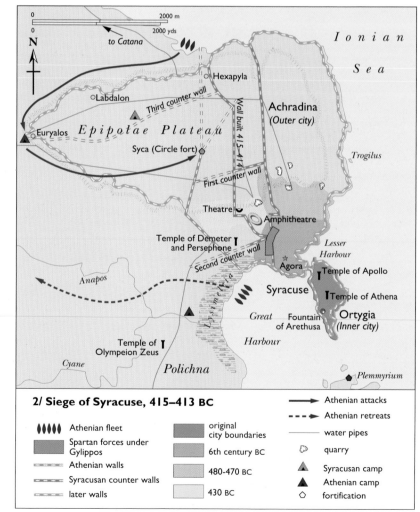

2/ Siege of Syracuse, 415–413 BC

- Athenian fleet
- Spartan forces under Gylippos
- Athenian walls
- Syracusan counter walls
- later walls
- original city boundaries
- 6th century BC
- 480-470 BC
- 430 BC
- Athenian attacks
- Athenian retreats
- water pipes
- quarry
- Syracusan camp
- Athenian camp
- fortification

*A view of one of the twin
Doric temples dedicated to
Hera and Concordia at
Akragas (modern Agrigento),
Sicily. This temple, dating
from the 5th—6th centuries
BC, was originally dedicated
to the goddess Concordia.*

Greece. Hostilities in Greece were breaking out again and in 415 three generals, Nikias, Alkibiades and Lamachus, were appointed to lead an expedition against Syracuse. Problems began immediately: Alkibiades, accused of profaning the Eleusinian mysteries, defected to Sparta rather than return to Athens to face trial. In Syracuse, the Athenians gained a foothold near the temple of Zeus by the great harbour. The Syracusans now sought aid from Corinth and Sparta; Alkibiades persuaded the Spartans to send troops. In 414 the main battlefield was Epipolae. The Athenians built walls to blockade the city, the Syracusans built counter-walls to break it. Lamachus was killed in action and Nikias was left in sole command. He fortified Plemmyrium at the southern entrance of the great harbour. The Spartan general, Gylippos, with Corinthian ships and allies from Himera, entered the city breaking the blockade. In desperation, Nikias wrote to the Athenian assembly. A new force was sent under the command of Eurymedon while Demosthenes prepared a larger force for the following spring. Before it arrived, Plemmyrium was captured along with its stores. Demosthenes' arrival changed the course of the war, and Athens gained the upper hand. A night battle then reversed the situation, with heavy Athenian losses. Demosthenes urged withdrawal towards Catana, but Nikias, on advice from soothsayers, postponed for a month. The enemy sealed the harbour and the retreat of the demoralised Athenian troops ended in catastrophe (413), some being massacred, some enslaved and the rest put into the quarries. The generals were executed. The expedition had been a total disaster and in Athens there was a reaction against those responsible, the democratic leaders. Sparta continued to involve itself in Sicily's affairs, and supported the tyrant Dionysios I who established power in Syracuse in 406.

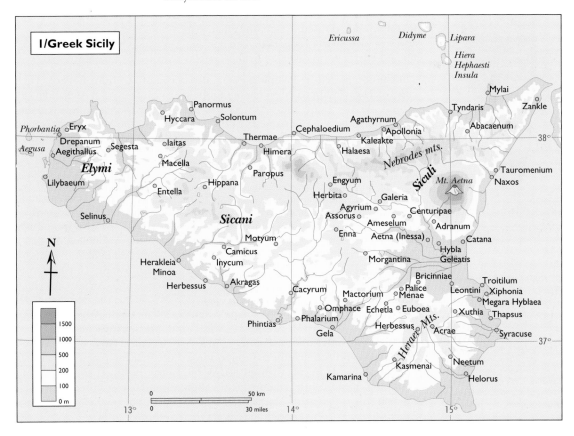

I/Greek Sicily

Ericussa *Didyme* *Lipara*

*Hiera
Hephaesti
Insula*

Mylai

Tyndaris Zankle

Phorbantia Eryx
Panormus
Hyccara Solontum
Agathyrnum
Cephaloedium Apollonia
Abacaenum
Aegusa Drepanum
Aegithallus Segesta
laitas
Thermae
Kaleakte
38°
Himera Halaesa
Elymi
Macella
Nebrodes mts.
Paropus
Tauromenium
Lilybaeum
Hippana
Engyum
Siculi
Mt. Aetna Naxos
Entella
Herbita
Galeria
Agyrium
Assorus
Centuripae
Selinus
Sicani
Enna
Ameselum
Adranum
Motyum
Aetna (Inessa) Catana
Camicus
Hybla
Herakleia
Minoa Inycum
Morgantina Geleatis
Bricinniae
Herbessus Akragas
Palice
Menae
Leontini Xiphonia
Troitilum
Cacyrum
Mactorium
Euboea
Megara Hyblaea
Omphace Echetla
Xuthia Thapsus
Phintias Phalarium
Heraeae Mts.
Herbessus Acrae
Syracuse
Gela
37°
Kasmenai Neetum
Kamarina
Helorus

N

1500
1000
500
200
100
0 m

0   50 km
0   30 miles
13°   14°   15°

Sparta and Thebes

Between 396 and 362 BC Sparta and Thebes became embroiled in a long and bloody trial of strength which would eventually result in both parties being seriously weakened.

The years following the surrender of Athens in 404 witnessed the consolidation of the Spartan hegemony with military and political activities in all regions. In Egypt, help was sent to the pharaoh Nefaurud's rebellion against Persian rule (396). Sparta also aided the rebellion of Cyrus against Artaxerxes II. In central Greece, Sparta supported Thessalian expansion, and in Sicily, Dionysios of Syracuse. These activities were a cause of concern to the other states of south Greece and ultimately led to the Corinthian War (from 395) in which Sparta was faced by a coalition of Boiotia, Corinth, Argos and Athens. The Corinthian war checked Spartan northward expansion for a time. The King's Peace (387/6) worked in Sparta's favour, and shortly afterwards she attacked democratic Mantinea (385). There was further interference in the north in 382, when Spartan troops marched to break up the Chalkidic League centred on Olynthos. On route, they were invited into Thebes by a pro-Spartan faction (382) and occupied the Kadmeia, the Theban citadel. The height of Spartan power came in 380 when Olynthos capitulated, Thebes was garrisoned, Corinth and Argos were inactive, Athens was still unpopular. The following year (379/8) Theban exiles, including Pelopidas, liberated Thebes with Athenian help. Athens, aware that she had provoked Sparta, entered into a number of alliances which were the beginning of the Second Athenian Confederacy. Thebes reunified Boiotia, an action which led to a peace conference in 371. The Theban leader, Epaminondas, refused to sign, the alliance of Athens and Thebes was ended, and war with Sparta reopened. The Spartan army marched against Thebes, but at Leuctra it was defeated by the Theban army led by Epaminondas.

Theban forces, led by Pelopidas, were also active in northern Greece. The cities of Thessaly appealed to Thebes for help against the tyrant Alexander of Pherai. At the same time Athens was attempting to regain control of Amphipolis and the Chersonese. In the Peloponnese, the Mantineans refortified their city and organized Arcadia into a federal state, building Megalopolis as its capital. When Tegea joined the league, Spartan intervention became inevitable and the Arcadians appealed to Athens for assistance (370). This was refused, so the Arcadians turned to Thebes. In the winter of 370/369, Epaminondas invaded the Peloponnese, liberated Messenia and fortified Messene. In response, Athens acted, but Epaminondas withdrew his army safely. A second invasion by Epaminondas (369) also withdrew. Two peace conferences (368 and 367) failed to resolve the problems. In 366, Epaminondas invaded the Peloponnese again: Thebes had deliberately started ed a war with the Achaeans and summoned Arcadian troops. The Thebans installed a garrison and imposed democratic government in Achaea. Arcadia re-opened a war with Elis (allied with Sparta) in 365. In 364 the Arcadian federal state fell apart and the Arcadians sought an alliance with Athens. By 362, Thebes had Tegea, Megalopolis, Argos and Messene as allies in the Peloponnese, with Euboea, Thessaly and Lokris in central Greece. Mantinea, Sparta, Elis and Athens stood in opposition. The final campaign was led by Epaminondas. It began with an attack on Sparta itself. At the Battle of Mantinea, despite his brilliant tactics, Epaminondas was killed, and the Theban forces defeated. Theban power was ended, but neither Sparta nor Athens looked strong enough to reassert their authority.

This bronze figure found at Sparta powerfully exemplifies the tense military pride for which Sparta was renowned throughout the Greek world. By the time of Leuctra, however, the number of fully-qualified Spartiates had considerably dwindled and Thebes, with generals such as Pelopidas and Epaminondas, was the rising star in Greece's military firmament.

The Battle of Leuctra was a disastrous action for the Spartan aristocracy who lost 400 men out of a total force of 700. At the onset the Spartans had obtained the initiative when, led by King Kleombrotos, they stole a march on the Thebans under Epaminondas. But despite being outnumbered the Theban general's tactical brilliance enabled him to win a victory of enduring significance.

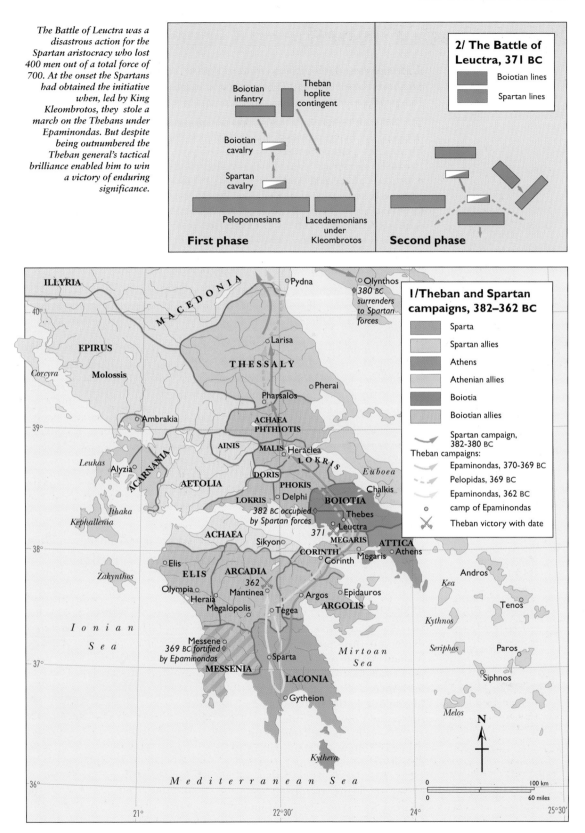

2/ The Battle of Leuctra, 371 BC

- Boiotian lines
- Spartan lines

Boiotian infantry

Theban hoplite contingent

Boiotian cavalry

Spartan cavalry

Peloponnesians

Lacedaemonians under Kleombrotos

First phase

Second phase

1/Theban and Spartan campaigns, 382–362 BC

- Sparta
- Spartan allies
- Athens
- Athenian allies
- Boiotia
- Boiotian allies

Spartan campaign, 382-380 BC

Theban campaigns:
- Epaminondas, 370-369 BC
- Pelopidas, 369 BC
- Epaminondas, 362 BC
- camp of Epaminondas
- Theban victory with date

ILLYRIA

MACEDONIA

EPIRUS

Molossis

Corcyra

THESSALY

Larisa

Pydna

Olynthos
380 BC surrenders to Spartan forces

Pharsalos

Pherai

Ambrakia

ACHAEA PHTHIOTIS

AINIS

MALIS Heraclea

Leukas

Alyzia

ACARNANIA

AETOLIA

DORIS

LOKRIS

Euboea

Ithaka

Kephallenia

LOKRIS

PHOKIS
Delphi

Chalkis

BOIOTIA

382 BC occupied by Spartan forces

Thebes
Leuctra
371

ACHAEA

Sikyon

MEGARIS
Megara

ATTICA
Athens

CORINTH
Corinth

Elis

ELIS

ARCADIA
362
Mantinea

Andros

Kea

Olympia

Heraia

Megalopolis

Tegea

Argos

Epidauros

ARGOLIS

Kythnos

Tenos

Zakynthos

Ionian Sea

Messene
369 BC fortified by Epaminondas

MESSENIA

Sparta

Mirtoan Sea

LACONIA

Gytheion

Seriphos

Paros

Siphnos

Melos

N

Kythera

Mediterranean Sea

0   100 km
0   60 miles

40°

39°

38°

37°

36°

21°   22°30'   24°   25°30'

Kingdoms of Northern Greece

Although frequently involved in wars against each other, the rulers of northern Greece shared the common aim of maintaining their independence from the imperialistic southern states.

"... at the beginning of winter, Sitalkes, the king of Odrysian Thrace, marched against Perdikkas, the son of Alexander, king of Macedonia, and against the Chalkidians. At the beginning of the war Perdikkas had been in difficulties and had entered into an undertaking with Sitalkes on condition that Sitalkes reconciled him with the Athenians and did not restore to the throne his brother Philip, who was opposed to him."

Thucydides, *History of the Peloponnesian War, Book II*

The Athenian siege of Poteidaia was one of the events which led to the outbreak of the Peloponnesian War. It also drew Perdikkas II of Macedonia and his eastern enemy, Sitalkes, King of Odrysian Thrace, into the conflict. Perdikkas sought aid from Sparta (unsuccessfully) and Corinth, which began a process of tactical manoeuvring to preserve his kingdom. Perdikkas became notorious as an unreliable ally. He tried to ensure no single South Greek state built up territory on his borders. He encouraged the cities around Olynthos to form the Olynthian (or Chalkidic) League. Athenian policy was to keep Macedonia weak but friendly—supporting opposition to the king, but maintaining Athenian interests and friendly relations with the non-Greek neighbours of Macedonia, notably the Thracian kingdoms.

Perdikkas' son Archelaos (413—399) sided with Athens: he delivered timber for the democratic fleet in 411, at the time of the oligarchic revolt and, in 410, he received Athenian assistance in capturing Pydna. Archelaos built up the military infrastructure of his kingdom, and constructed straight roads, forts and military supply depots. He centralized power and elevated Pella (which had direct access to the sea) to the role of royal capital. There was considerable Grecization at the court. The end of the Peloponnesian war saw the end of Athenian influence in the north Aegean, which was not taken up by Sparta. Following Archelaos' death, there was a period of instability in Macedon.

In the northwest, the Epirote kingdom of Molossis came to prominence and, further north, Illyria expanded rapidly in the 390s under the leadership of Bardylis from his base at Kosovo. Bardylis invaded Macedonia but Amyntas III (*c.* 392—370) soon recovered his throne. In 385/4 Bardylis invaded Epirus and defeated the Molossians. A Spartan army marched northwards and preserved Epirus from Illyrian takeover. There were further Illyrian invasions of Macedonia and Epirus in the following decades.

In Thessaly, Jason of Pherai expanded his power, making Alketas of Molossis (*c.* 390—370) his vassal, thereby extending his influence over the Pindos Mountains to the Adriatic. Both Alketas and his son Neoptolemos (*c.* 370—360) had alliances with Athens. Following the Spartan defeat at the Battle of Leuctra (371), Jason of Pherai, in support of the Thebans, destroyed the Spartan fort (Heraclea) defending Thermopylai and his route

into Greece. Jason annexed territory in Perrhaibia on the borders of Macedon, but was assassinated in 370 by his nephew Alexander who succeeded him. The death of Amyntas III of Macedon shortly afterwards, again opened up north and central Greece to intrigue and invasion: this time Thebes and Athens were the protagonists.

Following the Battle of Leuctra, Athens reasserted her claims to Amphipolis and the Chersonese. Pelopidas, who was responsible for Theban policy in the north, was called in by Thessalian cities against Alexander of Pherai and Alexander of Macedon (369). Pelopidas led a force to Thessaly where he captured Larisa (which Alexander of Macedon had garrisoned). He then went to Macedon where he made a settlement in favour of Alexander before returning to Thebes. Alexander of Macedon was murdered shortly after and further protests against Alexander of Pherai took Pelopidas north again in 368. Ptolemy, regent of Macedon, sought Athenian aid. When Pelopidas arrived, Ptolemy surrendered, perhaps because Athenian territorial ambitions in the region were a greater threat than Theban interests. Pelopidas was seized on his return through Thessaly by Alexander of Pherai. Two Theban expeditions (368 and 367) were needed before he was returned. For three years there was no further Theban intervention in the north. In 364 Pelopidas led an army north, in response to a further appeal from Thessaly against Alexander of Pherai. Pelopidas was killed at the Battle of Kynoskephalai, but Thebes sent another army, of 7000 men, which defeated Alexander, reduced his territory and made him join the Boiotian League.

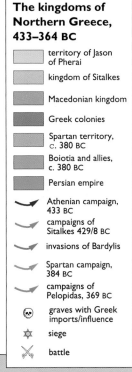

The kingdoms of Northern Greece, 433–364 BC

- territory of Jason of Pherai
- kingdom of Sitalkes
- Macedonian kingdom
- Greek colonies
- Spartan territory, c. 380 BC
- Boiotia and allies, c. 380 BC
- Persian empire
- Athenian campaign, 433 BC
- campaigns of Sitalkes 429/8 BC
- invasions of Bardylis
- Spartan campaign, 384 BC
- campaigns of Pelopidas, 369 BC
- graves with Greek imports/influence
- siege
- battle

Decline of Athens

As the flame of Macedonian ambition began to kindle in the north, a policy of continued militarism and the subsequent intervention of Persia resulted in a reduction of Athenian prestige and power.

During the years of Spartan and Theban ascendancy, Athens had generally sided against Sparta. In 379/8 Athens had antagonised Sparta by aiding the liberation of Thebes. In anticipation of a Spartan response, Athens formed a number of new alliances with the islands, notably Rhodes and Chios, and with Byzantion. These were the beginnings of the Second Athenian League, and seem to have prompted a Spartan attack on the Piraeus. Athenian policy was largely pro-Theban, but did not recognize Theban suzerainty over Boiotia. This was brought to an end when Thebes seized Oropos in north-east Attica (366). By a King's Peace of 366/5, Athens acknowledged Theban hegemony over Boiotia in exchange for Persian acceptance of Athenian rights in the Chersonese. Some of the islands joined the League because of a new threat from the east. In 377 Mausolos had succeeded as satrap of Caria and, from his new capital at Halikarnassos on the coast, began to expand his power through Lycia to the Greek coastal cities and the islands. Mausolos was now able to benefit from Athenian misjudgements in the eastern Aegean.

The satrap Ariobarzanes was in open revolt against Artaxerxes. In 366 Athens sent Timotheos to Samos to aid Ariobarzanes. The Persian garrison was evicted and the city besieged. When it fell, a cleruchy was established, but although the Athenians could claim some justification for this action, opinion was generally hostile. Theban naval actions followed, with some successes: Byzantion seceded from the confederacy, permanently. Her position on the corn-route was damaging to Athens' interests. Chios and Rhodes were also disaffected, but did not secede. On Keos anti-Athenian feeling culminated in revolt (363). Meanwhile, Persian influence was increasing in non-confederacy islands, such as Kos. This increasingly widespread discontent was due to the imposition of cleruchies and Athenian interference in commercial and judicial freedoms.

Events came to a head in 357, with the revolt of Chios, Kos and Rhodes against Athens. Mausolos stepped in. Athenian cleruchies on Lemnos, Imbros and Samos were attacked. Athens sent her general, Chares, with a fleet. He immediately put it to use aiding the Persian satrap of Phrygia, Artabazos. Full-scale war with Persia threatened. Artaxerxes wrote to the Athenians ordering them to recall Chares. They did, and the war came to an humiliating close in 355. The war saw the end of the Athenian empire, as many islands became independent with oligarchic rule and Carian garrisons.

Athenian activities in the eastern Aegean prevented her intervention in the north, with far-reaching results. In 359, Philip II ascended the throne of Macedon. Philip sought an alliance with Athens, withdrawing Macedonian troops from that perennial object of Athenian ambitions, Amphipolis. Then, suddenly, he attacked Amphipolis, capturing it after a siege. Having resisted Athenian aggression since 404, Amphipolis now appealed to Athens for aid. None was sent. The cities of the Chalkidike, led by Olynthos, also appealed to Athens, but, with the outbreak of the Social War, Athenian action was impossible. Philip himself entered into treaty with the Chalkidians, and captured Poteidaia (356). Athenian settlers were returned to Athens and the local population made into slaves. Athenian influence and ambitions in the north Aegean, as in the east, were at an end.

At his death in 353 BC the Carian satrap Mausolos was placed in a magnificent tomb at Halikarnassos, from which this statue is taken. The tomb, which became known as the mausoleum, was one of the wonders of the ancient world and revealed the impact of Greek culture on the Persian Empire in Asia Minor.

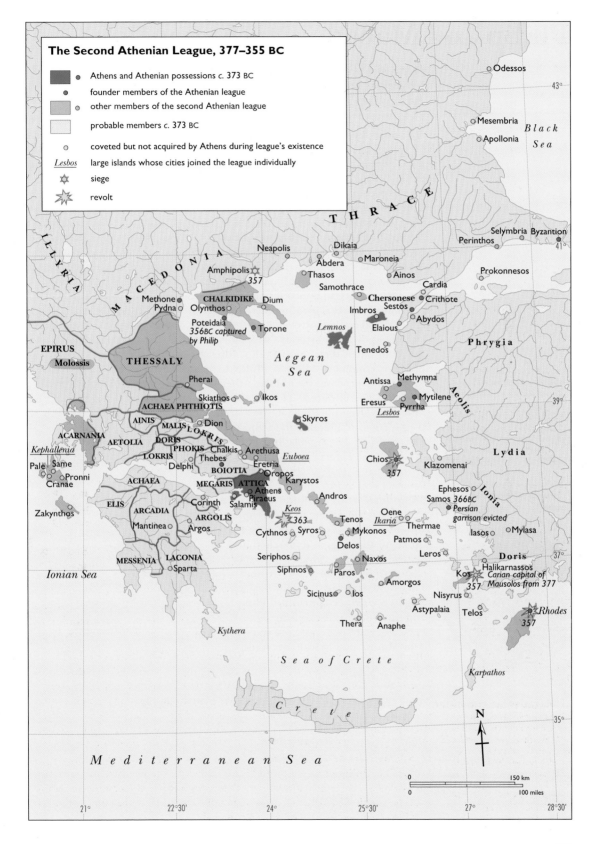

The Second Athenian League, 377–355 BC

- Athens and Athenian possessions *c.* 373 BC
- founder members of the Athenian league
- other members of the second Athenian league
- probable members *c.* 373 BC
- coveted but not acquired by Athens during league's existence
- *Lesbos* large islands whose cities joined the league individually
- ☆ siege
- ✷ revolt

ILLYRIA

THRACE

Odessos

Mesembria

Apollonia

Black Sea

Selymbria Byzantion

Perinthos

Prokonnesos

Neapolis   Dikaia

Abdera   Maroneia

MACEDONIA

Amphipolis ☆
357

Thasos   Ainos

Samothrace

Cardia

Chersonese Crithote

Sestos

Imbros   Abydos

Methone   CHALKIDIKE Dium
Pydna   Olynthos

Poteidaia
356BC captured
by Philip   Torone   Elaious

Lemnos

Tenedos

Phrygia

EPIRUS

Molossis

THESSALY

Pherai

Aegean Sea

Antissa   Methymna

Eresus   Mytilene
Pyrrha

Lesbos

Aeolis

Skiathos   Ikos

ACHAEA PHTHIOTIS

AINIS   Dion
MALIS LOKRIS
ACARNANIA   DORIS
AETOLIA   PHOKIS Chalkis Arethusa
LOKRIS   Thebes
Delphi   Eretria
BOIOTIA   Oropos
ACHAEA   MEGARIS ATTICA
Corinth   Athens
Piraeus
ELIS   Salamis
ARCADIA
Mantinea   Argos
ARGOLIS

Kephallenia
Pale Same
Pronni
Cranae

Zakynthos

Skyros

Euboea

Karystos

Andros

Chios ✷
357

Klazomenai

Lydia

Ephesos
Samos 366BC
Persian
garrison evicted

Oene
Ikaria   Thermae
Tenos   Mykonos
Keos ✷   Patmos
363   Delos
Syros

Cythnos

Leros

Mylasa

Iasos

Ionia

Doris

Halikarnassos
Kos ✷ Carian capital of
357   Mausolos from 377

Rhodes
357

MESSENIA   LACONIA
Sparta

Ionian Sea

Seriphos   Naxos

Siphnos   Paros

Amorgos

Sicinus   Ios

Nisyrus

Astypalaia
Thera   Anaphe   Telos

Karpathos

Sea of Crete

Mediterranean Sea

C r e t e

N

0   150 km
0   100 miles

Kythera

43°

41°

39°

37°

35°

21°   22°30'   24°   25°30'   27°   28°30'

Philip and Macedonian Expansion

Between 357 and 336 BC Philip of Macedon achieved ascendancy over all Greece and prepared the way for Alexander the Great's conquest of the Persian Empire.

"Before Zeus and all the gods, it is shameful and unworthy of you and of the history of Athens and the achievements of your fathers, to let all the rest of Greece fall into slavery."
Demosthenes

A gold medallion from Tarsus depicts an equestrian Philip II of Macedon. Though his reputation has often been cast into shadow by that of his son, Philip was a brilliant soldier, a fine speaker and an enormously charismatic leader. It was the mastery of Philip's diplomatic legerdemain that ensured the permanence of Macedonian hegemony in a united Greece.

Philip began his kingdom's expansion by taking the city of Amphipolis in 357, soon followed by Pydna. Further gains in Chalkidike (Poteidaia, 356; Methone, 354) gave Macedon control of the gold mines and much-needed ports. Philip also gained influence over his non-Greek neighbours, defeating the Paionians and Illyrians and winning successes against the Thracian kings. The expansion of Mausolos of Halikarnassos against the Second Athenian Confederacy drew Athens into the "Social War" with her former allies (357—355). In central Greece, the crisis was provoked when the Phokians seized Delphi, but it was not until it was clear that Athens, Phokis' chief ally, would lose the Social War that the enemies of Phokis were able to declare the "Sacred War"(355—346). In 353 Philip became involved in Thessaly against the alliance of Phokis and Pherai. He defeated the Phokians in 352 and took the port of Pagasai, but could not pass Thermopylai, due to the presence of an Athenian force. He moved his attention to Thrace. In 349 he again invaded Chalkidike and destroyed Olynthos (348). Athens had not sent aid to the city, being diverted by events in Euboea. The Phokians overran Boiotia and the Boiotians called upon Philip. Internal problems in the Phokian command allowed Philip to pass Thermopylai: southern Greece was his to take. Athens sought peace; the Phokians surrendered. The Sacred War was over and Philip was given the Phokian votes in the Amphictyony. By the Treaty of Philokrates (346), Athens abandoned her claims on Amphipolis. In 342 Philip moved once more against Thrace, finally crushing opposition. He moved further east, attacking Perinthos in 340. The Persians sent aid to the city, and the siege failed. Philip turned his attention to Byzantion. This threatened the Athenian grain supplies, and Athens again prepared for war. Philip broke off the siege and marched into central Greece where he was opposed by Thebes and Athens. They were defeated at Chaironeia in August 338. Peace concluded, Philip announced a full-scale war against Persia. An advance force was sent to Asia Minor, but before he could join it, Philip was murdered in his capital at Pella in 336.

ILLYRIA

Corcyra   EPIRUS   Dassare
Ores

Leukas   Ambrakia

Kephallenia   ACARNANIA   Pe
Pinios

Zakynthos   Naupaktos   C TH
Amphissa
Elis   Delphi   PHOKI
ACHAEA   Thermopylai
346
Mantinea   Chaironeia
338
Messene   Argos   BOIOT
Corinth   Thebes
Megara
Sparta   Athe
Gytheion
Mirtoan Sea
Kythr

1/Macedonian expansion, 359–334 BC

	kingdom of Macedonia in 359 BC		Athenian grain route
	Macedonian expansion to 336 BC		campaigns against Athens
•	Philip's garrisons in Greece		campaigns of Philip and Alexander
•	Athenian military base		342–341 BC
	member of coalition against Philip, 339–8 BC		340–339 BC
✕	battle		338–334 BC

The Battle of Chaironeia amply exemplifies the Macedonian supremacy in terms of training and generalship. Taking position on the right flank of his army Philip ordered a deliberate retreat thereby tempting the impetuous Athenians into an ill-considered and disastrous pursuit. Meanwhile, on the left, Alexander led his first great cavalry charge, smashing the weaker Greek cavalry and turning the flank of the Theban infantry.

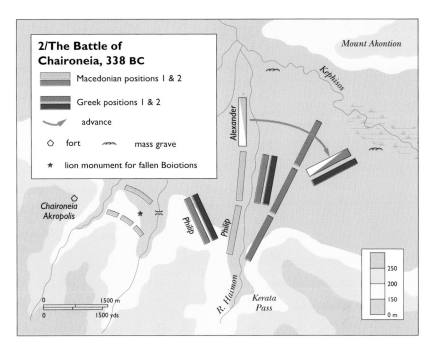

2/The Battle of Chaironeia, 338 BC

- Macedonian positions 1 & 2
- Greek positions 1 & 2
- ⌢ advance
- ⬠ fort
- ⁀ mass grave
- ★ lion monument for fallen Boiotions

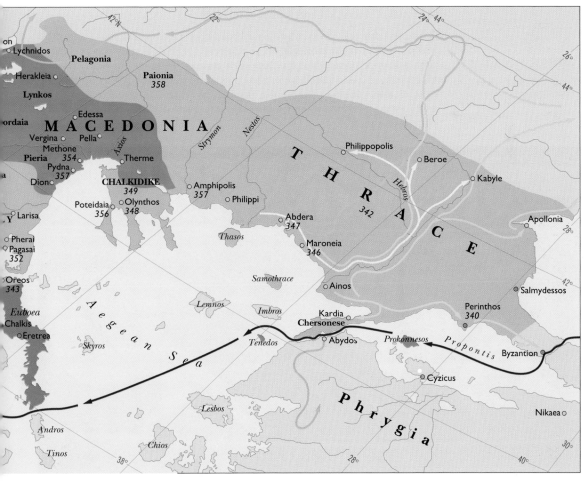

Greek Warfare

Perpetual bickering between the Greek states necessitated a condition of constant military readiness. Some states would use their forces for defensive purposes whilst others used them to enforce aggressive foreign policy.

"Military training ... has three purposes: (1) to save ourselves from becoming subject to others, (2) to win for our own city a position of leadership, exercised for the benefit of others ... (3) to exercise the rule of a master over those who deserve to be treated as slaves."
Aristotle, *The Politics, Book VII*

The first great innovation in Bronze Age warfare was the introduction of the chariotry which became a significant element in the armies of the kings of Egypt and western Asia. The chariot appears to have been brought to Greece at about the same time as it was introduced to Egypt, around 1600 BC, perhaps by the rulers buried in the Shaft Graves at Mycenae. It has been estimated that the ruler of Knossos may have had between two and three hundred chariots at his disposal. Exactly how they were used in warfare in Greece is still unclear. In the Homeric epics chariots are generally used to convey the combatants to the place of battle, but it seems probable that Mycenean warriors fought from their chariots using bows and arrows, as was common throughout western Asia.

There were some significant differences in warfare in the Iron Age, chariotry disappeared and the infantry became the main fighting force. The *phalanx*, a body of foot-soldiers (*hoplites*) with spears, requires organized formation and training. It seems to have been perfected in the 7th century. The wealthy who could afford horses rode to battle, accompanied by their squires, but they then dismounted and fought as infantry.

Evidence for weapons and armour comes from surviving examples, sculpture and from painting on pottery. The soldier's body was protected with a bronze breastplate, the legs with greaves. Helmets (of many varying shapes) had crests which were both protective and intended to intimidate. Shields also varied in shape, the hoplite carrying a large heavy one. The main weapon of the infantry was the thrusting spear, which had a reach of a little over a metre.

In the Classical period, the citizens formed the nucleus of the army in all city-states. In Athens, the young men served a period of compulsory military service, between the ages of 18 and 20, before entering civilian life and becoming citizens. In times of war the whole citenzry under the age of sixty could be called up. A similar system operated in most other states. In addition to the *phalanx* of *hoplites*, there could be contingents of sling-throwers and *peltasts* (the *pelte* was a light crescent-shaped shield). The *peltasts* were javelin throwers and their use became more common after the Peloponnesian war.

Sparta differed from the other states in that it organized its whole society along strongly militaristic lines and was on a permanent war-footing. The system was imposed on all full citizens, the Spartiates (*Homoioi* "Equals"). At the age of six, boys were removed from their mothers and put into a group in which they remained for fourteen years, undergoing strict training which included ritualized flogging. Other education was limited, although music and dance were considered important. From twenty he took charge of a group of younger boys. At thirty he became a citizen. The Spartiate's income was supplied from his family estates, which were worked for him by the *helots*. He could marry (indeed he was obliged to), but his life was devoted to military training. He dined and slept in a *sussition* (a mess) with his comrades and his visits to his wife were clandestine. Unlike the other states, Spartan women also trained, and these appearances in public gave them a reputation for immorality in other cities. A similar system, if slightly milder in form, operated on Crete in the Classical period.

Homosexuality, which was a universal practice in all Greek states (normally involving an older man and an adolescent boy), was institutionalized in the armies of Sparta and Thebes, Greece's two most formidable military states. In Thebes it was reputedly an intentional element in the composition of the "Sacred Band," it being believed that, placed side by side, lovers were ashamed to be disgraced in each other's presence, and that they would stand their ground to protect each other.

Philip II of Macedon initiated changes to the *phalanx* which brought about the first defeat of the Theban Sacred Band, at the battle of Chaironeia. He invented the very long pike, the *sarissa*. This was five metres long, and weighted so that nearly four metres were in front of the carrier. This allowed the points of four rows of pikes to project beyond the front line. It was a heavy weapon and was held with both hands. The light-weight shield was hung from the neck, and a closer formation was thereby achieved: two pikemen occupied the space of one *hoplite*. The size of the *sarissa* meant that the Macedonian *phalanx* required immense discipline, and if it broke up the soldiers were ill-equipped to defend themselves. Philip's training ensured that it became the most efficient of fighting machines and it was used to devastating effect both by himself and by his son, Alexander the Great.

The armies of the Hellenistic kings were professional and usually made-up of mercenary troops. There were many innovations in warfare and thinkers such as Archimedes were often involved in the invention of siege towers, engines and other weapons of destruction. An important introduction from the east was the use of elephants. Seleukos I obtained 500 from Chandragupta Maurya and used them with great effect at the battle of Ipsos in 301, but usually the numbers engaged were much smaller. The Ptolemies followed the example of the Seleukids, bringing their elephants from east Africa, and later, perhaps most notably, Hannibal included them in his force during his conflict with Rome.

Although the identity of the model for this fine 5th century Spartan sculpture is uncertain, it seems highly probable that it represents King Leonidas, the hero of Thermopylai. With a select force of 1,000 Spartiates, Leonidas defended the pass at Thermopylai against the overwhelming numbers of Xerxes' Persian invasion force. There were no survivors, but through their actions Leonidas and his followers came to symbolize the self-sacrificing heroism of the true Spartan warrior.

Opposite: Homer's Iliad, the greatest of the Greek military epics, concludes with the final confrontation between Achilles and Hektor. In this scene on an Attic vase dating from around 490 BC, Achilles lunges forward with his spear to deliver the coup de grace to the wounded Trojan hero.

V: Alexander and After

By 323 BC Alexander the Great was master of a vast heterogeneous empire. Its apparent unity was illusory but its disintegration would herald some of the greatest achievements of Greek culture.

"Alexandria is situated, as it were, at the crossroads of the whole world, of even its remotest nations, as if it were a market serving a single city, bringing together all men into one place, displaying them to one another and, as far as possible, making them of the same race."
Dio of Prusa,
Alexandrian Speech
(c. 69/79 AD)

The legend of Alexander is one of the most potent from the ancient world, influencing later political and military figures (such as Caesar and Napoleon) as well as providing subject matter to writers, artists and musicians. Many histories of Alexander's life and campaigns were written in the decades following his death. Some of these "histories" were essentially fantastic fabrications designed to enhance the Alexander myth, while others—such as that written by Ptolemy, Alexander's personal staff-officer and future king of Egypt—were detailed and authoritative. Arrian (fl. 130—175 AD), the author of the major surviving history, was certainly deeply indepted to Ptolemy's memoir. The later Roman empire saw the creation of the *Alexander Romance* derived from stories and fabricated letters written in Egypt in the 2nd century BC but attributed to Kallisthenes, a relative of Aristotle, who had written an account of the campaigns. Some episodes, such as the story of Alexander's journey to Aithiopia, were based upon a known "fact", in this case his interest in discovering the source of the Nile, but many others were pure fantasy (such as the bizarre tale of an encounter with a giant lobster). The *Alexander Romance* achieved enormous popularity and was the basis of a number of epics written in Europe in the Middle Ages. The deeds of Alexander also appear in Persian and other Asian literature, such as the *Shah-nama* of Firdawsi (*c*.935—*c*.1020 AD), a history of the kings of Persia.

Alexander's military success was due to his skill as a general and tactician, and particularly to the loyalty he inspired in his troops. Alexander was able to utilize the military machine created by his father, the core of which was the infantry *phalanx* with its five to six metre pikes, the *sarissa*, Philip's own invention. The traditional Greek *hoplite phalanx* carried spears which were about half the length of the *sarissa*, and the Macedonian formation meant that the front line was protected by the points of four rows of pikes and had far greater reach than the *hoplite* front line. However, the Macedonian *phalanx* needed to hold formation to be successful. Through rigorous training Philip had forged his units into a formidable fighting force and Alexander was to use the *phalanx* to great effect in his own battles. The cavalry, the archers and javelin throwers remained a major component of his army.

A willingness to conciliate Persian sensibilities ensured that Alexander's conquests lasted his own lifetime. On his advance through the Persian empire Alexander had re-ordered its administration, appointing both Macedonians and Persians as satraps. In Caria, he reconfirmed the female satrap Ada, a member of the indigenous Hekatomnid dynasty (the family of Mausolos); at Babylon, he installed Mazaeus, a former satrap of Darius and commander at the battle of Gaugamela. Such appointments assured the Persian elite of their position within the new regime and undoubtledly limited opposition. Alexander thus attempted to unite the eastern and western elements of his empire. However, Macedonian resentment of foreign officers and troops was one of the grievances which led to mutiny at Opis (324). Intermarriage between Macedonians and Persians was more successful. In a ceremony at Susa (324), Alexander married two Persian princesses, and arranged matches between his generals and members of the royal and satrapal houses. Arrian reports that 10,000 of the soldiers had contracted marriages in Asia.

This bronze statuette of an equestrian Alexander the Great dates from the Roman Imperial period but it is quite likely that it is a copy of a much earlier original. The scupltor has portrayed Alexander in an heroic pose and there is certainly no doubt as to Alexander's personal courage. Never avoiding danger he was wounded on a number of occasions and at a city "of the Mallians" (possibly modern Multan), he was wounded so seriously while storming the city-walls that his life was despaired of for days.

Alexander's adoption of some Persian royal customs received much more mixed reactions by his Macedonian followers. The attempt to introduce *proskynesis* (prostration) was abandoned because of the hostility of some of his courtiers; in Greece it was a practice reserved for gods. The assumption of divinity has been a problem for western scholars, as it was to the Greeks themselves, but Alexander was ruling ancient kingdoms in which the king had been divine, or was the earthly agent and representative of the gods. Royal divinity has perhaps been too easily dismissed—in both ancient and modern times—as megalomania and a sign of the "corruption" of Alexander's character.

One of the great features of Alexander's march through the Persian empire was the founding of cities which were to become the backbone of the eastern Hellenistic world (nearly all were east of the Tigris). The first, and greatest, was Alexandria in Egypt, which was to become one of the most important trading and cultural cities of the Mediterranean. A position on trade routes was an important factor in the siting of other cities (such as Alexandria ad Caucasum, at Begram, near Kabul), as was defence from external attack. The Macedonians and Greeks who were settled in these cities were not all content, and, following Alexander's death many tried to return to Greece. Initially the cities must have been inhospitable, little more than defensive garrisons, but within a century of the campaigns many of them were thriving, with elaborate public buildings and citizens drawn from Macedonia and the Greek world as well as substantial indigenous populations.

Alexander's death in 323, whether through illness, drinking or poison, brought the conquests to a sudden end and saw the inevitable, and rapid, dissolution of his enormous empire.

The Wars of the Successors

Following Alexander's death a conference of his generals at Babylon recognized his half-brother Philip III Arrhidaios and his son by the Sogdian princess Roxana, Alexander IV, as joint kings, with the general Perdikkas as regent. The generals (the *diadochoi*—"successors") divided the provinces amongst themselves and ruled as satraps. The most significant were Ptolemy, who had control of Egypt, Antigonos Monophthalmos ("the One-eyed") of Phrygia, Seleukos of Babylon and Lysimachos of Thrace.

Perdikkas wished to take Alexander's body to Macedonia for burial, but Ptolemy snatched it and took it to Egypt, claiming that Alexander had wished to be buried at Siwa. This was the beginning of the conflict between the successors. A coalition now formed to defy Perdikkas. One of its leaders was Antipatros, one of the most senior generals, having been a contemporary of Philip II. To seal the alliance, Antipatros gave daughters in marriage to Ptolemy and Lysimachos. Such marriage alliances continued to be arranged according to the changing situation. Many of these women took an active role in events and were not merely passive political instruments .

Perdikkas attempted an invasion of Egypt to recapture Alexander's body, but his troops mutinied and Perdikkas was murdered by his generals (321). Antipatros was declared the new regent, and arranged another marriage alliance with Demetrios, the son of the general Antigonos Monophthalmos.

Following the death of the elderly Antipatros (319), Antigonos moved to rebuild the empire under his own rule. To resist these ambitions, Ptolemy allied himself with Kassandros (son of Antipatros), Seleukos and Lysimachos. In the next decade there was much conflict with successes and failures for both sides. Ptolemy gained control of Cyprus and secured Kyrene, both of which were to remain important Ptolemaic possessions. Antigonos and his son Demetrios also had some considerable success, and were active in Greece. Shortly after the death of Philip III (317) Kassandros gained control of Macedon. He acted as regent for Alexander IV, but imprisoned the young king and his mother until their deaths (which were anounced in 306). Kassandros, having married a daughter of Philip II, could now claim to be the legitimate heir of the Macedonian royal house and became king.

In 306 both Antigonos and Demetrios were proclaimed "king"; but not of anywhere in particular. The other *diadochoi* soon followed suit. The conflict continued and eventually Antigonos was defeated and slain at the Battle of the Kings at Ipsos (301) and his territory carved up. Demetrios fled.

Kassandros did not survive long, both he and his eldest son, Philip IV, dying from disease in 297. When his two younger sons, Antipatros and Alexander V, were elected joint kings, Macedonia became the centre of violent conflict, as each king sought to oust his brother. Demetrios, meanwhile, returned to Greece and captured Athens which he made his base for an attack on Macedonia. Seleukos, Ptolemy and Lysimachos attempted, by a series of complex dynastic marriages, to neutralize Demetrios, who still retained control of a large fleet. The crisis between the two young kings grew deeper: Alexander sought the help of Demetrios and of Pyrrhos, king of Epirus, Antipatros sought that of Lysimachos. Pyrrhos sent aid in return for some western areas of the kingdom, but with the arrival of Demetrios, Alexander V was promptly killed and Demetrios himself hailed as the new king of Macedonia. Demetrios ultimately emerged as victor in 294, but he was not an effective ruler and his former rivals now joined again in coalition to defend their interests, with Pyrrhos as an ally. In 288, both Lysimachos and Pyrrhos marched into Macedonia. Demetrios' army was defeated at Beroia and he was again forced into exile, dying of drink at the court of Seleukos some years later. Macedonia was ruled jointly by Lysimachos and Pyrrhos, until, in 285, Lysimachos succesfully ousted Pyrrhos. But Lysimachos was not to enjoy the kingdom for long, he was murdered by a Ptolemaic prince, Keraunos ("Thunderbolt") who ruled until his own death in battle with the invading Celts. In the conflict which followed it was the Antigonids who finally achieved their ambition of ruling Macedonia, the victor being Demetrios' son, Antigonos II Gonatas (perhaps meaning "Knock-Kneed").

By 280 BC the scramble for kingdoms was over and a number of dynasties was securely established: the Antigonids in Macedonia, the Seleukids in Syria and the Ptolemies in Egypt. By the European mind, for which the Athens of Perikles was the model by which Greek culture should be judged, these Hellenistic kingdoms and the culture of their courts have been viewed as decadent—this applies particularly to the Seleukids and the Ptolemies. Now the importance of the three hundred years of the Hellenistic world are more fully appreciated.

Macedonia and Greece

Not all of the events of the Greek world concentrated on the Aegean and the successor kingdoms. Pyrrhos, the king of Epirus, had been an active participant in the struggle for supremacy in Macedonia. He was one of the ablest generals of the day, but some of his later victories were gained with such enormous losses to his own troops that they have become proverbial. Pyrrhos was invited to help Tarentum against Rome (281) and took his armies to Italy. In the next year he defeated the Roman army and advanced on Rome itself. Although most of the Roman Senate was inclined to peace, the elderly statesman, Appius Claudius, harangued them, and Pyrrhos' overtures were rejected. At the battle at Asculum—the proverbial Pyrrhic victory—in 279, the Epirotes suffered heavy losses. News now arrived of the death of the Macedonian king Ptolemy Keraunos, but instead of returning to Greece to seize the vacant throne, Pyrrhos decided to accept the offer from the cities of Sicily to aid them against the Carthaginians (one of Pyrrhos' wives was the daughter of Agathokles ruler of Syracuse). He lost many of his ships in a sea battle with the Carthaginian fleet and returning to the mainland he was defeated by the Romans at Beneventum. In 274 he crossed back to Epirus. The episode had revealed the power and ambition of Rome, and Ptolemy II soon agreed a treaty with the city, perhaps for trade (273).

Pyrrhos' army was severely depleted, but he defeated Antigonos Gonatas and seized Macedonia. He did not rest for long, being invited by Kleonymos of Sparta to help him regain his throne. After another dubious victory, Pyrrhos turned his attention to Argos. Antigonos and his troops were close-by. Pyrrhos was let into the city at night, but the alarm was raised when some of his elephants got stuck in the gateway. According to one version of events, the king was killed when an old woman hurled a tile at him from a roof, stunning him: he was then decapitated by a soldier. Pyrrhos' unfortunate demise gave Antigonos control of the south.

Antigonos II Gonatas (276—239) rebuilt Macedonian strength, but Ptolemaic ambitions in the Aegean made conflict inevitable. The Ptolemies had strengthened their ties with the cities of mainland Greece, particularly with Athens and Sparta. Athens relied on corn supplies from Egypt, and an alliance was concluded. In 266 Antigonos invaded Attica. The Macedonian garrison at Corinth prevented the southern armies joining together and the Egyptian fleet off Cape Sounion was unable to assist. A revolt of Antigonos' Galatian mercenaries forced him to withdraw, but he returned the next year and defeated the Greek army at Corinth. The Egyptian fleet withdrew. At Ptolemy's instigation, Alexander of Epirus invaded Macedon, and Antigonos had to give up the siege of Athens. But he was soon able to return: the Peloponnesian League collapsed and Athens was besieged until she surrended (263/1). Macedonia once again dominated the states of southern Greece.

Antigonos' control of southern Greece did not last long. The Aetolian League slowly expanded its power until, by 245, it controlled central Greece. It then gained influence in the Peloponnese and Aegean. Conflict between the Aetolian League and Macedonia broke out in the reign of Antigonos' successors Demetrios II (239—229) and Philip V (221—179), but Philip's main opponent was Rome.

Philip's actions made enemies in Greece, which was unable to present a united front against Rome when it was most needed. Following the first Macedonian War (214—205), the Aetolian League sought help from Rome, and in 201, due to naval activities by Philip in the Aegean, so did Rhodes and Pergamon. The Roman settlement following the second Macedonian War (200—196) left the Aetolian League discontented and they sought the help of the Seleukid king, Antiochos III, to liberate Greece. Renewed Roman action in Greece ended the power of the League for good. Although the Romans withdrew, they had become inextricably involved in the affairs of Greece and it required little provocation for them to declare war on Philip's son, Perseus (171). There was little Greek support for Perseus, but none for Rome. Perseus was victorious at Larisa, but at the battle Pydna (168) the Macedonian army was almost annihiliated. The Roman Senate partitioned Macedonia into four republics and Perseus was taken to Rome. A pretender reunited the country (150) but war was renewed. Following their victory the Romans turned Macedonia into a province and added Epirus to it. Further conflict in Greece ended in defeat, the destruction of Corinth and enslavement of its habitants and the annexation of Achaea (146). Rome was now on the doorstep of the Hellenistic kingdoms of Asia.

The Seleukid Empire

The empire of the Seleukid dynasty was the largest of the successor states, reaching from the coast of Anatolia to India. The focus of the Seleukid empire was the "fertile crescent" stretching from Mesopotamia to the coast of North Syria. The rich cultural traditions of this region, in themselves an influence on Greece, had been absorbed by the Assyrian and Babylonian and then the Persian empires. Although the Seleukids were often preoccupied by the affairs of the other successor states of the eastern Mediterranean, and by the rise of Rome, the eastern part of their empire was equally important.

The Seleukid influence and possessions in Anatolia, at times contested by the Ptolemies, were eroded first by the growing independent Hellenised kingdoms of Pontos, Cappadocia and Bithynia. Antiochos III was drawn into events in Greece and direct conflict with Rome. Following his defeat by the

Roman armies at Magnesia (190) Antiochos was deprived of all of Asia Minor west of the Taurus mountains. Rome did not annex this territory, but divided it between its allies Rhodes and Pergamon. The Seleukids also lost control of Armenia where the governors installed by Antiochos set themselves up as kings. Pergamon became one of the great powers of Anatolia under the Attalid family, and a renowned literary and artistic centre. On the death of Attalos III in 133, the kingdom was bequeathed to the Roman people.

The reigns of Antiochos III's son, Seleukos IV (187—175) and Antiochos IV (175—164), saw both loss and regaining of territories, before the dynastic crisis which erupted between the descendants of the two kings. This was exploited by Rome for its own ends.

In the eastern part of the Seleukid empire, centred on the cities founded by Alexander the Great, new dynasties and kingdoms arose. At times their expansion was checked by the Seleukids, notably under Antiochos III, but ultimately large parts of the empire became partly, or completely independent. Shortly after Alexander's campaigns, the Indian ruler Chandragupta Maurya had absorbed some of the eastern borders of the Seleukid empire. Under his descendants the Mauryan empire came to rule much of the subcontinent and had close trade and cultural contacts with the Seleukid and Ptolemaic kingdoms.

The kingdoms of Bactria and northern India were ruled by dynasties of Greek (in the broadest sense) origin. The Bactrian king Demetrios (c. 185—175) expanded his rule into India, but shortly afterwards the Seleukids temporarily regained control of parts of Bactria (169—167). Later, the Greek kingdoms of Bactria and India were divided amongst a number of different rulers, in some cases with territories overlapping. Invasions from the north brought further crises although a diminished kingdom around Kabul continued with Chinese support until 30 BC.

Parthia emerged as the greatest rival to Seleukid power. Mithridates I (170—134) managed to annex significant parts of Bactria (159—141), and following the death of the Seleukid king Antiochos IV, added the region around Susa to his expanding kingdom. By 141 Mithridates I was in possession of Babylon. The internal dissensions of the Seleukids divided Syria, and although attempts to reconquer the east had some success, they were short-lived. The Parthian king Phraates II regained Babylon and by 100 Mithridates II had probably absorbed the rest of Mesopotamia.

This portrait bust has been tentatively identified as Kleopatra VII, last of the Ptolemaic rulers of Egypt. A woman of considerable intelligence, Kleopatra made use of her physical charms to strengthen her position in Egypt and to ensure independence from the rapidly expanding Roman empire.

The much reduced Seleukid kingdom in the west struggled through continuous dynastic crisis, much of it involving Ptolemaic princesses. It suffered further erosion of its territory from the northward expansion of the Nabataean trading kingdom of Petra, which absorbed Damascus, and from the emergence of a Judaean kingdom based on Jerusalem.

Following his defeat of Mithridates of Pontos, the victorious Roman general, Pompey, set about reorganizing the east (64), confirming and installing client rulers and creating a string of Roman provinces around the coast of Anatolia. Syria now became a Roman province. Although the Seleukid monarchy had come to an end, Syria was one of the most important Roman provinces, and her capital of Antioch one of the foremost of the empire.

Ptolemaic Egypt

Egypt under Ptolemaic rule, rather like Seleukid Syria, is often viewed as undergoing a long process of degeneration and decline. The earliest rulers were authoritative and patrons of the arts, but the constant dynastic bickering, internecine feuding and murders which characterize the last century and a half has been dismissed as a sign of the inbreeding of the family. While it cannot be denied that dynastic quarrels were significant and that the Alexandrian populace was a key player in events, the colourful history of the Ptolemies is rather different from the history of Egypt under Ptolemaic rule.

Egypt was the richest of the successor kingdoms. It was the first to enter into agreement with Rome, and, despite the involvement of Rome in its internal politics, was the last to be subjected. For much of the three hundred years of the Hellenistic world, Egypt was also the most powerful of the kingdoms, having extensive control of the Aegean, Cyprus and coastal cities of Anatolia.

Even today the temple complex at Edfu acts as a potent reminder of the wealth and power of the Ptolemaic dynasty which ruled Egypt for nearly 300 years. Amongst their Hellenistic subjects the Ptolemies sponsored the hybrid Graeco-Egyptian cult of Serapis, although the older native cults were imbued with a vitality which enabled them to survive the annexation of Egypt by Rome.

The Ptolemies turned Alexandria into the most magnificent and important city of the eastern Mediterranean, which it continued to be under Roman rule until supplanted by Antioch in Syria. The rule of the first Ptolemies saw the founding of the great library, one of the leading centres of literary and scientific endeavour in the Hellenistic world. Trade flourished, and Ptolemy II sent expeditions both up the Nile to the wealthy kingdom of Meroë, and along the Red Sea. Ptolemy IV brought elephants from the Aithiopian highlands via the Red Sea routes and later development of the Red Sea resulted in the opening of the sea route to India.

Within Egypt itself, there were many Greek settlers and new towns, particularly in the Faiyum region, which became extremely prosperous. The

Egyptian elite was Hellenised and incorporated, but the peasant class undoubtedly suffered. The new cities built in Egypt were modelled on the Greek pattern, but there was considerable Egyptian influence on architectural and artistic styles. The Ptolemies were also responsible for building many of the largest surviving temples to the Egyptian deities, in traditional style.

There was opposition to the Ptolemies at many times, the most significant being the rebellion which broke out in 207/206 BC. For about 20 years, the whole of Upper Egypt came under the rule of indigenous kings, Harwennefer and Ankhwennefer, who probably had support from Meroë. Ptolemy V regained control of Upper Egypt (187), but his death (by poison) left an infant king on the throne. The ruling ministers made a move to regain Coele-Syria in 170. The Seleukid king, Antiochos IV, retaliated, pushed into Egypt and was proclaimed king by his troops at Memphis. In 168, Antiochos re-entered Egypt, but at Alexandria the Roman ambassador Popillius Laenas, forced his withdrawal.

Rome was now frequently appealed to to resolve dynastic conflicts. The Senate ended the long feud between Ptolemy VI and his brother by giving the younger king, Ptolemy Physkon ("Pot-belly"), control of Kyrene. On the death of Ptolemy VI, Physkon returned to Egypt, murdered his nephew and assumed power. Decades of bloody dynastic dispute followed, with increasing reliance upon Rome. At his death (116) the king bequeathed Kyrene to a son, Ptolemy Apion, who in his turn bequeathed it to Rome (96).

During the last century of the Ptolemaic dynasty, the formidable queens and princesses were as politically active as their male relatives. A number of princesses married their Seleukid cousins, and controlled events in Syria. Kleopatra VII was not an exception, she was the most successful of a line of almost equally influential royal women. Following the death of Physkon, Kleopatra III ruled with her elder son, Soter II (nicknamed "Chickpea"), until they quarrelled. Chickpea went to Cyprus and was replaced by his brother, Alexander I. The new king soon fell out with his mother as well, and had her murdered. He then married his niece, Berenike III, but was driven into exile and killed in battle. Chickpea returned and ruled again until his death (80). Berenike III, popular with the Alexandrians was again queen, but, forced to take a husband, she married her stepson, Alexander II. It was a fatal decision. The new king killed his wife after 19 days, only to be torn to pieces by the Alexandrian mob. The reign of Chickpea's son, Ptolemy Auletes ("the Oboe Player"), brought an ever greater Roman involvement in Egypt's affairs. In 58 BC, Auletes too, was exiled, his eldest daughters Kleopatra Tryphaina (d. 57) and Berenike IV reigning in his place. Restored with Roman support, Auletes put Berenike to death. Following his own death (51) there was further conflict amongst his remaining children, Ptolemy, Arsinoe and Kleopatra VII. This ended with Julius Caesar's arrival in Alexandria, the death of Ptolemy, Arsinoe's capture and Kleopatra's accession with the youngest brother (yet another Ptolemy) who was soon removed.

Following Caesar's assassination, Mark Antony and Octavian defeated the conspirators at Philippi (42) and shortly afterwards divided the control of the Roman provinces between themselves. Antony took Greece, Asia, Syria and Kyrenaica. Having summoned Kleopatra to meet him at Tarsus, Antony obligingly put the captive princess Arsinoe to death. Alliance was advantageous to both Antony and Kleopatra: the wealth of Egypt could support his army, his support would ensure her rule. The campaign he now led against Parthia and Armenia was only partly successful, but was celebrated with a triumph in Alexandria (34). On this occasion, Antony announced the "Donations of

Alexandria" by which Kleopatra's son by Caesar, Kaisarion, was recognized as joint ruler of Egypt. Antony's own children by Kleopatra received some of the Roman provinces: Ptolemy, Syria and Cilicia, Kleopatra Selene, Kyrenaica and Libya, Alexander Helios was supposed to have Parthia, Media and Armenia. The break with Octavian was now inevitable, but Antony still had considerable support in Rome. Octavian set out on a campaign of vilification, claiming that Antony intended to remove the capital to Alexandria: Rome was to become a province of Egypt. The ensuing war was fought in Greece. The defeat at Actium (31) was soon to be characterized as the victory of the West over the East: the virtuous Roman Republic had triumphed over Egypt, just as the democratic Athenians had defeated Persia.

The Culture of the Hellenistic World

Greek culture spread across the Hellenistic kingdoms and into the regions surrounding. The culture of Gandara in India and of the kingdom of Meroë in Africa combined strong Hellenistic influence with indigenous styles. Within the Hellenistic cities, the gymnasium and theatre were an important focus for Greek education and culture, and were found in such "remote" centres as Ai Khanoum in Bactria.

In literary terms, the Hellenistic period built on the Classical tradition, particularly that of Athens. The first kings encouraged the writing of histories of their new kingdoms by members of the indigenous elite. In Egypt, the priest Manethon compiled such a history from Egyptian sources for Ptolemy II (all that survives are the king lists and a few fragments in the work of later writers). Similarly, in Babylon, Berossos used cuneiform historical texts in his work. There were clearly cross-cultural influences in literature. These are best-documented from Egypt, where texts in the native language include episodes which are modelled upon Greek myth. Hellenism was much more than a cultural veneer. There are also examples of Egyptian stories in both Greek and Egyptian versions. Ptolemy II himself summoned Jewish scholars from Jerusalem to produce a Greek translation of the *Pentateuch*.

In the great library of Alexandria, founded by Ptolemy II, half-a-million scrolls were gathered. Here a new form of critical scholarship developed, analyzing and interpreting earlier literature. Notable work was done on the Homeric texts, and an authoritative edition of the *Iliad* was produced. The period is renowned for bucolic poetry (as in the work of Theokritos) and the origination of the "novel". These were usually tales of separated lovers, who eventually reunite after numerous adventures in exotic locales. Most novels which survive are products of the Roman period, but written, and set in the Greek-speaking east. The Alexandrian style of poetry was typified by the work of Kallimachos (*c.* 280—240). With a skilful use of metre, it addressed subject matter which was exotic, allusive and frequently erotic. The library was also notable for the focus on the sciences. Eratosthenes of Kyrene (275—194), librarian to Ptolemy III, calculated the circumference of the earth, with tolerable accuracy, while Aristarchos of Samos expounded the radical theory that the earth moved round the sun: it was not generally accepted.

Later the city of Pergamon, under the rule of the Attalids, came to rival Alexandria as a literary centre, and its library was almost as great. Athens too remained culturally important, particularly in the field of philosophy: the Epicurean and Stoic schools developed at this time.

In architecture there was a monumentality not generally found in the earlier period, reflecting the wealth and splendour of the kingdoms. Alas, little survives of ancient Alexandria, and its role in architectural development (often called Hellenistic Baroque) is disputed by scholars. Nevertheless, it is certain that the buildings of Alexandria combined Greek with Egyptian elements. Something of this style may be seen in the rock-cut buildings at the Nabataean city of Petra (in modern Jordan). Alexandria (or perhaps Antioch) served as the prototype for all the great cities of the eastern Roman empire. Laid out on a grid-plan, the main streets were lined with colonnades to protect pedestrians from the glare of the sun. The old cities of the Ionian coast were particularly spectacular in their new guise, many of them, like Ephesos and Pergamon, in commanding positions on mountains overlooking the sea. The sea, indeed, was at the centre of the Hellenistic world: control of the sea and islands was important economically and politically. One of the most notable buildings of the age was the imposing 120-metre tall Pharos lighthouse at Alexandria.

Many of the most noted sculptures of the Greek world belong to the Hellenistic age (although some survive only in Roman copies): the Venus de Milo, the Nike (Victory) of Samothrace, the Laocoon, the Apoxymenos. There is great emotional and dramatic energy in these sculptures. The scale of the figures and the emphatic shadows on the frieze of the Great Altar of Zeus from Pergamon are far removed from the sculptures of the Parthenon.

In religion, local deities were identified with those of Greece. There was also a spread of some "oriental" cults, particularly from Egypt. The worship of Isis was the most notable, and these Mystery religions (which had strong connections with Greek cults such as the Eleusinian mysteries) were to be a potent force in the Roman empire.

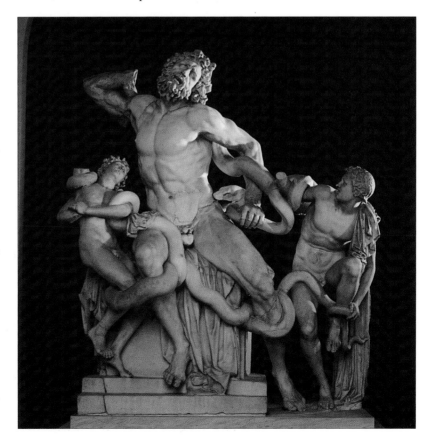

According to Greek mythology, Laocoon was a Trojan prince and priest of Apollo who argued against bringing the Trojan horse within the city's walls. To prevent him foiling the Achaean plan Poseidon sent two sea serpents to destroy both Laocoon and his sons. This magnificent statue based upon the legend is the work of three Greek sculptors, Athenodoros, Agesander and Polydoros and amply exemplifies the flourishing condition of the arts in the Hellenistic period. It is first mentioned by Pliny the elder who describes it as standing in the palace of the emperor Titus. Discovered in Rome in 1506 it is uncertain whether this is the original statue, completed towards the end of the 2nd century BC, or a copy of the 1st century AD.

Campaigns of Alexander

Upon Philip's assassination in 336 BC, Alexander inherited both his father's veteran army and his plans for the subjugation of Persia. By 323 BC Philip's plans had been carried out in full.

"It is my belief that there was in those days no nation, no city, no individual beyond the reach of Alexander's name; never in all the world was there another like him … I have, admittedly, found fault with some of the things which Alexander did, but of the man himself I am not ashamed to express ungrudging admiration."

Arrian, *The Campaigns of Alexander*

The campaigns of Alexander were the culmination of two centuries of inter-action between Persia and the Greek world. The surviving ancient accounts of the Macedonian defeat of the Persian empire were written long after Alexander's death and it is at times difficult to distinguish what might be historical reality from myth. The problem is further complicated by Alexander's conscious emulation of the Homeric heroes, particularly Achilles.

Alexander crossed the Hellespont in 334 and won the first of his victories, against the Persian satraps, at the Battle of the River Granikos. He soon gained control of Asia Minor, the only delay being the siege of Halikarnassos. He then confronted, and defeated, the army of Darius at Issos. The Persian king fled, but rather than pursuing Darius to the heart of the empire, Alexander marched down the Levantine coast, besieging and capturing its cites, notably Tyre and Gaza. This enabled him to control the Phoenician ports, thus hampering the Persian fleet which was still active in the Aegean. Egypt was taken without Persian resistance (332). After founding a new city, Alexandria, on the Mediterranean coast, Alexander made a detour to the oracle of Amun at Siwa in the western desert, where he was acknowledged as the son of the god Amun. The army now marched back through

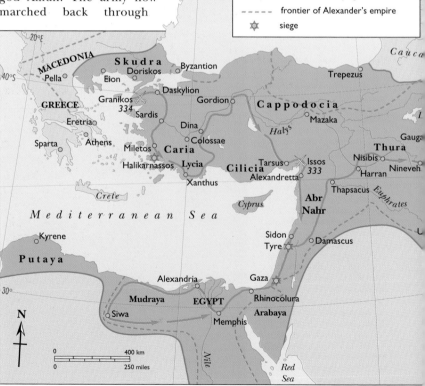

Alexander's campaigns, 334–323 BC

- Achaemenid empire
- the Persian Royal road
- Alexander's campaigns
- frontier of Alexander's empire
- siege

A bronze coin depicts Alexander the Great attacking Persian troops astride an elephant. Alexander clearly believed in leading from the front and he was wounded on a number of occasions. It was these injuries, coupled with over-exertion and over-indulgence in wine, that brought on the fever from which he died in Babylon, in his thirty-third year.

Phoenicia to Mesopotamia and the final great confrontation with the Persians, at Gaugamela. Following his defeat, Darius fled, but instead of pursuing him, Alexander marched south to Babylon and Susa, before advancing on Persepolis. The city fell to the Macedonians after they stormed the narrow pass of the "Persian Gates". Alexander resided for five months at Persepolis (330), which was set on fire before he marched north in pursuit of Darius. Darius fled further east, but was murdered by a Persian nobleman in his entourage, Bessus.

The campaigns in Bactria and Sogdia which occupied the next two years (329—328), were against Bessus and another opponent, Spitamenes. Throughout his march, Alexander continued to found new towns, which were settled with Greeks and Macedonians. In 326, he turned south, intent on the conquest of India. The subjugation of the Punjab was achieved in one great battle, at the River Hydaspes (Jhelum) (326), but further advance into India was prevented by a mutiny of his troops. Alexander began the march back to Susa, first down the Indus to the Arabian Sea (326—325). Alexander led the army across the Gedrosian Desert (Beluchistan), an error which resulted in a large number of deaths. He reached Susa in 324. The whole enterprise was brought to a sudden and unexpected end with Alexander's death at Babylon, aged 32, in 323 BC.

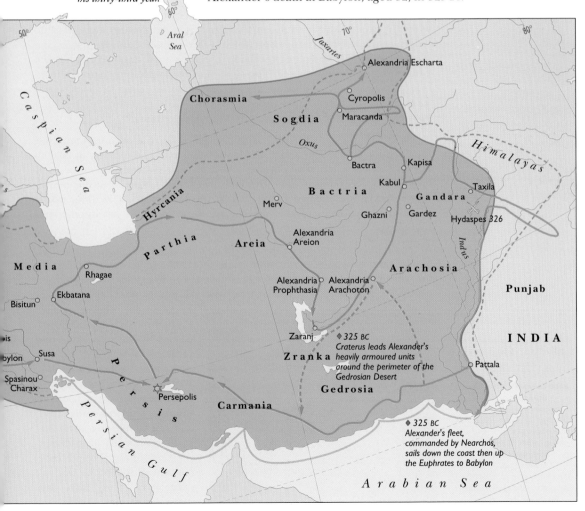

Alexander the General

Throughout his military career Alexander consistently proved his ability to gauge the strengths and weaknesses of his foe with unfailing accuracy.

"... they tipped water into a helmet and gave it to him. Alexander, with a word of thanks for the gift, took the helmet and, in full view of his troops, poured the water on the ground. So extraordinary was the effect of this action that the water wasted by Alexander was as good as a drink for every man in the army."
Arrian, *The Campaigns of Alexander*

Alexander's victories owed much to the Macedonian *phalanx* of pikemen developed by Philip II. Alexander's skill as a strategist ensured that the phalanx's speed and manoevrability were used to the greatest advantage against the far larger, but more disparate Persian forces. He was aware that the elements of his army, Greek, Macedonian and Balkan, could not be mixed as they had different languages and weapons. He also recognised the potential disunity of his army: the alliances were very recent, and any weakness in the Macedonian troops might lead to insurrection. His deployment of units and personal involvement in the action overcame these difficulties.

At Granikos, the first of his battles in Asia, Alexander confronted the Persian satraps. In this conflict Alexander used only a small portion of his strength. Parmenio, Philip's most experienced general, was given command of the 5,100-strong Thessalian cavalry, Alexander himself took command of the 13,000 Macedonians. The Persian force was much larger—perhaps 20,000 cavalry and 20,000 mercenaries. Alexander placed the *phalanx* at the centre, with the cavalry and archers on the wings. The battle line was the same length as the Persian cavalry line which it faced, about 3km. By placing the *phalanx* at the centre against Persian cavalry Alexander ensured that his own cavalry was not outnumbered. The *phalanx* armed with long pikes had considerable advantage against the javelins and scimitars of the Persians, and it was a tactic which Alexander repeated. In the resulting victory, Macedonian losses were insignificant compared to those of the enemy.

In his first confrontation with Darius himself, at Issos, Alexander employed much larger forces, with a total cavalry of 5,300 and total infantry of 26,000. Darius adopted a defensive position. Alexander again arranged his line, 4km long, with cavalry and infantry on the wings and the *phalanx* at the centre. Again the centre pushed through with the advantage of its long pikes. Alexander was able to advance directly on Darius' position, putting the king to flight: the rout of the army followed.

At the final confrontation on the level plain of Gaugamela, Darius showed he had learned from the defeat. Some of the chariots were fitted with scythes on the wheels to break up the *phalanx*, and some of the cavalry were equipped with pikes and swords of Macedonian type. Alexander now deployed even

A detail from a mosaic of the Battle of Issos depicts a spear-wielding equestrian Alexander. A soldier bent upon conquest rather than a diplomat or politician, Alexander's talents were not, perhaps, as many-faceted as those of his practical and far-seeing father. Pouring all his energy into his military campaigns, Alexander apparently spared little or no thought for the establishment of a secure dynastic future.

larger forces. Alexander and Parmenio each had comand of 3,500 cavalry and the infantry totalled 40,000. Alexander arranged a double *phalanx*, the back was to turn about-face if it was attacked in the rear. The centre advanced at an angle, parting when the scythed chariots bore down, then reforming. The advance continued and broke Darius' centre: he fled, with the inevitable result.

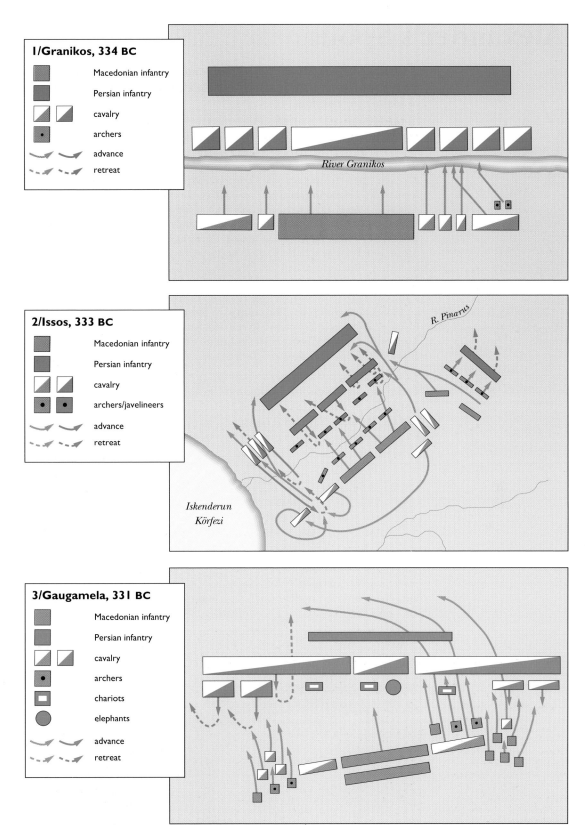

1/Granikos, 334 BC

Macedonian infantry

Persian infantry

cavalry

archers

advance

retreat

River Granikos

2/Issos, 333 BC

Macedonian infantry

Persian infantry

cavalry

archers/javelineers

advance

retreat

R. Pinarus

Iskenderun Körfezi

3/Gaugamela, 331 BC

Macedonian infantry

Persian infantry

cavalry

archers

chariots

elephants

advance

retreat

Alexander's Spoils

Following the early death of their commander, Alexander's marshals quickly became involved in a long and bloody power struggle in an attempt to secure their positions.

"In my view it is beyond dispute that Seleukos was the greatest king of those who succeeded Alexander, of the most royal mind, and ruling over the greatest extent of territory, next to Alexander himself."
Arrian, *The Campaigns of Alexander*

In the two decades after Alexander the Great's death there were several different divisions of the empire following major confrontations amongst his generals. In 321 the most powerful of the generals were Ptolemy, ruler of Egypt and Kyrenaica; Seleukos, the Satrap of Babylon; Antigonos who held Phrygia; and Antipatros who controlled much of Asia. Antipatros now returned to Macedon with the new kings, Philip III and Alexander IV, and Asia was placed under the authority of Antigonos. Civil war broke out in Macedonia when Alexander the Great's mother, Olympias, again seized control. In 317 Philip III was assassinated. Olympias, with Roxana and the infant Alexander IV, now sole king, were besieged by Kassandros, Antipatros's son, in Pydna. Kassandros, hailed as the liberator of Macedonia, celebrated the funeral rites of Philip III and married a daughter of Philip II, thereby establishing a claim to the throne. By 316 Kassandros was virtual master of Greece and Macedon; Antigonos had control of most of the satrapies of Asia as far as India, Ptolemy held Egypt and Kyrenaica. Seleukos stirred up trouble against Antigonos who now became the common enemy. The Battle of Gaza (312) allowed Ptolemy to seize much of Syria and enabled Seleukos to regain control of Babylon.

The treaty of 311 brought temporary peace: Antigonos retained Asia; Lysimachos, Thrace; Ptolemy, Egypt and Cyprus; Kassandros was to be regent of

Macedon until Alexander IV achieved his eighteenth year (305) and the Greek cities were to have their garrisons removed. Shortly after, probably in 308, Alexander and Roxana died. Propaganda claimed that Kassandros had had them murdered. With Alexander's death the male line of the royal house came to an end.

In 307, Antigonos' forces succeeded in taking Athens, Kassandros' principal base in Greece, and captured Cyprus from Ptolemy. Alexander IV's death was made public only in 306, and Antigonos and his son Demetrios were elected kings by an assembly of soldiers in Syria. The following year, Ptolemy, Lysimachos, Kassandros and Seleukos were all acclaimed kings in their own territories and formed a coalition against Antigonos and Demetrios. Lysimachos crossed into Asia Minor against Antigonos, Seleukos marched from the east. Demetrios now abandoned Greece and took his army to Asia to help his father. The decisive moment was the Battle of the Kings at Ipsos in 301. Antigonos was killed, Demetrios escaped but received little support in Athens or Greece.

At the time of his murder in 280 bc, the empire of Seleukos I Nicator stretched from Babylon to the Indus. Originally the commander of Alexander the Great's footguards, Seleukos was one of the first field commanders to appreciate the value of elephants in warfare; he would use them to devastating effect during the battle of Ipsos in 301 bc.

Antigonos' domain was carved up amongst the victors: Seleukos got Syria; Kassandros' brother received Caria and Cilicia; Lysimachos, the rest of Asia Minor. Ptolemy had been absent from the battle, and so received no new territory. During the campaign, however, Ptolemy had occupied Syria south of Damascus, and the Lebanon. As yet, Seleukos did not insist on the return of this land, but he preserved his claim to it.

The successor states, 303 BC

- Kassandros
- Lysimachos
- Antigonos
- Seleukos I
- Ptolemy I
- Chandragupta Maurya

Consolidation of the Kingdoms

As the first generation of Alexander's successors died, whether through natural causes or through murder, their heirs revealed no inclination to end the struggle for supremacy.

"After the battle (of Ipsos) had been decided ... the victorious kings proceeded to carve up the realm which Antigonos and Demetrios had ruled, like the carcass of some great slaughtered beast, each of them taking a limb and adding new provinces to those they had already possessed."

Plutarch, *Life of Demetrios*

The kingdoms of Asia Minor, Syria and Egypt were wealthy in natural resources and through trade, but despite Macedonia's peripheral position and its relative poverty, it was prestigious as the heart of Alexander's empire. Macedonia therefore became the focus of the ambitions of Demetrios, Pyrrhos of Epirus and Lysimachos. After his reign in Macedonia (294—288), Demetrios failed in his attempt to regain control of his father's Asian empire. This was in part due to the desertion of his admiral and the best of the fleet to Ptolemy I, who thereby gained control of the sea, of the Island League and some coastal cities of Asia Minor and Phoenicia. Ptolemy died peacefully in his bed, the only one of the generals to do so, and was succeeded by a younger son Ptolemy II (282—246). Seleukos I now regarded the aged Lysimachos, ruling over Macedonia and Thrace as a threat and marched his army against his former ally, defeated him at Korupedion in Lydia (281) and then continued into Europe. For a moment it seemed as if it was Seleukos who would reunite the major part of Alexander's Asian and European empire, but he was stabbed to death at Lysimacheia by Ptolemy Keraunos, the eldest son of Ptolemy I. Lysimachos' Macedonians hailed Keraunos as Lysimachos' avenger and as the new king of Macedonia. But there were rivals, Antigonos Gonatas, son of Demetrios and Ptolemy son of Lysimachos. There were also Celtic invasions. The events of the next years are complex; a succession of kings was defeated or

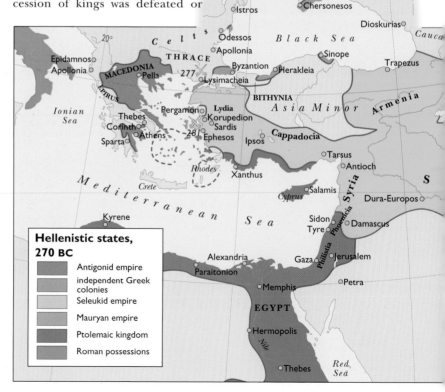

Hellenistic states, 270 BC

- Antigonid empire
- independent Greek colonies
- Seleukid empire
- Mauryan empire
- Ptolemaic kingdom
- Roman possessions

An Egyptian tetradrachm bears the portrait of Ptolemy I. Although his conflicts with the other successor kings involved Ptolemy in a number of military campaigns, he survived them all and eventually died in his bed—the only one of Alexander's successors to enjoy such a peaceful fate.

ousted until the Celtic armies were crushed near Lysimacheia (277) and Antigonos Gonatas emerged as undisputed ruler of Macedonia (277—239).

During the lives of Seleukos I and Ptolemy I the question of Seleukid control of Phoenicia, Philistia and southern Syria had been left unresolved. The ports were important for control of the sea, and of trade, the mountains for the supply of timber for the fleets. With the accession of a new generation the conflict broke out. From 276 until 272, Egypt and Syria were engaged in the First Syrian War. The end of the war left Egypt with extensive control of the coast of Asia Minor, the islands and Phoenicia. Ptolemy II also expanded his trade interests in Arabia and along the Nile to the kingdom of Meroë, supplier of ebony, ivory, elephants and incense.

The Seleukids had also lost territory on their eastern borders. With the help of Macedonian mercenaries, Chandragupta Maurya had established a kingdom in the Ganges Basin. Seleukos had abandoned his lands east of the Hindu Kush to the new king, in exchange for the elephant corps which helped to win the Battle of Ipsos. Good relations continued under the successors, Chandragupta's grandson Asoka (*c.* 275) bringing much of India into his empire. The following century was to see the appearance of more Hellenised states on the periphery of Alexander's former empire.

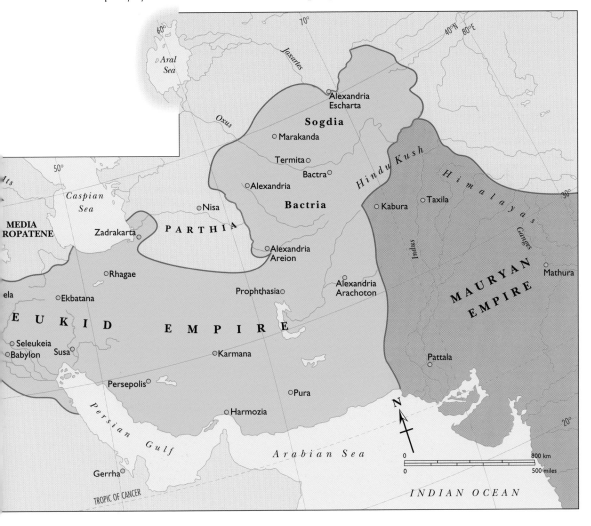

New Kingdoms, New Rivalries

The years leading up to 200 BC witnessed a lengthy power struggle between the Ptolemies and the Seleukids. On the outskirts of their world, meanwhile, the power of Rome was gradually expanding.

"Antiochos crossed the Caucasus and renewed his friendship with Sophagesenos king of the Indians and received more elephants, raising their number to a total of 150."
Polybius, *Histories, Book XI*

Ptolemy I and II had established Egypt as one of the most stable and wealthy of the Hellenistic kingdoms. Their acquisitions and influence in the cities of coastal Asia Minor and Phoenicia gave them control of the Aegean, and their corn supplies established good relations with Athens. The Chremonidean War was essentially a conflict between Egypt and Macedonia for influence in southern Greece.

In Asia Minor Ptolemy II meddled in the affairs of the Seleukid kingdom to increase his own influence. Eumenes the Seleukid governor of Pergamon (263—241) declared himself king, attacking and defeating the armies of Antiochos I at Sardis with mercenaries paid for by Egypt. Eumenes expanded the Pergamene state and Ptolemy was able to gain control of Miletos and Ephesos. Further rebellions saw the erosion of Seleukid territory in other parts of Asia Minor, and the creation of new Hellenised monarchies ruled by non-Macedonians. In Cappadocia, Ariarathes established an independent kingdom which was eventually recognized by the Seleukids through dynastic marriage. Pontos too had become an independent state under the rule of a Persian, Mithridates. Seleukid attempts to regain control ultimately failed and again dynastic marriage secured its recognition. Bithynia had always been independent and now became a kingdom successfully fending off Seleukid attempts to control the region. The kings adopted Greek customs and founded cities on the Greek model, the principal being Nikomedia. In Media Atropatene, a native dynasty had ruled since 323 and in Armenia descendants of the Persian satrap held power. The importance of all of these states was to increase as Seleukid power diminished.

The conflict between Antigonos, the Ptolemies and the Seleukids continued, with the Aegean as its main arena. Antigonos' naval victory over the Egyptian fleet at Kos in 258, brought an end to the Second Syrian War. The peace of 255 gave the western seaboard of Asia Minor to

The Hellenistic states, 200 BC

- kingdom of Macedonia
- allies / dependents of Macedonia
- kingdom of Pergamon
- Seleukid empire
- technically subject to Seleukid kings
- Ptolemaic kingdom
- Roman possessions

After a lengthy period of Seleukid weakness and decline, Antiochos III enjoyed comparative success in his military campaigns against his neighbours. Between 212–205 BC, for instance, he successfully reduced the Parthian king to vassaldom, thereby earning for himself the title of "Great".

Antiochos II (261—246) and Ptolemy surrendered the Cyclades to Antigonos. Ptolemy now began to meddle in Greece again and events allowed him to regain control of the sea.

Both Ptolemy II and Antiochos II died in 246, and the Third Syrian War soon broke out between the new kings Ptolemy III and Seleukos II. Antigonos, allied with Rhodes, defeated the Egyptian fleet off Andros, but by the end of the war in 241 Egypt still possessed a large number of bases in the Aegean.

From the middle of the third century, Macedonia became increasingly involved in events in Greece, the conflicts of the Leagues of city states, and with Rome; the Ptolemies were preoccupied with dynastic disputes, while the Seleukids remained distracted by the continuing disintegration of their Asiatic empire. More distant regions had seceded during the conflict in the west with Ptolemy II. Soon after 250, a large part of the Seleukid territory in Iran was formed into two new kingdoms. A Macedonian, Diodotos (c. 245—230), created his own kingdom in Bactria, and Arsaces established the beginning of the Parthian kingdom in 247, which was consolidated by his successor Tiridates.

Antiochos III (223—187) restored some prestige to the Seleukid throne, although the Fourth Syrian War concluded with an Egyptian victory at Raphia in 217 and Antiochos had to give up his claim to Coele-Syria.

In 219, the new king of Macedon, Philip V (221—179) attacked the Aetolian League as Hannibal entered Spain in his war against Rome. The following year the Roman army was defeated by Hannibal at Lake Trasimene and Philip took the opportunity to expand his kingdom into Illyria. He also entered into alliance with Hannibal. Direct conflict with Rome was inevitable, but the First Macedonian War went in Philip's favour.

Internal and dynastic problems afflicted Egypt following the Fourth Syrian War and Antiochos III and Philip V each absorbed some of the Ptolemaic overseas possessions. Philip took Samos and Miletos, Antiochos took Coele-Syria. Rhodes and Attalos, ruler of Pergamon, were now threatened by the expansion of the Seleukid kingdom and the activities of Philip in Caria. In 210, Attalos joined Rhodes in an appeal to the Roman Senate for assistance. Rome, having defeated Hannibal the year before was ready for action and in 200 declared war on Macedon.

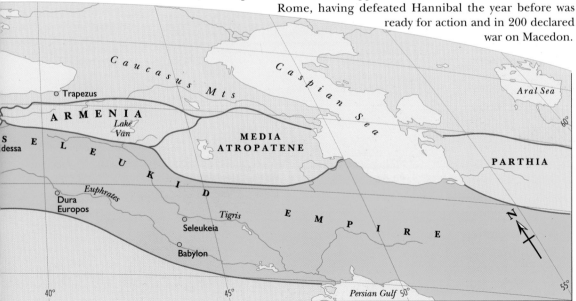

Kingdoms in Crisis

The actions of Philip V would eventually result in the Roman subjugation of not only Macedonia but of all of Greece as well.

"Popilius handed him the tablets containing the Senate's resolution... After reading the decree, Antiochos said that he would summon his friends and consult with them about his course of action; at which Popilius... drew a circle round the king... and said 'Before you step out of this circle, give me an answer to report to the Senate'. The king hesitated for a moment; then he replied: 'I shall do what the Senate decrees'."
Livy, *Histories,*
Book XLV

Roman intervention in the affairs of the Hellenistic kingdoms increased, resulting first in the annexation of Macedonia and Greece. In 200 Rome declared war on Philip V. The Macedonian defeat at Kynoskephalai in 197 brought this, the Second Macedonian War, to an end but war broke out again in the reign of Philip's son Perseus in 171. It seems that Rome was now determined to destroy Macedonia. Perseus gained some victories, but at the Battle of Pydna in 168 the Macedonian army was annihilated. Macedonia was divided into four republics, but the struggle continued. Following a further Roman victory in the Fourth Macedonian War in 150, Macedonia was turned into a province, in 148. Shortly afterwards, conflict in Greece ended in the defeat of the Achaean League, the destruction of Corinth and the enslavement of its inhabitants. Achaea, too, became a Roman province in 146.

The Seleukid empire was revitalized by Antiochos III. The king marched his army into Greece in response to an appeal from the Aetolian League. Having declared war on Antiochos in 191, Rome inflicted a devastating defeat on the Seleukid army at Heraclea. Antiochos was forced to flee back across the Hellespont with the Roman armies in pursuit. Antiochos suffered three further defeats in Asia Minor during 190, at Side, Myonessos and Magnesia. The resulting Peace of Apameia in 188 deprived the Seleukid kingdom of all of Asia Minor west of the Taurus Mountains. Rome did not annex

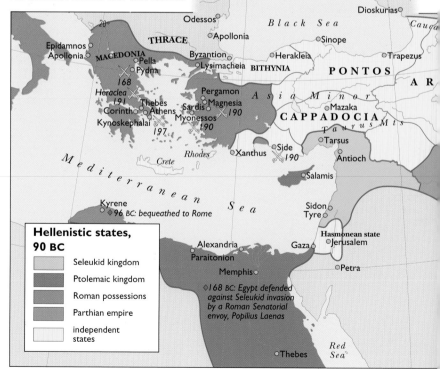

Hellenistic states, 90 BC

Seleukid kingdom
Ptolemaic kingdom
Roman possessions
Parthian empire
independent states

◇96 BC: bequeathed to Rome

◇168 BC: Egypt defended against Seleukid invasion by a Roman Senatorial envoy, Popilius Laenas

The ruins of the temple of Apollo at Corinth. In 146 BC the city was sacked by the Roman general Mummius. The majority of the male population was slaughtered but Mummius was able to amass a considerable fortune through the sale of the women and children into slavery.

this territory, but divided it between her allies, Rhodes and Pergamon.

Pergamon was the beneficiary of the conflicts, and the Attalids frequently appealed to Rome to intervene. On the death of Attalos II in 133, the kingdom was, quite inexplicably, bequeathed to Rome.

The successors of Antiochos III, his sons Seleukos IV (187—175) and Antiochos IV (175—163) retained much of the empire, but dynastic crisis erupted amongst their descendants. In the east, Bactria was still ruled by an independent Macedonian dynasty. In 167 the Seleukids temporarily regained control of parts of Bactria, but it was Mithridates I of Parthia who managed to annex much of it. Parthia made further gains from Seleukid territory, first taking Susa, then Babylon in 141. Attempts to reconquer the east *c.* 140 resulted in some success, but this was shortlived and the Parthians regained Babylon and then absorbed the rest of Mesopotamia. The Seleukids also lost control of Armenia when its governors set themselves up as independent kings.

Egypt, too, became more reliant upon Rome. The attempt of Antiochos IV to take Egypt in 168 was prevented by Popilius Laenas, who forced his withdrawal. Decades of bloody dynastic dispute followed the death of Ptolemy VI, with increasing reliance upon Roman support. At his death in 116, Ptolemy Euergetes II bequeathed Kyrene to a son, Ptolemy Apion, who, in his turn, bequeathed the small kingdom to Rome in 96.

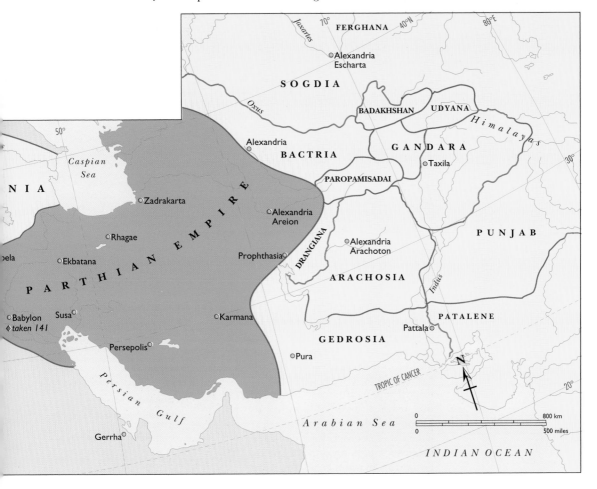

Roman Conquest

When Rome absorbed the kingdoms of Macedon and Pergamon as provinces she gained an even greater interest in the affairs of the Hellenistic east.

As the Seleukid and Ptolemaic families were torn apart by dynastic feuds appeals to the Roman senate became more frequent and the Hellenistic east became the focus of the increasing rivalries of the Roman generals. The crisis in the Seleukid kingdom allowed the powers on its fringes to expand. Some territory fell to Mithridates VI of Pontos who had also extended his kingdom around the northern shore of the Black Sea and established a new capital at Panticapaeum. Mithridates now claimed to be the champion of the Hellenistic and Greek world against "barbarian" Rome. Invited by Athens to "liberate" Greece, Mithridates came into direct conflict with Roman armies (88—85) and was forced back into Asia. There were two later conflicts (83—82 and 74—63), the second prompted by the bequest of Bithynia to Rome and its conversion into a province. Mithridates was eventually defeated at Dasteira by Pompey who now reorganized Anatolia and Syria into Roman provinces and client kingdoms. These kingdoms were to form a buffer against Parthia, the other beneficiary of Seleukid collapse.

In Egypt the dynastic rivalries continued until, in 80 the Alexandrians offered the crown to Ptolemy Auletes. A will was eventually produced which claimed that Egypt (like Pergamon and Bithynia before it) had been bequeathed to Rome. The will may have been a forgery and the Senate took no action until 65 when Crassus (perhaps for his own ambitions) called for the annexation of Egypt. Cyprus, ruled by Auletes' brother, was taken and added to the province of Cilicia (58). Auletes' failure to send aid outraged the Alexandrians who forced him to flee. In 55 Aulus Gabinius, governor of Syria, and Mark Antony escorted Auletes back to Alexandria. They were accompanied by a large military unit which was left in the city to protect the king. The next year the Roman army suffered a crushing defeat, at Carrhae in Mesopotamia, at the hands of the Parthians. Events at Rome were soon to lead to civil war, with Greece as one of the main arenas of action. In Egypt, the death of Auletes (51) led to war between his appointed successors, Ptolemy and Kleopatra. Following his defeat at Pharsalos

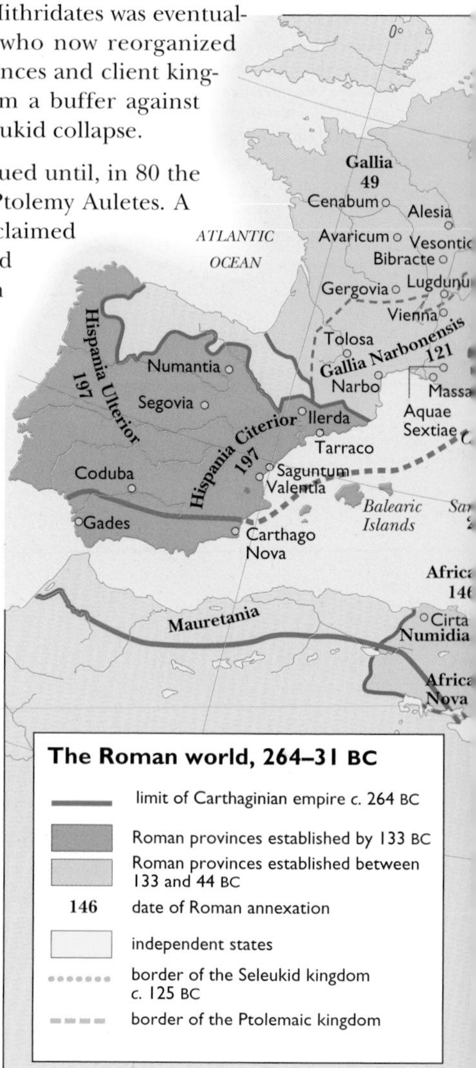

> *"Gabinius was approached by Ptolemy Auletes who appealed to him to join forces, invade Egypt, and recover his kingdom, for which services he offered a bribe of ten thousand talents. Antony ... who longed to undertake some ambitious enterprise, was eager to gratify Ptolemy's request and so threw his weight on the king's side and persuaded Gabinius to join him."*
>
> Plutarch, *Life of Mark Antony*

The Roman world, 264–31 BC

— limit of Carthaginian empire c. 264 BC

▨ Roman provinces established by 133 BC

▨ Roman provinces established between 133 and 44 BC

146 date of Roman annexation

☐ independent states

······ border of the Seleukid kingdom c. 125 BC

– – – border of the Ptolemaic kingdom

Map labels: Gallia 49, Cenabum, Alesia, Avaricum, Vesontic, Bibracte, Gergovia, Lugdunu, Vienna, Tolosa, Gallia Narbonensis 121, Narbo, Massa, Aquae Sextiae, ATLANTIC OCEAN, Hispania Ulterior 197, Numantia, Segovia, Hispania Citerior 197, Ilerda, Tarraco, Saguntum, Valentia, Coduba, Gades, Carthago Nova, Balearic Islands, Sa, Mauretania, Africa 146, Cirta, Numidia, Africa Nova

(48), Pompey fled to Egypt, and on his arrival was murdered on Ptolemy's orders. Caesar arrived shortly after. The Alexandrine war ended with the death of Ptolemy, leaving Kleopatra sole ruler of Egypt. Following Caesar's murder (44), Antony became pre-eminent in the east. The Parthians invaded Syria (41), one of the repercussions being the overthrow of Hyrcanus in Jerusalem and the seizure of power by Herod. Antony later (37) installed Herod as king of Judaea. Antony's Parthian war (36) was a failure, but on his return to Alexandria he announced a settlement of the east. Kleopatra, and her son by Julius Caesar, Kaisarion, were declared joint rulers of Egypt and Cyprus and Antony's own children by Kleopatra also received vast—if theoretical—kingdoms: Alexander Helios was to rule Armenia, Parthia and Media, Ptolemy was to have Syria and Cilicia, Kleopatra Selene to have Kyrenaica and Libya. Antony himself assumed no royal style. Shortly after, Octavian declared war on Kleopatra. Antony's defeat at the decisive battle of Actium (31) was followed by the capture of Alexandria and the death of Kleopatra. The vast empire of Alexander the Great was now divided between Parthia and Rome.

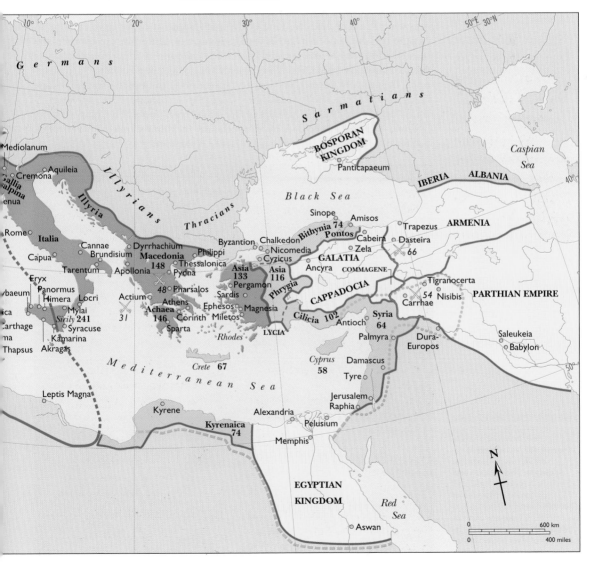

Architecture of Ancient Greece

The architectural legacy of ancient Greece is rich and varied, ranging from the maze-like complexities of Minoan Knossos and the massive defensive structures of Mycenae to the Classical elegance of Periklean Athens.

"And this is the more cause to marvel at the buildings of Perikles, that they were made in so little time to last for so long ... Such a bloom of newness is there upon them, keeping them, to the eye, untouched by time, as though the works had blended into them, an evergreen spirit and a soul of unfading youth."
Plutarch, *Life of Perikles*

The influence of Greek architecture on that of western Europe has been immense, although largely at second hand, through the architecture of Rome. Our perception of Greek architecture has also been deeply influenced by even later reinterpretations: Renaissance and Neoclassical.

The surviving architecture of the Mycenaean world is largely monumental, such as the Cyclopean walls of the fortifications at Mycenae and Tiryns. Domestic architecture of the period, which survives in Minoan sites on Crete and Santorini reveals sophisticated drainage systems and elaborate frescoed decoration. There were some influences on later architecture, notably, the layout of the classical temple derived from the Mycenaean *megaron*.

In the cities of the Classical and Hellenistic periods, the main public buildings were the temples, the theatre, the gymnasium and the *agora*. The houses were relatively modest and inward looking: they generally presented blank facades to the street and opened onto a central courtyard. Although many of the cities of mainland Greece were of ancient origin and seem to have developed organically, town planning was introduced quite early in the Asiatic cities. Many of the Hellenistic cities were planned: some were new foundations, others extensively rebuilt under royal patronage. The plan was the *gridiron*, reputedly invented by Hippodamos of Miletos (mid–5th century), but used much earlier in some parts of the Near East.

Although none of their palaces achieved the astonishing complexity of Minoan Knossos, the Mycenaean kings did live in considerable splendour. Their wealth and influence is amply indicated by their construction of massive fortifications such as the Cyclopean walls of Mycenae which acted both as symbols of their power and as very effective defences.

Undoubtedly the most influential aspects of Greek architecture have been the three Classical orders—Doric, Ionic and Corinthian. The Doric and Ionic, developed about the same time (the earliest surviving Doric temple, of Hera at Olympia, is of the late 7th century BC). Doric was found all over Greece, Sicily and southern Italy, whereas Ionic appears first in the coastal cities of Asia Minor. The Ionic order certainly has predecessors in the architecture of Egypt and western Asia and a form of "proto-Doric" column (although without capital) was also common in Egyptian architecture. The Doric order was used for many of the largest and most imposing of the suriving temples—at Paestum, Corinth, Aegina and, at Athens, the Parthenon. The most majestic of the Ionic temples must have been that of Artemis at Ephesos, with 117 columns, each over 18 metres high. Ionic, however, lent itself to graceful rather than monumental buildings, such as the Erechtheion and temple of Nike, both on the Akropolis at Athens. The Corinthian order was supposed to have been invented rather later, in the 5th century. It was essentially an elaboration of the Ionic, surrounded with sprays of acanthus leaves. Corinthian was particularly favoured by the architects of the Hellenistic and Roman periods.

Sculpture was an integral feature of Greek architecture, both as decoration (friezes and pediments) and free-standing. Colour was also extensively used. Although the columns were left white (and freshly-cut marble must have been very white), red and blue was added to accentuate certain details of the cornices and architraves, and the background of the sculptured metopes and pediments. The sculptures were also painted, and would have had some features (such as diadems) added in bronze. The whole effect must have been rather more dazzling than the impression of mellow stone and a certain simple elegance, even austerity in Doric temples, conveyed by the ruins.

The caryatid porch of the Erechtheion, completed around 406 BC on the site of Athens' earlier Mycenaean palace. This complex temple commemorates the mythical struggle between Athena and the trident-wielding sea-god Poseidon for the possession of Attica. Inside the temple stood the ancient wooden statue of Athena which had, according to tradition, fallen from the skies. It was to this crude effigy, and not to the glittering colossus created by Pheidias, that the Panathenaic procession annually brought a robe of sumptuous and costly workmanship.

The tholos of the sanctuary of Athene Pronaia at Delphi. Originally possessing a peristyle of 20 Doric columns the temple has been repeatedly damaged by successive earthquakes. Delphi became a treasure-house of the various styles of ancient Greek architecture as the competing city-states built monuments to commemorate their victories at the Pythian games and constructed temples sacred to the site's principal deity, the sun-god, Apollo.

Further Reading

ANCIENT WRITERS

Aristotle, *The Politics*, tr. T.A. Sinclair, Penguin, 1962

Arrian, *The Campaigns of Alexander*, tr. A. de Sélincourt, Penguin, 1971

Collected Ancient Greek Novels, ed. B.P. Reardon, University of California Press, London, 1989

Herodotos, *The Histories*, tr. A. de Sélincourt, Penguin, 1972

Livy, *Rome and the Mediterranean*, tr. H. Bettenson, Penguin, 1976

Pausanias, *Guide to Greece*, tr. P. Levi, Penguin, 1979

Plutarch, *Parallel Lives*, tr. I. Scott-Kilvert as *The Rise and Fall of Athens*, Penguin, 1960; *The Age of Alexander*, Penguin, 1973

Thucydides, *The Peloponnesian War*, tr. R. Warner, Penguin, 1972

Xenophon, *The Persian Expedition*, tr. R. Warner, Penguin, 1972

MODERN SOURCES

Boardman, J., *The Greeks Overseas: their early colonies and trade*, Thames and Hudson, London, 1980

Bowman, A., *Egypt after the Pharaohs*, Oxford University Press, 1990

Burkert, W., *The Orientalizing Revolution: Near Eastern influence on Greek culture in the early Archaic age*, Harvard University Press, 1992

Cartledge, P., *The Greeks: a portrait of self and others*, Oxford University Press, 1993

Coldstream, J.N., *Geometric Greece*, Methuen, 1977

Cook, J.M., *The Persian Empire*, London, 1983

Davis, J.K., *Democracy and Classical Greece*, Fontana, 1978

Dickinson, O.T.P.K., *The Aegean Bronze Age*, Cambridge World Archaeology, Cambridge University Press, 1994

Dover, K.J., *Greek Homosexuality*, London, 1978

Drews, R., *The Coming of the Greeks*, Princeton University Press, 1988

Drews, R., *The End of the Bronze Age*, Princeton University Press, 1993

Ehrenberg, V., *Frem Solon to Socrates*, Methuen, 2nd edn., 1973

Finley, M.I., *The Use and Abuse of History*, The Hogarth Press, London, 1986

Forrest, W.G., *History of Sparta 950—192 BC*, London, 2nd edn., 1980

Green, P., *Alexander of Macedon*, Penguin, 1974

Grimal, P., *Hellenism and the Rise of Rome*, London, 1978

Hammond, N.G.L., *The Miracle that was Macedonia*, Sidgwick and Jackson, London, 1991

Hoddinott, R.F., *The Thracians*, Thames and Hudson, 1981

Hooker, J.T., *Mycenaean Greece*, Routledge, 1976

Hood, M.S.F., *The Minoans*, London, 1971

Hornblower, S., *The Greek World 479—323 BC*, Routledge, London and New York, 1991

Humphreys, S.C., *Anthropology and the Greeks*, London, 1978

James, P.J., *Centuries of Darkness*, Jonathan Cape, 1991

James, P.J., *The Sunken Kingdom: The Atlantis Mystery Solved*, Jonathan Cape, London, 1995

Momigliano, A., *Alien Wisdom*, Cambridge, 1975

Onians, J., *Art and Thought in the Hellenistic Age. The Greek World View 350—50 BC*, Thames and Hudson, 1979

Richter, G.M.A., *Handbook of Greek Art*, 7th edn., London and New York, 1974

de Sainte Croix, G.E.M., *The Origins of the Peloponnesian War*, Duckworth, London, 1972

Sherwin-White, S. and Kuhrt, A., *From Samarkhand to Sardis: A new approach to the Seleucid empire*, Duckworth, 1993

Snodgrass, A.M., *The Dark Ages of Greece*, Edinburgh University Press, 1971

Taylour, W., *The Mycenaeans*, (2nd edn.), Thames and Hudson, London, 1983

Walbank, F.W., *The Hellenistic World*, Fontana, 1981

Wilkes, J., *The Illyrians*, Blackwell, Oxford, 1992

Index

References shown in **bold** are maps or pictures. Quotes are in *italics*.

Acknowledgements

Picture Credits

Front Cover

(clockwise from top right)

Michael Holford: The Dolphin Fresco

Michael Holford: Greek Sculpture—Apollo Kouros

Michael Holford: Corinth, Temple of Apollo

Michael Holford: Greek vase—Achilles fighting Hektor

Michael Holford: Athens, The Parthenon

Michael Holford: Bust of Perikles

Werner Forman Archive: The Temple of Apollo

Sonia Halliday Photographs: A detail of the Alexander Sarcophagus from the Royal Cemetery at Sidon

Internal

Author's Collection: 31

Michael Holford: 15, 18, 21, 29, 36, 41, 43, 45, 46, 54, 89, 108, 111, 115, 116, 121, 131

Sonia Halliday Photographs: 27, 35, 57, 60, 61b, 84b, 109, 125, 135t, 135b; 17, 24, 94, 122, 134 (F.H.C. Birch); 67, 71, 78 (T.C. Rising); 119 (Jane Taylor); 65 (James Wellard)

Werner Forman Archive: 13, 61t, 87, 99; 76 (Archaeological Museum, Teheran); 90 (British Museum, London); 69 (Musum Ostia, Italy)

Quotations

The author and publishers gratefully acknowledge the following translations from ancient writers used in this atlas:

Aristotle, *The Politics,* trans. T.A. Sinclair, Penguin, 1962: p 80

Arrian, *The Campaigns of Alexander,* trans. A. de Selincourt, Penguin, 1971: pp. 120, 122, 124

Herodotos, *The Histories,* trans. A. de Selincourt, Penguin, 1972: pp. 32, 58, 70, 72, 78

Homer, *The Iiad,* trans. E.V. Rieu, Penguin, 1963: pp. 34,60

Livy, *Rome and the Mediterranean,* trans. H. Bettenson, Penguin, 1976: p. 130

Pausanius, *The Guide to Greece,* trans. P. Levi, Penguin, 1979: p. 26

Plutarch, *Parallel Lives,* trans. I. Scott-Kilvert as *The Rise and Fall of Athens,* Penguin, 1960: pp. 48, 86, 126, 132, 134

Thucydides, *The Peloponnesian War,* trans. Rex Warner, Penguin, 1964: pp. 50, 54, 62, 94, 96, 98, 102

FOR SWANSTON PUBLISHING LIMITED

Concept:
Malcolm Swanston

Editorial and Map Research:
Stephen Haddelsey

Illustration:
Julian Baker
Ralph Orme

Cartography:
Andrea Fairbrass
Peter Gamble
Elsa Gibert
Stephen Haddelsey
David McCutcheon
Kevin Panton
Peter Smith
Nick Whetton

Typesetting:
Jeanne Arnold
Charlotte Taylor

Picture Research:
Stephen Haddelsey
Charlotte Taylor

Production:
Barry Haslam

Separations:
Central Systems,
Nottingham.

Index:
Jean Cox
Barry Haslam